METAPHORS FOR THE MUSICIAN
Perspectives from a Jazz Pianist

Edited by Sandra Burlingame

Cover Design by Janis Mann and Bill Olmstead

Deepest thanks to Jay Clayton, Jerome Gray,
Laura Kaminsky and the many others who have
touched me with their words and music.

Special thanks to Chuck Sher, Attila Nagy, Chuck Gee,
Susan Muscarella, Alan Steger, and Dick Hindman

Contact Randy Halberstadt by email at randy@randyhalberstadt.com
or visit his website at www.randyhalberstadt.com

Randy Halberstadt

©2001 Sher Music Co., P.O. Box 445, Petaluma, CA 94953
ISBN 1-883217-12-1

For Chris and Robin

CONTENTS

Part V **Theory Demystified**

Part VI **Incomparable Comping**

Part VII **At the Gig**

Part VIII **Paths to Success**

Preface

How To Use This Book

The inspiration for this book came from my twenty-five years of teaching jazz piano. During that time I've seen hundreds, perhaps thousands of students. Although I don't remember all their names and have probably even forgotten a few faces, certainly each student has been unique in some way and required individual attention. Yet in all those years I can't say that I've seen hundreds or thousands of unique problems; there simply aren't that many. I've watched as student after student encounters the same common pitfalls and hurdles. In fact, I still remember confronting most of them myself. In this book I try to address several of those issues and offer some strategies for dealing with them.

When you study jazz piano, you have to learn music, you have to learn jazz, you have to learn piano—and you have to learn about yourself. It should come as no surprise, then, that the typical issues you'll face cover a wide spectrum. Some of the chapters in this book are very philosophical in nature; others are so specific as to be concerned with fingerings for scales. Some chapters cover issues faced by any jazz musician, while others deal with purely pianistic challenges.

One of the hurdles I encountered in writing this book was simply what to name it. As it's not just a piano book or a jazz book, this was a thorny problem. My students learn very quickly that I love metaphors. A difficult concept often becomes very simple if you can relate it to something familiar. Over half the chapters in this book use this device at least once. This is why I chose the title *Metaphors for the Musician.*

This is not a comprehensive how-to book. It's a collection of my special insights, "nuggets" if you will, designed to supplement books dedicated to jazz piano or jazz theory. Approach it as you would a unique department store that specializes in one-of-a-kind items for your musical house, not a huge warehouse that includes everything required to build and furnish it. For one thing, it presumes that you've already laid a foundation: you've learned to play your instrument, studied some basic theory, listened to lots of music, and tried your hand at jazz. You can amble through this store at will—look, buy, put something in layaway, even stop by the cafe for nourishment. You won't buy everything in this store. But if you can leave with a few choice items—some helpful practice techniques, fresh approaches to improvising or new theoretical perspectives—then my efforts were well worth it.

On the other hand, it's not my wish that you read this book without stopping along the way to apply what you've learned. You'll see that I've highlighted several of the exercises with gray boxes like this one:

You can measurably improve your musicianship if you practice the exercises to perfection before you continue. Good luck!

Introduction

Crooked Road

It wasn't the first time. Oh no. My exposure to music—learning to play it—began years earlier with three weeks of piano lessons with Mr. Gambino (I gave them up for Cub Scouts) and continued through six years of playing the trombone in the school band. But that was another life. I had put that all behind me in 1971 when I came to the University of Washington from Texas to become an oceanographer. Yet here I was, sitting at a piano in my college dorm at three in the morning, and I felt as if I were discovering music for the first time. There were no rules, no pressure to be good, no people listening. There was just the piano, myself, and pure sound. I fell in love.

The next day I showed up at the office of the music department and declared, "I want to be a composer!" I'm not sure why the receptionist wasn't as impressed with the enormity of my decision as I was. She merely yawned, flipped open a scheduling book, and droned, "Fine, your audition is next Tuesday at three." "Audition?" I asked. I had said composer, not performer. I couldn't play anything. She was sorry but an audition was required for admission into the music department.

In a daze I walked back to my dorm and called home. "Mom, do you still have my trombone? Can you send it up to me? Well, because I want to be a composer, and I…. yes, I know…I know…well, it didn't make any sense to me either, but that's what the lady said…thanks, Mom." Now what? I didn't know what to think. Back in high school I was a big fish in a small pond. My band director had tried to convince me that I was the "second coming of Tommy Dorsey." The part of me that believed him was annoyed that I was being put through the formality of an audition. Didn't they realize how lucky they'd be to have me in their music school? But there was another part of me that remembered I hadn't played the trombone in almost two years—and that part was petrified.

A few short days later I appeared at the trombone professor's studio (nervous already: "trombone professor"?) and played my audition. There were a couple of mistakes along the way, but overall I was quite pleased with how it went. Well, I thought as I put the horn away, I haven't lost it after all. I guess it's like riding a bicycle, you just…

"Ahem…"

It took a full twenty minutes for the professor to catalog all the crimes I had committed during my seven-minute audition. Finally, and with great reservations, he accepted me into the program. "But boy, do we have a boatload of work to do…" I mumbled a thank you and slunk out of his office.

I spent the next four years struggling in vain to be the world's greatest trombonist. I don't know why. I had already quit the instrument once before because I didn't like it. And I was shaken by how shaken the professor was by my bad trombone playing. I wasn't used to being called "bad" at anything, and I suppose I felt I had something to prove. And over the next four years I did prove something: I was a bad trombonist. Each year I watched helplessly as the new crop of freshman trombonists entered the school with more talent than I. Years later, shortly after graduation, a jazz improvisation teacher asked me point-blank, "Now Randy, you've had four years of training with Stuart Dempster over at the University, right? Then help me out here, because I'm obviously missing something: why aren't you better?"

During those years I took one brief and forgettable course in composing as part of the normal program of music classes. But there were high points. I had a singularly inspiring theory teacher who took great joy in playing through Bach's "Well-Tempered Clavier" while singing an analysis of the harmonic framework. I loved the way he introduced a new topic. He would talk non-stop for ten or fifteen minutes, apparently oblivious as more and more confused faces and raised hands appeared throughout the classroom. Then he would suddenly stop and announce, "All right, now here are the answers to all of your questions." Then he would begin again. And one by one the hands would go down and the faces would relax. He didn't need to hear the questions—he already knew just what the inherent problems were.

I will also never forget his method of questioning individual students. When one confidently and correctly answered a question, Mr. Babb would counter with, "That's the right answer, but what did you mean by [a particular term]?" The student responded with slightly reduced certainty and accuracy, then: "That's still basically correct, but why did you phrase [one part of the answer] like you did?" Now the student was on shaky ground. His next response would reveal a basic flaw in his thinking. Mr. Babb would nod kindly and say, "Here's where you went wrong..." As he carefully explained the particular theoretical point, you could fairly hear the thud as the basic foundation of the student's knowledge settled firmly into place. I witnessed at least a dozen cases of Mr. Babb worming his way down into the depths of a student's psyche to troubleshoot a weak link (including a time or two when the "worm" was aimed at me).

During this time I also took piano lessons. They were required for all music majors, but I loved them. My teachers didn't load me down with endless Hanon exercises or other technique drills. I was a trombonist, and they knew that (they just didn't know how bad!). They saw that I was developing a real love for the piano, and they nurtured that by giving me some great music to play: Gershwin, Ginastera, Chopin—quite a mixed bag. Meanwhile, I continued to develop my own private relationship with the instrument— staying up until all hours of the night, composing and improvising my own sounds. Somehow I managed to keep this relationship remarkably pure and free of the pressure-driven neuroses that I associated with the trombone. It still hadn't occurred to me that I could become a pianist. I was simply playing because I loved it, and in a strange way I didn't even care if I got to be good at it. It wasn't about me—it was about the music and how good it felt to play it. And of course, that's why I began to get good very quickly.

As graduation neared, I was confronted with a stark realization: I had no marketable skills. I was a bad trombonist in a world where good trombonists can't make it without a day gig to support them. My, how my dreams had collapsed. Four short years earlier, I had marched into college with my guns blazing, confident that I would be the next Jacque Ives-Cousteau (the only oceanographer I knew of, growing up in West Texas). Now I seriously wondered how I could avoid being the next homeless bum on the street.

A girlfriend asked me, "Why don't you teach piano?" Now I had heard some bad ideas in my time, but this was lunacy. I knew what it took to be a piano teacher. You needed to be old, preferably German, you needed to know the preferred fingerings for every Bach invention, and it helped if you knew which edition of Beethoven's piano sonatas was more historically accurate.

"No," she told me. "All you need in order to teach is the ability to play some type of music well and the ability to show others how to do it." I decided that she was probably wrong, but I was in no position to argue. So I placed an ad in the paper. Then a most unforeseen and frightening event happened. Someone answered it.

As soon as I put down the phone, I reached frantically for a pencil and paper. I made a list of about forty items:

Everything I Know About Music

1. Scales
2. Chords
3. Improvising
4. Blues
5. Reading music
6. .... etc., etc.

When my student showed up for her first lesson, I kept my list close at hand (hidden from her view, of course). My plan? I thought I could probably make it through one hour without running out of things to teach. Then I'd have a whole week to run out and learn some new things before her next lesson! This is how little I valued the worth of what I knew and could play. I actually thought that someone else might be able to learn it all in a week. Of course, we barely scratched the surface of item #1 during the lesson. Not only did I realize that day that I could teach, but I also came remarkably close to enjoying it.

Over the next few weeks, I took on a few more students. Before long I was supporting myself (albeit in a very modest lifestyle), and I was both proud and relieved that I had stemmed my impending slide into homelessness and hunger. Let me stress at this point: I had yet to play my first gig as a pianist! I probably taught for almost two years before I performed for the first time. It's a little embarrassing to admit that I was the poster child for the slogan, "Those who can't do, teach." Eventually, though, I began to play around town in various bands, including my own trio.

My playing and my teaching improved tremendously over the next few years. The trombone? I sold it within a year of graduation. Years later, I was on a gig with a trombonist. As I looked at his instrument, I thought, I still remember the slide positions, the embouchure, the breath support, everything it takes to play that instrument. Now that the pressure's off and I don't have to be good at it anymore, now that all my neuroses are gone, I know I can pick that trombone up and play it, no question. "Steve, mind if I play your horn a little? Thanks, man." I grabbed the instrument by the still familiar grip and raised it to my lips with anticipation. But as I took my first breath, I had a tangible sense of breathing in all the old demons. By the time I released it, I was an insecure, bumbling college kid again, and the only sound that came out of the bell was reminiscent of digestive gases being released. "Well, er, hmm...thanks, Steve..." I had never questioned my decision to give up the trombone for a second time, but now I congratulated myself for it.

I don't regret my years of playing the trombone. It was during this time that I developed many of my melodic sensibilities as an improviser. When I switched to the piano, many of those impulses remained intact, resulting in a horn-like melodic style that remains to this day a trademark element in my playing.

It's now almost thirty years since that early-morning epiphany at the piano in my dorm. I'm a jazz pianist now. There have been honors and achievements along the way. I've played at the Monterey Jazz Festival and at the Kennedy Center; I've made recordings of my own and performed on countless others; I've performed with the likes of Herb Ellis, Buddy DeFranco, Ernestine Anderson, and Bobby Shew; and I've become a full professor at Cornish College of the Arts in Seattle—as well as a sought-after private teacher. I'm proud of the honors, but most of them don't have much effect on my day-to-day world. Here's what does have an effect: I still love the piano. I love it today as freely and openly as I did then. I love it much more deeply, in fact, because I can express so much more of myself through it.

Because I started learning music at such a relatively late age, I knew I wouldn't get very far by just hanging out and picking things up by osmosis. I used my analytical skills to process information about voicings, improvising, and time. It bothered me whenever I heard someone say that it will kill your passion for something if you analyze it. I certainly hoped that wasn't true because I felt I had no other option. Now I can say with certainty that the analytical approach has only increased my fascination with and love for music. Not that it doesn't have its own drawbacks. When you learn music in little boxes, you tend to be trapped by them for a while. But ultimately the intuition catches up.

After a recent solo gig I told my wife Chris that I've never enjoyed music as much as I do now. I described my experience metaphorically, of course. "I have a big tank of fish which are my musical resources. Some of them are scales [she rolled her eyes at the pun], some are voicings, some are licks. Now when I play, it's like watching the tank as these fish swim around in a constantly changing pattern. Even though it's basically the same population of fish that I know very well, they continually combine in unpredictable ways. I really don't know exactly what's coming next, and sometimes I have to laugh because my hands will figure out a wonderful new sound before my mind can think it or my ear can hear it. I never could have predicted that playing would become this much fun."

Chris loves her work (social work administration) as much as I do mine. Our biggest problem by far is that we both work too hard. We have a wonderful eighteen-year-old daughter named Robin. She hasn't found her thing yet, but she's heading off to college next year to begin her search. One of the clearest lessons in her young life has been in seeing the contrast between jobs (she's had a few) and passions (such as her parents'). She definitely won't be a musician, and she probably won't be a social work administrator. But she'll leave this nest with a clear purpose: to find something that she loves—something that doesn't feel like work at all.

As I review the past thirty years, it occurs to me that my musical development has taken a crooked road, not at all how I would have drawn it up. Yet I don't think my story is particularly unusual or unique. Every musician has some strange tales to tell about the path that led him to this point. I've intentionally focused here on my early years, on my struggles to find myself. I wanted to share my confusion, my fears, my wrong turns, as well as my joys and successes. That's because I'm trying to send a message to those of you who are currently confused, fearful, and prone to taking wrong turns. It's going to be all right. It really is. There are joys and successes ahead for you. Almost all the successful, effective people who surround you every day were once as clueless as you are now. And some of the best roads you'll ever travel are the ones you find when you're hopelessly lost. So just sit back and enjoy the ride as much as you can. It's...going...to ...be...all...right. Believe it.

Part I **Picturing Jazz**

As you dig into this book, you'll get down into the trenches and deal with many specific issues. But first you should glimpse the larger terrain, the overall picture of jazz, so you'll know why the details are important.

Chapter 1

Jazz Quilt

This quilt is you, it's all the things you are.
Jimmy Rowles on the corner, talking shop with Frishberg.
Miles of squares of Miles, cool blue, no wrinkles, offsetting Trane's sheets of sound.
Bebop checkerboard, Thelonious strips breaking the pattern.

Flag of Brazil stitched in with Jimi's bandana,
Ludwig's cape speckled with bangles of Mariah.
Renaissance madrigals scrawled on Springsteen denim,
And still room for Louie's handkerchief.

Tattered squares in the center, childhood photos, old man's cap,
The well-oiled palm of a catcher's mitt,
A faded letter from first love, still with her scent,
A speeding ticket.

Bring this quilt to the bandstand, unfurl it, let it be seen.
Drape it over Cole's melodies,
Spread it over Jerome's harmonies,
Wrap it around Monk's rhythms.

This quilt is all the things you are,
And it belongs to everyone.

– Randy Halberstadt, March 2001

Chapter 2

Jazz Concert Tonight!

The usher hands you a program as you walk into the concert hall. You take your seat and begin to read.

Tonight's concert will feature two groups, the Backstage Jazz Quartet and the Front and Center (F&C) Jazz Quartet. The Backstage derives its name from the fact that it never actually performs in public; it only performs backstage, out of earshot. The F&C Jazz Quartet, consisting of some of the best jazz musicians in the country, will perform onstage. Each quartet consists of bass, piano, drums, and tenor sax.

The two quartets will play the same program simultaneously, but their treatment of the music will be very different. Each Backstage musician will have a very specific role to play:

> **PIANO:** Play rooted chords, right on the downbeat.
> **BASS:** Play roots only, right on the downbeat.
> **DRUMS:** Play standard swing with repetitive ride cymbal and no surprises.
> **SAX:** Play the melody exactly as written. Improvise in strict time over the original chord changes.

These musicians will only be able to hear themselves. Each member of the esteemed F&C quartet, on the other hand, will wear an earphone through which he can hear the Backstage musicians. Then he will respond in this way:

> **PIANO:** Listen to the Backstage pianist (and the rest of his quartet) through the earphone and simply play along. Make musical comments that agree or in some cases disagree with that performance. Make no special effort to overtly produce the harmony of the tune because the Backstage pianist already has that covered.
>
> **BASS:** Similarly, just play along with the Backstage bassist. Don't feel at all obliged to play the root of every chord because he's already doing that.
>
> **DRUMS:** Play along with the Backstage drummer. Make no special effort to overtly produce the time since it's already there.
>
> **SAX:** Play the melody but feel free to leave it and come back to it since the Backstage saxophonist is already playing it. Improvise freely, and simply be aware of when your improvisation agrees or disagrees with the harmony and/or time.

Each F&C musician will listen and respond to his fellow onstage band members with his uncovered ear, often with great energy and joy. At no point, however, will he remove his earphone. He'll always be able to hear his Backstage counterpart quite clearly. Although he will have total freedom to play whatever he wants, he will always experience the convergence or conflict with his backstage counterpart.

The saxophonist may take only an occasional detour from the written melody then quickly resolve back into it. On the next tune he may leave out half the melodic phrases, opting instead to add comments to the Backstage saxophonist's straight version of the melody. The drummer may love the gritty feeling of one sound against another, so he may fight the Backstage drummer's beat with one of his own for several bars at a time. Perhaps the F&C pianist will intentionally voice his chords ambiguously, simultaneously implying multiple tonalities rather than delineating the home key as clearly as the Backstage pianist does. The F&C bassist may slur up to the roots to achieve a temporary tension against the solid note he hears from backstage; or he may leave almost all the roots to his counterpart and choose instead to improvise a line in his upper register. Each F&C musician will respond to conflicts in his own way, maintaining or resolving tensions as the mood hits him.

We hope you enjoy the concert!

The lights dim and the curtain opens. The quartet launches into the first tune, "Autumn Leaves." It quickly becomes evident that this is not like any "Autumn Leaves" you've ever heard. At any one moment as few as one musician and as many as four are in disagreement with the tune as played by the Backstage Quartet. Just when the saxophonist is returning from a melodic side trip, the pianist is embarking on a harmonic one. Just when the drummer superimposes five against the Backstage drummer's four, the bassist is investigating an alternative route to lead to the first chord in the next phrase.

An accomplished jazz musician hears harmony, melody, and time in his head as profoundly and accurately as if they were actually being played. Then he simply plays what he hears. Whether he plays in accord or in conflict with the elements of a tune doesn't matter. As long as he's responding to those elements, he's playing that tune.

Imagine that the F&C bassist's earphone goes dead in the middle of the performance, and he can no longer hear the roots being played by the Backstage bassist. Without the original tune to anchor him, his playing loses all intelligence. Similar problems arise if the drummer can't hear the beat, the saxophonist can't hear the melody or the pianist can't hear the chords. Very simply, a musician can only play and improvise over a tune maturely if he hears all the elements of a tune accurately in his head.

Each of the F&C musicians seems to be freely playing whatever he hears at the moment. The music has an exhilarating sense of immediacy. Suddenly you come to an astounding realization: you're not lost! Somehow you know exactly where the musicians are

Chapter 2

with respect to the harmony, melody, and time. In other words, you can deduce exactly what the Backstage musicians are playing solely by the responses of the F&C musicians! In fact, you realize that the overlapping tensions and releases between the two quartets are an integral part of your enjoyment of the music. If you couldn't hear the Backstage performance in your mind, the F&C music would sound like so much chaos.

And so the concert goes, with each tune more fascinating than the last. You actually feel that you're a part of the music—and in a very real way, you are. The raw data being sent to you by the F&C quartet is encrypted, disguised. They include just enough hints in their playing so that you can reconstruct the harmony, melody, and tempo of each tune. In that sense, you become a fifth member of the group. The F&C quartet supplies you with a connect-the-dots puzzle that only becomes a beautiful landscape when you complete it.

This then is jazz at its best. It is what jazz musicians strive for—the magic that occurs between musicians and the music, between musicians as individuals, and between musicians and listeners.

Part II **In The Practice Studio**

Building something is much easier if you have the right tools. In this section you'll learn basic practice approaches to help you process information, set priorities, and avoid pitfalls.

Chapter 3

Jazz Is Freedom, But...

You just learned a tune—or did you? How are you playing the melody? Do you take some rhythmic or melodic freedoms with it? After all, no one wants to hear a stiff version of the melody that comes out the same way each time. And what about the chord progression and the specific voicings that you use—do they vary each time? After all, jazz is about personal expression and spontaneity, isn't it?

It's time to be brutal with yourself. Do you know how the melody really goes? Does it come out different each time because you hear it that way, or is it just that you don't really know exactly how it goes? Are you changing your voicing approach at the bridge for musical reasons, or is it just too physically awkward to continue the same approach once the key changes? And why are you playing the tune in a rubato style? Is that a purely musical decision, or is it because you can't quite play the tune in steady time?

One of the most wonderful aspects of jazz is its sense of freedom, the potential for anything to happen at any time. A good jazz musician rediscovers a tune each time he plays it—not just in his improvised solo but also in the way he phrases the melody and voices the chords. But be very clear on this point: that same musician knows the tune in its original form. Only after he pays homage to the composer by learning the exact notes, rhythms, and harmony of the tune does he proceed to re-interpret it in his own style. Those original facts of the tune represent the center line around which a good musician will take freedoms. If you don't know those facts, then you're essentially passing along a rumor every time you play the tune.

Then how should you learn a tune? Multi-dimensionally. Get your hands on the original published version of the song. Get a lead-sheet version or two from some reputable fake books (such as Sher Music Co.'s New Real Books). By all means, listen to and transcribe a recording or two, especially if there's an early definitive recording. These versions will rarely agree with each other, but if you're familiar with them all you'll be able to reconcile them intelligently. Yes, this is a lot of work just to learn one tune, but that's the price of maturity. At this point you can say that you've done your homework and you know how the tune really goes. Now you can deviate from the original tune with confidence, secure in the knowledge that your variations are coming from the right place.

A young jazz musician often struggles to reconcile the opposing concepts of freedom and discipline in jazz. He will convince himself that he's exercising his freedom when he's really just being undisciplined. Watch out for this trap. Be brutal with yourself. Learn the tune precisely. Then do your thing.

The Censor in the Brain

From very early on in my development as a jazz musician, I have placed a tremendous amount of importance on being able to play exactly what I hear. I think of myself essentially as a scat singer. To that end I've studied theory, worked on ear-training drills, practiced improvising at very slow tempos, picked out melodies in twelve keys, and transcribed and learned to play my own scat solos. The end result is that I've become very adept at playing what I hear. The piano strings are like my vocal cords.

Of course, the key to expanding what you hear is to listen, listen, listen. Listen to jazz played on your instrument as well as on other instruments, and listen to singers. Listen to other styles of music: classical, rock, ethnic, etc. The more listening you do, the richer and more interesting your own improvising will become.

But I've noticed a strange phenomenon in my own development as an improviser—one that has nothing to do with listening. Unbeknownst to me, it begins when I start practicing some technically challenging material, perhaps for an upcoming performance. Usually this is music that is fully written out. In the course of practicing, I introduce my hands to patterns that don't occur naturally during my normal improvising. I work out the fingering for these new shapes and I practice them until I can play them in polished form, up to speed. After the performance I usually move on to the next challenge and leave that material behind. But here's the curious thing: a month or two later I find that my improvising has become more interesting. Almost overnight I seem to be hearing a lot of new ideas, and I can execute them cleanly.

What happened? I was so busy practicing the specific material that I didn't really listen to much other music, so I obviously didn't get my new ideas from listening. Where did they come from? The answer is that those ideas were not new at all. I'd probably heard them with my inner ear for years, but only now that my technical ability had improved could I gain access to them.

It's as if I have a censor in my brain. As I'm improvising, a specific line spontaneously comes to me. This is not something I create with my knowledge of theory or by any other means. It simply comes into being as an organic synthesis of all the music I've heard, combined with the sound of the prevailing harmony, and several other factors. It's a microcosm of my musical personality. This line is sent to the censor for examination. He may decide, "No problem: I'll allow this through." He sends it on to my conscious mind. Only then do I actually know that I'm hearing the idea. Just as that happens, it comes out on the keyboard, fully realized.

Or the censor may examine the idea and say, "Yeah, right—in his dreams! I'm not letting this thing through. It's a great idea, but he can't play it yet. He doesn't have the chops. I'll send another idea through instead. It's not exactly what he's hearing, but it's pretty close, and he can play it." So I play the substitute idea, never even knowing that I

Chapter **4**

settled for second best. I think I'm playing what I hear, but I'm really playing what my hands are willing to execute. And this is precisely why I seem to be hearing so many new ideas after my technique improves. The ideas are not new at all. They are old ideas that my censor is finally willing to let through.

Practice music that expands your technical abilities in many ways. Listening to jazz will enrich and deepen what you're hearing in your inner ear. Developing your technique will serve to lull your censor to sleep so that more of that wonderful music will actually see the light of day.

How Slow Is Slow?

Practicing is the means by which you progress from imperfection to perfection. You select something that you can't do and you work on it until you can do it. Perhaps your definition of perfection looks something like this:

1) Right notes
2) Accurate rhythms
3) Correct tempo

Or maybe you also insist on the right articulation and dynamics. After all, the music doesn't really come to life until you shape it. And what about fingering? If your fingering isn't consistent, the line will feel different to your hand every time. So let's add those elements to the list.

4) Good articulation and dynamics
5) Consistent fingering

That should be enough, right? Not quite. The final item on the list should be this one:

6) Right state of mind

To play a line of music perfectly, you must be able to toss it off as if it were no challenge at all. You should be bored. If you have to make the first five elements happen instead of simply letting them happen, then you don't know that line yet. You may stumble on it in performance because you're thinking about other things. The line needs to run itself.

Is it really necessary to add that element to the definition? After all, your state of mind will settle down the more you practice the first five elements. Well, perhaps this is true. But to some extent, your practicing mind works like a camcorder. It records every action that you intended to record, plus everything else that you didn't. If you practice too fast, your state of mind will best be described as panic. In addition to practicing the right notes, rhythms, tempo, articulation, dynamics and fingering, you'll also be practicing panic—as if you intended to learn it. That line may sound unsettled for months or years because of the way you initially practiced it.

So the alternative is to consciously practice the correct state of mind. As you play the line you need to be thinking, "This is so easy. I could play this line all day and never make a mistake." To achieve this you only need to alter one of the elements: the tempo.

You already know that you should practice slowly. Few students, however, understand what a truly slow practice tempo is. Instead, they practice at what I would call a slow performance tempo, which may be three times as fast. A slow practice tempo is one at

Chapter 5

which you can consciously control all the various elements with ease. That means that you have time to send individual messages from the brain to the hand to control the notes, rhythms, articulation, dynamics, and fingering—and you even have time left over to think how easy it all is!

Most students have a tough time counting off such slow tempos. Playing this slowly can be very challenging at first because it's difficult to feel the beat. Try this exercise:

Choose a short melodic line, four measures or so. Set your metronome to one beat per second (sixty beats per minute). At first, count "1 2 3 4" until you're comfortable with the tempo. Now, without changing the tempo, just change your words to "1 and uh 2 and uh 3 and uh 4 and uh," thereby tripling the actual length of each beat.

Seconds	1	2	3	4	5	6	7	8	9	10	11	12
At first, count	1	2	3	4	1	2	3	4	1	2	3	4
Then change the count to:	1	and	uh	2	and	uh	3	and	uh	4	and	uh

Now you're counting very slow eighth note triplets, one per second. Each quarter note takes three seconds, and a measure of 4/4 takes twelve seconds! Make sure you can also count swing eighth notes:

Seconds	1	2	3	4	5	6	7	8	9	10	11	12
Count:	1		uh	2		uh	3		uh	4		uh

Now play the line of music at this tempo, making sure to align every note with the appropriate subdivision. It may be unsettling at first to play this slowly, but at least you should find it easy to get to the notes on time with the right fingering. Practice it at this tempo until all the elements are in place and you're a little bit bored, then gradually inch up the tempo. Maintain the same sense of ease throughout.

Now let's re-examine the opening sentence in this chapter: "Practicing is the means by which you progress from imperfection to perfection." I know I wrote it, but I don't really believe it. Here's what I really think: practicing is the means by which you progress from one form of perfection to another—from conscious-control perfection to autopilot perfection.

Everyone knows how good it feels to play fast. When you tear through a piece at break-neck speed, it can be very exciting. But the trick here is to discover how equally good it can feel to play very slowly. To play a piece of music with total control can provide its own form of exhilaration. It can make you feel like a well-oiled machine. The problem is that most musicians think of slow playing as a "should" (as in, "I'll play this slowly because I should, then I'll speed it up so I can enjoy it"). If that's how you feel about it, you won't play slowly for long enough, and the tempos you choose won't be slow enough.

Chapter 5

Don't think of slow playing as a beginner's issue. When I am first learning to improvise over a tune, I take the tempo way down. I could probably play a competent solo at a much faster tempo, but it wouldn't be a rewarding experience for me. Slowing down the tempo allows me to find my own personal song over the chord changes—it allows me to taste the chords. You've probably heard the axiom, "There are no wrong notes in jazz." It's true that every member of the chromatic scale can be made to work over any chord. It is also true that each chord implies a certain set of notes that are inside (and right) or outside (and wrong, meaning "use them at your own risk"). But the most rigorous perspective is that there is only one right note: the one that I hear at that moment. If the chord is Cmi7 and the correct improvising scale is Bb major, the note G is usually a perfectly valid note to play. But if the sound in my head is an F, the G is a wrong note. It's not what I'm hearing. So by slowing the tune down, I'm able to play exactly the notes that I hear.

Your reasons for playing slowly may be different (staying within the correct scales, playing with solid time, etc.). But whatever the motivation, slow tempos are a vital practice tool for players at every level. So how slow is slow? A teacher once said to me, "Anyone can play Grieg's Piano Concerto perfectly the first time—as long as he plays it slowly enough."

Chapter **6**

The Sequencer

> **Treat this whole chapter as a practice box. Don't just read it—do it!**

Here's a no-nonsense method for practicing new material. Master it and you'll be able to learn in fifteen minutes what used to take two hours.

Cole Porter's "Everything I Love" begins with these five chords:

Here's what most students play in order to learn those chords:

They may need to play it fifty times to overcome the mistakes—that's 200 measures!

Here's how I recommend learning that same progression:

EXERCISE 6.1

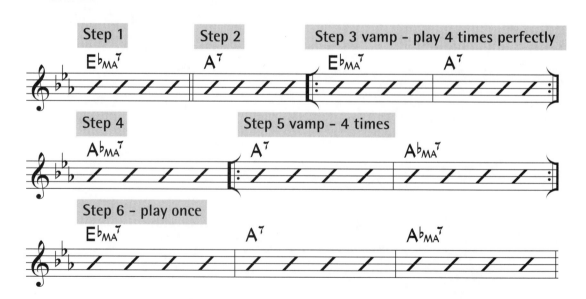

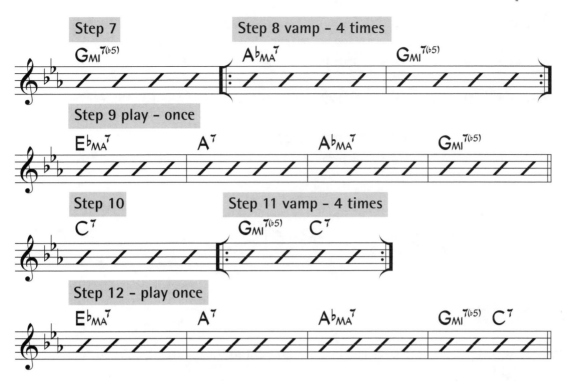

If you play each vamp four times, that's still only 44 measures altogether—quite an improvement on 200!

Each time you add a new chord to the sequence, take the time to observe its appearance on the keyboard. For example, C7 in second inversion (G Bb C E) is "white-black-white-white on G, clustered in the middle." (Observing the cluster will prevent you from confusing the chord with Gmi7, which is another white-black-white-white chord on G.)

Before you practice a two-chord vamp, take the time to observe which of your fingers move and which don't. Let's say that you just learned the C7. Now you're going to play a Gmi7(b5) C7 vamp. If you learned the Gmi7(b5) in root position (G Bb Db F), make this observation: "In going from Gmi7(b5) to C7, I move only the top two notes: Db and F both come down a half-step to C and E. The bottom notes (G and Bb) are anchors." Then play the vamp. Play it without looking at the keyboard.

So here it is, the **"Sequencer!"**:

Learn each chord in three ways:

1. By itself (observe the white-black picture)
2. In conjunction with the previous chord (observe "anchors" and "movers," and then play without looking at the keyboard)
3. In the context of the entire progression up to that point (again, don't look at the keyboard)

Chapter 6

Why don't I call this the "Chord Sequencer?" Because it's much bigger than that: it's a way of learning any sequence of events, musical or otherwise. You could use it to learn a written melody, measure by measure.

Measure #   (1)   (2 / 12)   (3 / 23/ 123)   (4/ 34/ 1234)   (5 / 45/ 12345) etc.

You could even apply it to improvising. Here's the "Everything I Love" progression again with recommended scales for improvising:

EXERCISE 6.2

Improvise with each scale over the appropriate chord (or chords) until you feel comfortable.

EXERCISE 6.3

Now practice the transition from the previous scale to the current one.

Now go back to the beginning and improvise through the current scale.

Maybe you don't like using scales as an approach to improvising, opting instead to outline the notes of each chord. Obviously the Sequencer still works. Just outline the first chord, then the second, then the first two, then the third, then the second and third, then the first three—you get the idea.

For that matter, you can use the Sequencer to learn a sequence of dance steps, a list of names, a set of instructions—any fixed order of events.

If you try the Sequencer you'll be convinced of its value. I won't need to sell you on it. But if you do need to be persuaded before you give it a try, consider this:

You were probably brought up to believe that hard work is a virtue. "If at first you don't succeed, try, try again." Well, that's a hard philosophy to argue with, isn't it? Not at all, not once I paraphrase it: "Pick something difficult and try to do it. Fail. Don't worry if it's terrible today because you already knew it would be. It doesn't have to be perfect until you sweat at it for three weeks. Sloppy effort and unfocused concentration are O.K. for the time being, because you're just getting started. Fail again and again. Fail tomorrow. Fail every day—just a little less. Finally, after three weeks and 999 failures, succeed. Be very impressed with attempt #1000. Stop practicing it, now that you've achieved your goal. Try it again in a month and be devastated to discover that your chances of success are approximately 1 out of 1000." After all, that's what you did: you played it 1000 times and only one of them was perfect.

Now compare that to the philosophy behind the Sequencer: "Chew off a small bite and learn it well. Chew off another and do the same. Glue the bites together until they feel like one thing. Learn a third small item. Glue it to the first pair until it becomes a unit. Just keep learning one small thing at a time and integrating it into a whole." That's it!

Chapter **7**

Balancing Act

Improvise over a I VI II V progression in Eb major, using your best tone and a solid groove. Play right notes, whatever that means to you (staying within the correct scales, outlining the chord tones, or just carefully playing the pitches you hear). Try to express coherent ideas, not just notes. This usually involves playing short motifs and developing them through repetition or by shifting them up or down within the scale (Refer to "You're Repeating Yourself (hopefully)" on page 49.)

Now improvise again over the progression. This time play with the right notes, good tone, and coherent ideas but with terrible time. Skip beats, add beats, drag, rush, hesitate—you get the idea. See what it does to the quality of your playing.

Now try it again. Restore the good groove to your playing and keep the right notes and the coherent ideas but play with a bad tone. (This may be an easier assignment for horn players than for piano players.) So how does this sound?

O.K., now play the right notes with great tone and great time, but no ideas. Don't repeat any motifs and don't use many rests. Just wander around. Remember to try for the best note choice you can (such as a bebop-oriented line which clearly communicates the harmony underneath). Again, see what happens to the quality of your overall sound.

So you must know what's up next: great time, great tone, great ideas — but all wrong notes. This may be a little disconcerting at first. Just play a wrong scale or outline a wrong chord. But play like you mean it. All the other elements (time, tone, and ideas) must be strong. What do you think?

This exercise is about setting priorities. It's about knowing what's most important so that you can make intelligent choices if something's gotta give in your solo. I have my own feelings about those priorities, but you can come to your own conclusion.

To me there's no question that time is the single most important element. If I hear a solo with bad time, I have to leave the room (at least figuratively speaking). No matter how intelligent the ideas are or how elegant the language is, that solo will just make me feel agitated and irritable. If I can tap my foot or snap my fingers to a solo, if there's a real pocket to the time feel, then I'll enjoy it no matter what other problems arise. I'd much rather hear wrong notes than bad time.

I also can't appreciate a solo if it sounds like it's coming from the pinched mouth of a balloon. Imagine trying to listen to Coltrane's "Giant Steps" solo performed by a kazoo player with a sinus infection. I can be swept away by a musician's beautiful tone and not care whether he improvises or even expresses coherent ideas. I just want him to keep making that beautiful sound.

When ideas are removed from the mix, it doesn't sound too bad. It wanders, yes, but improvised lines often do that while the musician is searching for the next nugget to mine. If the tone and time feel are good and if the notes reflect both the underlying harmony and the history of the music, the sound works quite well for a while. It's as if the improviser is making a speech, using beautiful diction and making eloquent use of the language. The listener is happy just to hear the words flow from his mouth for a while, but eventually he'll want him to say something important. That's where the ideas come in.

I hope you discovered something when you played with all wrong notes. When I do it, I make a point of playing with very good time and using a lot of very clear motivic development. What I find is that the sound can be strangely refreshing. Wrong notes are usually accompanied by shaky time and a complete lack of direction in the line. But when you play them like you mean them, it has a remarkable effect. You discover the power of intent. If you came to a similar conclusion, then ask yourself why you would ever play with bad time in order to get the right notes.

While I'm elevating time, tone, and ideas to a higher status, I'm not for a moment minimizing the importance of correct notes. My personal bar graph looks like this:

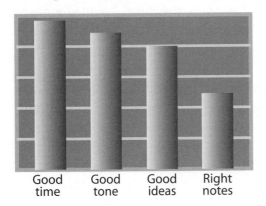

Good time   Good tone   Good ideas   Right notes

Again, yours may be different, either in the actual order of priorities or in the relative degrees of importance. All I care about is that you spend some time thinking about these issues.

Chapter **8**

Target Bombing

There is no substitute for practice. By spending a couple of hours with your instrument every day you develop a special relationship with it. You need to have a regular practice routine that contains certain constant elements (such as warm-up exercises) as well as variable elements that address your current avenue of study. And performing doesn't count as practice. Although playing gigs is an essential part of your musical development, it won't replace time in the practice room.

There are times, however, when you just can't maintain a regular practice routine. All the other elements of your life crowd in and you find you have to grab a spare hour of practice wherever you can. It seems futile to embark on any long-range practice projects that will require weeks or months of steady work, because you know it won't happen. So should you just give up? Must you put off the idea of improving your musicianship until you have more time (and are you sure that time will come)? Here's an alternative—I call it "target bombing."

You have an hour to practice. Find something to practice that is not currently in your arsenal. It could be a lick, a scale, a set of chord voicings, a section of a tune, a transcribed solo, anything. But this is important: it must be small. Don't set a general goal (e.g., mastering the McCoy Tyner style of pentatonic scale improvisation). Instead, select a little piece of business (such as a particular pentatonic lick to be learned in 12 keys). Assume that this is the only opportunity you'll have to learn this particular item. Tomorrow you'll move on to something else.

Approach the hour's practice with this attitude: "What can I do within the next hour to permanently improve my musicianship in one very small but measurable way?" More specifically, "What can I do to master this one item so that it will be self-reinforcing, so that it will immediately begin to show up in my actual performances?" Your plan is to devour this one small thing so completely that it can't slip away. If it's a lick, make it a short one and learn it in several keys. Work out the fingering. Play it over random II-V progressions. Solo over a few tunes and work that lick in wherever you can. If it's a chord voicing, practice it in 12 keys, work it into tunes, and make sure you can make smooth transitions to and from other voicings. If you don't get it by the end of the hour, you lose it forever. But if you ingest it fully enough, then it will immediately begin to show up in your performances. It will become a small element of your style and you'll never lose it.

This is target bombing. It's intense, focused, and can be tremendously effective and satisfying. Although at first it may be a method that you use because you can't find time for the more traditional, routine-oriented practice, you may find it so successful and fun that you make it your primary approach. After all, you climb a mountain with thousands of small steps. Take each step so well that you never have to take it again.

Chapter **8**

I've seen this approach work wonders for many students, and I use it all the time myself. I've also seen it fail miserably for others. It requires a type of tunnel vision, a willingness to gnaw on one thing for one hour without letting other concerns intrude. You might feel as if you are playing when you should be working or that focusing on a tiny area is not productive when there are so many major areas to be covered. But once you successfully target bomb a few small items, you'll realize the needlessness of your concerns. Anyway, try this method on—see if it fits your style.

Chapter **9**

Don't Sing While You Play

I've heard the rationales several times:

Singing while you improvise will develop your melodic sensibilities. Because you have to breathe, you'll develop a natural sense of phrasing. You'll play more natural lines, like a scat singer. Not to mention, a lot of people think it's cool. (After all, George Benson was a big hit when he did it.) Even Keith Jarrett does it.

Well, sorry, but I don't buy it. I find that someone who sings while he improvises is playing first and singing second; that is, the notes are coming out just as they would without the singing. The voice is simply getting pulled along. In many cases, the player is not even singing coherent pitches but only the general outline of what he's playing more clearly on his instrument. So singing doesn't develop your melodic concept because it doesn't change what you play in the first place. It's an add-on.

But what if I'm wrong? What if you decide that you really are singing first and playing second and that you really can improve your phrasing by singing? Then I need to warn you that if you sing and play at the same time the two behaviors will become permanently linked. You won't be able to play your instrument without singing along. You may have originally intended to sing only as a practice method, but suddenly you'll find it showing up on your gigs, in your recording sessions, as you accompany singers—everywhere!

The solution is simple. When you practice, sing the sound first. Then go back and play it. This way you know that your voice is leading your instrument and not the other way around. You'll retain all the benefits to your note choice and phrasing, and since you never sing and play at the same time there's no threat of linkage.

Are you wondering why I am so adamant about this, why I feel so strongly? Because I sing when I play. I've tried to stop, but my best efforts have met with only partial success. It's a bad habit, and I'd get rid of it in a second if I could. So don't get into the habit of singing while you play.

Part III **Painless Piano**

Whether you're a singer, saxophone player, bassist or
composer, a rudimentary knowledge of the piano can be
of great benefit. This section presents some quick ways of
learning inversions and scales on the piano. It will also
help you gain a sense of how to connect physically with the
instrument.

Chapter **10**

Inversions

Remember the early screensavers? Maybe you still have one on your computer. The words march across the screen from left to right, where they disappear only to show up again on the left. Fine, but what do screensavers have to do with inversions? Imagine chord tones instead of words marching from left to right. When you run out of fingers instead of screen, your chord tones show up an octave to the left and continue their march to the right.

Finger numbers

Before we continue, let's clear up some fingering terminology. This chapter deals specifically with inversions played with the left hand. In "piano speak," the thumb is referred to as the first finger. The index is the second finger, the middle finger is the third, the next finger is the fourth, and the pinky is the fifth.

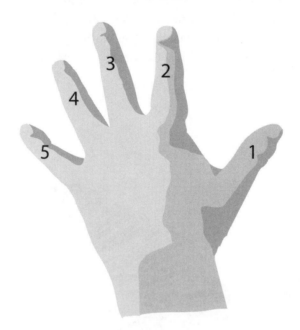

Screensaver inversions

Most people are taught to produce a second-inversion Bb7 in this time-consuming way:

1. Place your left pinky on the note Bb.
2. Build a root-position Bb7 from that note (Bb D F Ab)
3. Invert the chord by bringing Bb up an octave (D F Ab Bb). You'll need to pick up your hand and re-finger the chord.
4. Invert the chord again by bringing the D up an octave (F Ab Bb D). Again, you'll need to pick up your hand and re-finger the chord.

Here's a more streamlined approach — the screensaver way:

1. Place your 2nd finger on the note Bb.
2. Build the chord up to D (with the thumb).
3. Find the next chord tone above D (the fifth, F), but play it down an octave (with the pinky), then build up to the Ab (with the 3rd finger).

That's it — you're done! The first approach requires that you place your hand on one shape (Bb7 in root position), change it to another shape (first inversion), then change it again to get to second inversion. The new approach places your hand immediately on the final product.

Try another chord in second inversion: Abma7. Place your 2nd finger on Ab. Put your thumb on C. Look to the right of that C: the next chord tone is Eb. Play Eb down an octave with the pinky. Now finish building the chord from that Eb, placing your 3rd finger on the G. It's easy to remember: to produce a second inversion chord, reach for the root with the 2nd finger.

Now how about a first inversion chord C7? You guessed it: put your 1st finger (the thumb) on C. Find the next chord tone above C (the third, E). Play the E down an octave with the pinky. Finish building the chord from that E (G and Bb with the 3rd and 2nd fingers, respectively).

Try it with Dmi7(b5). "Thumb" the D, find the F above but play it down an octave with the pinky, then finish off with Ab and C. So, for first inversion chords, reach for the root with the 1st finger.

So guess how you start a third inversion chord? In a fair world, you'd begin with the 3rd finger. Instead, you need to reach for the root with the 4th finger. In fact, you won't use the 3rd finger at all. Let's try it with F#mi7. Place your 4th finger on F#. Build the chord up, placing the 2nd finger (not the 3rd) on A and the thumb on C#. Find the next chord tone (the 7th, E), but play it down an octave with the pinky. That's it.

Try a DbMa7 in third inversion. Place the 4th finger on Db, then build up to F and Ab (with the 2nd finger and the thumb). Find the C above, but play it underneath the Db with the pinky.

If you review what you've learned so far, you'll realize that the fingering is 5321 for chords in root position, first inversion, and second inversion. Only for third inversion chords, where you begin by placing your 4th finger on the root, do you end up with a 5421 fingering.

Chapter 10

To produce any inversion in the left hand:

1. Place the appropriate finger on the root:

Inversion	Root finger
Root position	5
1st inversion	1
2nd inversion	2
3rd inversion	4

2. Build the chord up until you run out of fingers.
3. Looking further up the keyboard, decide what the next note should be, then play it down an octave with the pinky.
4. Finish building the chord from the pinky.

> Play Eb7 in all its positions (root position, first inversion, second inversion, and third inversion). Do this with several chords of different types (for example, GMa7, Abdim7, C#mi7).

If you can play inversions with your left hand and a single note line with your right, you can play a simple tune. A professional pianist uses more sophisticated voicings (refer to "Voicings 101", page 227), but this is a good, straightforward way to get started playing tunes from lead sheets.

Choosing the right inversion

But which inversions should you play? You need to play the chords in a fairly narrow range just below middle C so that they flow together smoothly and don't sound muddy or thin.

> Play FMa7 in root position (F A C E) so that your index finger ends up on middle C. This is a perfect example of the ideal range.
>
> Play the same FMa7 in second inversion, so that your pinky is on middle C. This is too high. While it may not actually sound too thin, you'll find it difficult to play melodies with your right hand because the left-hand chord is often in the way.
>
> Now play that second inversion FMa7 down a full octave, so that the entire chord is below middle C. For most situations this is too low. It sounds a bit muddy.
>
> Play the FMa7 in third inversion, with your thumb on middle C. This is not far from the root position placement, and it would be fine to play the chord in this way.
>
> Play the FMa7 in first inversion, with the third finger on middle C. This would also be fine.

Here's a neat little system for choosing the single best inversion for each chord. Once you understand the system, you can loosen the strings to include other acceptably close inversions.

With your left hand play a chromatic scale from E below middle C to Eb above middle C, using this fingering: 5 5 5 5 4 4 2 2 2 2 1 1:

Now here's how you should use this scale. Let's say you wish to play a Bb7 in the ideal range. Simply consider what finger you used to play the note Bb in the chromatic scale. You used the second finger—so place the second finger on Bb and build the chord in second inversion. That's the ideal range for that chord.

Now try F7. The pinky goes on F, so that will result in a root position chord. Try Ab7. The fourth finger goes on Ab, so it should be played in third inversion. For D7 place your thumb on D and play the chord in first inversion.

Play all four of these chords in succession, with the appropriate inversions.

Bb7 (second inversion)   F7 (root position)   Ab7 (third inversion)   D7 (first inversion)

Observe how smoothly you can move from one chord to the next. All the chords are in the ideal range, so there's very little transitional movement. Not only is it easier to play the progression this way, but it also sounds better. We say that the progression now features smooth voice leading.

Now play this chord progression with appropriate inversions:

Gmi7 (root position)   C7 (second inversion)   FMa7 (root position)   D7 (first inversion)

Very smooth, isn't it? Not only does it sound better to place all the chords in the same range, but they're also much easier to play. In fact, you can probably play this chord progression without having to look at the keyboard. Work out the chord inversions in this way for a few of your favorite tunes.

Chapter **10**

There are times when you'll want to use a different inversion than the system suggests. Sometimes the melody dips into a lower range and the chord gets in the way. One way to solve this problem is to lower the chord by one inversion (for example, from third to second). Be careful, though: don't move the chord down so low that it sounds muddy. You may have to play the correct inversion instead, and simply leave off a note or two in order to fit in the right-hand melody.

One of the purposes of the system is to produce smooth voice leading, but sometimes it does the opposite. Consider the progression: Emi7 Gmi7. According to the system, you should play both of these chords in root position. That requires a jump from the first chord to the second. But if you play the Gmi7 in third inversion (F G Bb D), you'll find that it's in the same range as the Emi7. This is easier to play, and it sounds better.

Limitations

This system is to be used for one thing only: to choose the best inversions for left-hand chords that are played below a right-hand melody or improvisation. If you're playing a bass line in the left hand and chords in the right hand, you'll find that you can play some of your chords higher than before. It's not so much that the higher left-hand chords sound thin; it's just that they tend to get in the way of your right-hand melody. Now that the chords are in your right hand, you'll find that the octave above middle C is not so bad after all.

User-friendly Scales

> **Treat this whole chapter as a practice box. Don't just read it – do it!**

Scales are an essential part of a pianist's toolbox. Like any tool they can be misused or used too primitively, but in the right hands they can lead to some great music. Unfortunately, they present a barrier to many young musicians. That's partly due to the way that scales are often taught, as if they are such complex structures that each one requires a week to learn. In this chapter I want to demystify scales--major scales, to begin with, and then the minors—so that you can learn them easily.

You probably already know how to find the notes of a major scale. If not, use the "two-wholes-and-a-half, three-wholes-and-a-half" technique. For example, start on A and build those intervals (whole step, whole step, half step, whole step, whole step, whole step, half step). You should find the notes A B C# D E F# G# A. You can also probably find the right notes by ear.

Right-hand fingering for C, D, E, G, A, and B major scales

Using both hands, hold down these six notes on the piano (C D E G A B):

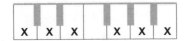

These are the starting notes for six major scales that use the same fingering: 1 2 3 1 2 3 4 5 (where the thumb is the first finger and the pinky is the fifth finger). Practice each of these scales up and down for one octave.

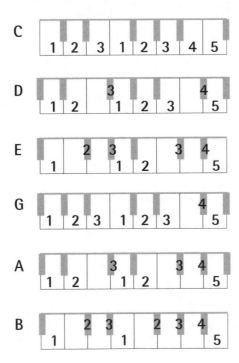

Chapter **11**

Right-hand fingering for Db, Eb, F, Gb, Ab, and Bb major scales

Now hold down the other six notes (Db, Eb, F, Gb, Ab, Bb):

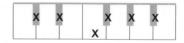

It would be convenient if I could now show you a fingering which works for these six scales, but the truth is that each of them has its own fingering. For example, Db major is fingered 2 3 1 2 3 4 1 2, while Gb major uses 2 3 4 1 2 3 1 2. But fear not: there's a way to learn all six fingerings without having to memorize them. Touch the group of two black notes (Db and Eb) with the second and third fingers. Then pick up your hand and set it on the group of three black notes (Gb, Ab, and Bb) with the second, third, and fourth fingers:

Remember, we're discussing the fingering for the second group of six scales (Db, Eb, F, Gb, Ab, and Bb). Each of these scales has at least one black note; some have all five blacks. Here's what you need to know: every Db gets the 2nd finger, every Eb gets the 3rd finger, every Gb gets the 2nd finger, every Ab gets the 3rd finger, and every Bb gets the 4th finger, just as the last diagram shows. This rule doesn't tell you what black notes will occur in a particular scale, but it does explain how to finger the ones that do. Let's call it the black note rule.

Here's the white note rule: as you go up the keyboard, always place your thumb on each white note that follows a black.

If you follow this rule, your black-note fingering will take care of itself. Here's how the six scales look with these two rules in effect:

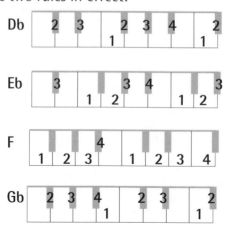

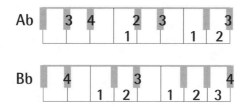

Practice each of these scales up and down for one octave.

Playing scales beyond one octave

Here's one final fingering rule: when you play a scale for more than one octave, begin each octave with the same finger. That's already happening for the scales that begin on black notes. The Db major scale, for example, begins and ends with the 2nd finger, so it's very natural to continue into the second octave:

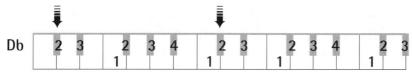

The one-octave fingering for the F major scale begins with the thumb but ends with the 4th finger. Replace the fourth finger with the thumb if you want to continue for another octave:

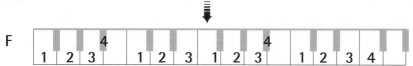

A similar adjustment is necessary for the first six scales we discussed (C, D, E, G, A, and B). The one-octave fingering begins with the thumb but ends with the pinky. Replace the pinky with the thumb to continue for another octave:

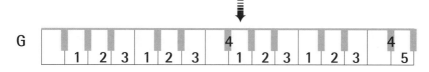

Chapter **11**

In summary, the fingering rules for major scales are:

1. For C, D, E, G, A, and B major, use a 1 2 3 1 2 3 4 5 fingering.
2. For Db, Eb, F, Gb, Ab, and Bb major, follow two rules:
   a) Use these fingers on the black notes: Db-2, Eb-3, Gb-2, Ab-3, Bb-4
   b) On the way up, thumb the first white note after a black.
3. When you play a scale for more than one octave, begin each octave with the same finger.

Slowly practice all twelve major scales up and down for three octaves.

The magic of 3-groups and 4-groups

If you don't already know your major scales fairly well, you're probably still missing some notes. You're almost certainly making some fingering mistakes. It's one thing to intellectually understand how to get to the right notes with the right fingers. It's another thing to make it happen in real time.

Imagine that you are playing a computerized keyboard. When you want to play an Ab major scale, you press the Ab button on a built-in console. Instantly, the five notes in each octave which are not members of the Ab major scale (D, E, F#, A, and B) recede into the bed of the keyboard, so that you can't even see them, much less play them. Meanwhile, each remaining note lights up with the correct finger number, just like the diagrams in this chapter. If you had such a magical keyboard, it would be impossible to play wrong notes, and it would be very difficult to use the wrong fingering. Here's a way of visualizing scales that will virtually have such an effect.

I'll start with an outrageous claim: the fingering for all twelve major scales is the same. This seems to directly contradict what I just taught you about fingering—i.e. that six scales share the same fingering, but that each of the other six scales has a different fingering. How can I reconcile these two points of view? Take a look at these six major scales, each presented in a three-octave range:

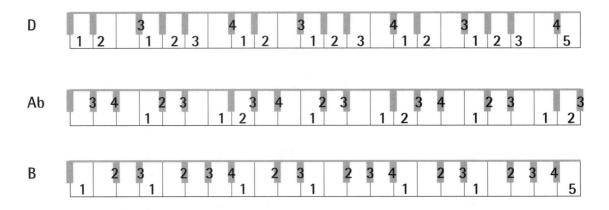

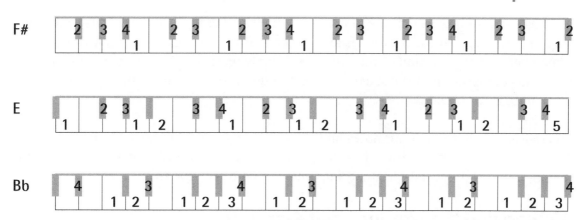

Now recite out loud the fingering for each of these scales. What do you hear? That's right: 123 1234. My point is that all twelve major scales do in a sense have the same fingering (123 1234 123 1234 etc.). Six of the scales (C, D, E, G, A, and B) begin that cycle right at the beginning, while the other six scales pick it up somewhere along the way. The reason that those six scales appear to have six different fingerings is that they pick up the cycle at six different places:

The Universal Fingering Chart

Db: 1**23 1234 12**3 1234 123 1234 123 1234

Eb: 12**3 1234 123** 1234 123 1234 123 1234

F: 123 **1234 123 1**234 123 1234 123 1234

Gb: 123 1**234 123 12**34 123 1234 123 1234

Ab: 123 12**34 123 123**4 123 1234 123 1234

Bb: 123 123**4 123 1234** 123 1234 123 1234

If you understand this, then you're beginning to see what my visualizing system is all about. Learn to think of a Bb major scale as a simple combination of these two note-groups:

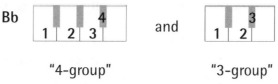

"4-group"   "3-group"

There is only one aspect of this scale-learning system that students often find challenging: starting a scale in the middle of a group. It can be disorienting at first to view a

Chapter **11**

scale as a pair of groups that are unrelated to the starting note. It's easy to fall into the trap of believing that the 3-group is always the first three notes of the scale. Just remember that the location of the groups is directly related to the fingering for the scale, not the location of the starting note. Any group that results in the thumb on a black note is wrong.

You're learning both the right notes and the right fingering all at once. Each of the twelve major scales has a distinct 3-group and 4-group. Find them and commit them to memory. There are several specific things you can do to achieve this:

Memorizing the 3-groups and 4-groups

1. Write them down on a keyboard chart (I've included one on page 307 in the appendix; make several copies before you fill it out so you can also do ones for the harmonic minor, melodic minor, etc.)
2. Speaking out loud, name and describe each group as a series of black and white notes. For example: "The 4-group for the Bb major scale has three whites and one black built on F." Verbalizing these descriptions will help lock them in.
3. Play the groups as clusters up and down for three octaves: i.e. play all the notes of the 3-group together like a chord, then play the 4-group, then the next 3-group, etc.
4. Same as 3), but play the notes one at a time. For example, set your hand on the Bb major scale 3-group (C, D, Eb) and play the notes in that order, one at a time. Then pick up your hand, set it on the 4-group (F, G, A, Bb), and play the notes one at a time."
5. Play the scale smoothly, saying "3-group" or "4-group" out loud as you enter each group. On the way up, you'll speak each time you play your thumb. On the way down, you'll speak each time you play the 3rd finger (entering the 3-group) or the 4th finger (entering the 4-group).
6. Improvise in the scale, jumping from one group to another. You can do this with just your right hand or you can add some appropriate left-hand chords. Always keep track of which group you're in.
7. Observe the patterns that emerge when you look at the completely filled-out keyboard chart:

> For C, D, E, G, A, and B major scales: the 3-group is always made up of the first three notes of the scale, and the 4-group is the last four notes. Also, every 3-group and 4-group is completely made up of whole steps (the half steps occur between the groups, not within them).

> For Db, Eb, F, Gb, Ab, and Bb major scales: The 4-groups all use the thumb on F and the 4th finger on Bb. All you need to do is figure out whether the G's and A's are flat or natural. In four of the six scales (Db, Eb, Ab, and Bb) the 3-groups use the thumb on C and the 3rd finger on Eb. Just decide whether the scale has a D or Db. The exceptions are F major (3-group: C D E) and Gb major (3-group: Cb Db Eb).

Chapter 11

Applying groups to improvising

This is a way of processing both the notes and the fingering for your scales so that you can play them up and down the keyboard with ease. But you'll mainly be using these scales for improvising. When you do, you won't often be running them up and down in straight lines. You'll select notes in various orders to create many different shapes. Sometimes you'll leap up and down using large intervals instead of scale steps. At this point the scale fingering will become irrelevant. You'll need to improvise a fingering that is appropriate to the shape of your line.

If the scale fingering is irrelevant when you improvise, doesn't that mean that the 3-groups and 4-groups are irrelevant as well? Nothing could be further from the truth. I referred to this approach as a visualizing system. When you improvise with the scale in a more jagged, large-interval fashion, you need to see all the notes of the scale at once so you can leap from one note to the next with confidence. If you visualize the scale as two clumps instead of seven individual notes, then you'll know where you're going. So the 3-group and 4-group help you to visualize the scale, even when you're not using the scale fingering.

Now you understand my computerized keyboard metaphor. When you know the 3-group and 4-group for a scale, it's as if the five non-scale tones simply disappear and you feel that you could play all day without missing a note. And if you do have the occasion to run the notes up or down as a smooth scale, it's as if the finger numbers magically appear on the notes.

Minor scales

You may already be aware that there are several types of minor scales:

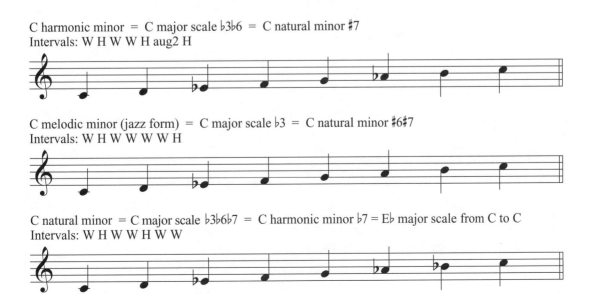

C harmonic minor = C major scale ♭3♭6 = C natural minor ♯7
Intervals: W H W W H aug2 H

C melodic minor (jazz form) = C major scale ♭3 = C natural minor ♯6♯7
Intervals: W H W W W W H

C natural minor = C major scale ♭3♭6♭7 = C harmonic minor ♭7 = E♭ major scale from C to C
Intervals: W H W W H W W

Chapter 11

If you know the 3-groups and 4-groups for your major scales, you can learn all your minor scales quickly. The trick is to think of a minor scale as having the same groups as the parallel major scale, with an alteration or two.

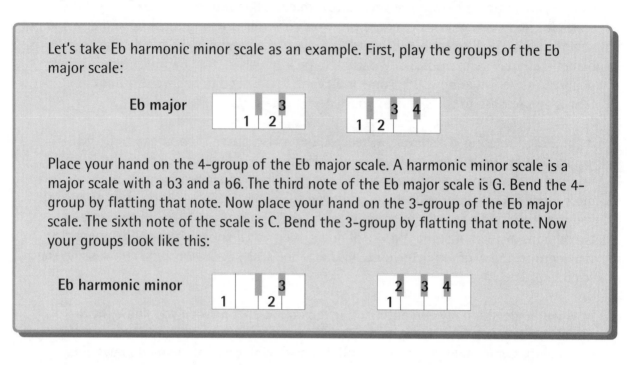

Let's take Eb harmonic minor scale as an example. First, play the groups of the Eb major scale:

Place your hand on the 4-group of the Eb major scale. A harmonic minor scale is a major scale with a b3 and a b6. The third note of the Eb major scale is G. Bend the 4-group by flatting that note. Now place your hand on the 3-group of the Eb major scale. The sixth note of the scale is C. Bend the 3-group by flatting that note. Now your groups look like this:

You can think of almost all your minor scales as bent major scales: simply place your hand on the major scale groups and flat the required notes. Once you've found the new groups, commit them to memory by writing them down on keyboard charts and verbalizing their descriptions. There are only three scales for which this bending process won't work. Here they are, with their correct fingering and groups:

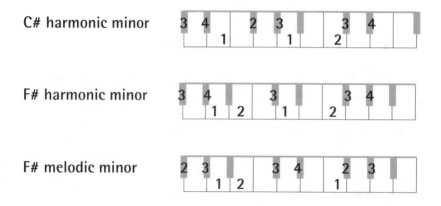

You'll have more luck with your natural minor scales if you learn the harmonic minor scales and their groups first. Then use this definition for the natural minor:

Natural minor: Harmonic minor b7

In every case, simply bend the harmonic minor groups by flatting the 7th note of the scale. In some cases, you'll arrive at the groups of the relative major scale. For example:

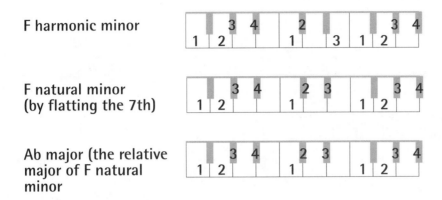

F harmonic minor

F natural minor
(by flatting the 7th)

Ab major (the relative
major of F natural
minor

In other cases, the groups will be new. For example:

G harmonic minor

G natural minor
(by flatting the 7th)

Bb major (the relative
major of G natural
minor)

It's because of this inconsistency that I don't recommend learning the natural minors in terms of their relative major scales. Instead, just bend the groups of the parallel harmonic minors by flatting the 7th. You'll always arrive at the correct groups.

> Find the 3-groups and 4-groups for a few harmonic and melodic minor scales by bending the parallel major scale groups. Now find the 3-groups and 4-groups for a few natural minor scales by bending the parallel harmonic minor groups.

You should fill out keyboard charts for your major, melodic minor, harmonic minor, and natural minor scales. Then memorize the 3-groups and 4-groups. You'll be able to play and improvise with the scales with much greater ease.

> Try improvising with a minor scale of your choice, always keeping track of which fingering group you're in.

Chapter **11**

Other scales

You can use groups to learn other scale types as well. Of course, if the scale doesn't have seven notes it won't have a 3-group and a 4-group: it may have two 3-groups, two 4-groups, or some other configuration. Here are some samples:

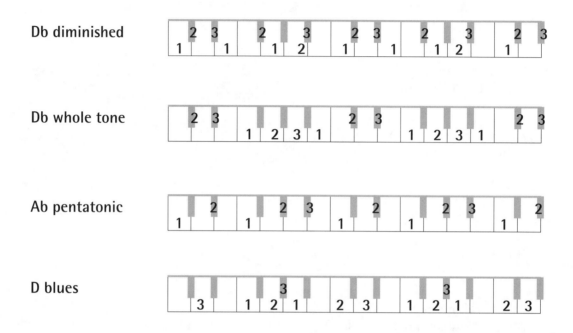

Db diminished

Db whole tone

Ab pentatonic

D blues

Again, try improvising with these scales while thinking in groups.

Weighted Keys

Here's a fairly simple thing to do which can improve your tone on the piano significantly. Hear the sound of a scale in your head, nice and slow. Imagine each note as a deep, full tone (as if sung by a warm, rich tenor voice). Now play that scale while imagining that the surface of each key is about 1/2" lower than it actually is. Drop each finger right through the actual key, as if it weren't there, to get to the imaginary key. Experience the feeling of weight into each note, and notice the effect on the sound.

Now try the same thing with a chord in the left hand. Pre-hear the chord in your head, resonant and warm, then drop all your fingers right through the actual surface of the keys as if they were lower than they are. Try a few different chords, repeating each one until it has the right weight. Now try it with some right-handed chords. Now do it with some two-handed chords. Now play the melody to a song with your right hand (start with a ballad) and try to get the same sense of weight into each key. Now play the melody in your left hand, then in octaves. Finally, play the chords and melody together, all on the imaginary lower keyboard.

As you can see, I've combined two techniques here that are designed to help you get the richest, deepest sound. One of them is to suspend your sense of the physical barrier of the keyboard surface, so that you can get "inside" the piano. The other one is to pre-hear the tone you want to produce. If you have the right sound in your head before you play, your body will make the adjustments necessary to get that sound as if by natural selection.

If you find this to be difficult, don't be discouraged. Come back tomorrow and try it again. If you've been playing a different way, your body is going to fight this change. It may take a few days or weeks before you really make the switch.

Chapter **13**

The Piano Is A Drum Set

Too many pianists seem to have forgotten that their instrument is classified as part of the percussion family. They spend so much energy and focus on the minute details, such as which note goes where, that they lose (or never get) the visceral connection with their instrument, the relaxed physicality that drummers have. It's no mystery why drummers often make the best jazz pianists. Listen to the great Cuban pianist Gonzalo Rubalcaba. He was originally a drummer, and you can always hear it in his playing.

In the following metaphor I have used absolutes to make a point strongly. I've minimized the importance of individual notes in favor of the larger elements of rhythm and shape. Certainly this is an injustice to a more complex truth. Undeniably, tension and release, occurring as one melody note moves to the next, is a vital and emotional part of music. To be able to spontaneously craft beautiful melodies on the piano while functioning also as a percussionist is just one of the many tightropes you must learn to walk as a musician.

However, much of the emotional content in music is to be found in its larger elements: the rhythms and the contours of the line as opposed to the individual notes. If you want to express your emotions freely, you need to be able to focus your attention on those elements. And you can only do that when the smaller, mechanical tasks have been hard-wired into your hands. For instance, shifting scales as the harmony changes is not a creative act. It is largely a bookkeeping issue that should be delegated to your hands—it should become automatic.

In order to thoroughly program your hands to handle the mechanical aspects of playing you need to spend years focusing on them—working out note-choice, fingering, and technique minutiae. And you need to know theory: the task of analyzing a tune for scale-choice (another non-creative act) should feel automatic. But all of this disciplined detail work is a means to an end, and you'll progress much more quickly if you have a clear image of that end.

Imagine a very odd-looking piano—an electronic keyboard without keys, just two touch-sensitive drumheads where the keys used to be.

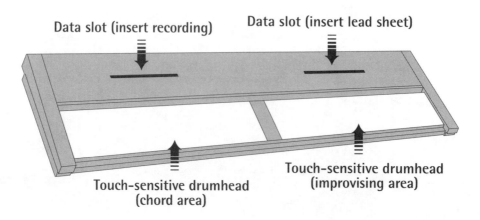

Data slot (insert recording) Data slot (insert lead sheet)

Touch-sensitive drumhead (chord area) Touch-sensitive drumhead (improvising area)

Not only are the drumheads digital, there's also a built-in computer that can instantly analyze chords to determine the most appropriate improvising scales. When you first plug in this instrument, you are asked to insert a recording of your playing so that the computer can adjust its scale analysis to match your style.

Before you play a tune, you must insert the lead sheet into the data slot. During your solo, you tap rhythms on the right drumhead, shifting your hand right and left to indicate higher or lower pitch. When you want to create a line with a particular shape, you simply move your right hand through that shape much like a conductor, unhampered by the details of specific pitch. The computer simply translates your rhythmic and melodic input into actual notes that make musical sense over the chords. You are able to concentrate on the more fundamental issues of time and shape, while the piano's brain attends to the details.

While your right hand is busy tapping, you comp on the other drumhead with your left hand—again, just by tapping the rhythm you want. The computer selects one of your favorite voicings for each chord. Your only concern is the rhythm.

Playing this piano is almost as easy as playing a set of bongo drums. You can express your rhythmic impulses freely through the instrument without the usual complications of being in the right key, making transitions from scale to scale, or searching for the right voicing.

Are you sold? Shall I direct you to the company's website so you can place your order for the next piano off the assembly line? Sorry—this instrument has not yet been invented. I'm afraid you'll have to get by with the old Model 88 brand—you know, the one with the keys.

The point of this newfangled piano is to get you to envision what being a pianist is like after you've learned all your theory, scales, voicings, and other structures thoroughly. It's a way for you to imagine the physical, loose, big-movement, conductor-like, drummer-like way of being at the instrument. It's to help you keep that end vision in mind so that you don't end up boxing yourself in. And it's to remind you that the piano is a percussion instrument.

Part IV *Ways to Develop Your Improvising*

Here is a wide array of practical exercises that will improve your continuity, phrasing, time, range, rhythm, note choice, and ability to hear changes. Don't just read about these exercises—play them.

Chapter **14**

This is a fictional account. The names have been changed to protect the nonexistent

The Uninvited Fan

There's a fellow here in town by the name of Zass who always goes by his first initial, Y. Mr. Y. Zass is a jazz aficionado of sorts, but the local jazz musicians cringe when he walks in the club. You see, Y. is very knowledgeable about music, knows what he wants to hear, and is remarkably willing to share his criticism of your playing (to your face) at every opportunity.

Several years ago he called me over after a set. "So, Randy," he began, "here's what I'm hearing: your solos have all these holes in them—'rests,' I think you call them—and they all line up with the shifts in the harmony. Every time there's a change of key, your improvising stops for a beat or two. So I'm thinking, 'Is he choosing these rests based on what sounds best, or is it just because he can't make the transitions into the new keys smoothly?' So I don't trust your phrasing decisions. What do you have to say about that?"

I just shook my head, thanked Y. Zass for his input, and walked away. But as I drove home that night, I realized that he had nailed me: I wasn't making my transitions. So I cooked up an exercise for myself and called it the **endless 8th drill**. Simply put, I improvised through a set of changes using eight 8th notes in every bar. I took special care not to hesitate at the seams between the scales. Even if I had to miss a few notes, I kept my fingers moving. Actually I didn't miss too many notes because I took the drill at a very slow tempo so I could look ahead to the next scale. First I practiced the exercise over the random II-V chart (page 303 in the appendix). Then I applied it to standard tunes such as "It Could Happen To You":

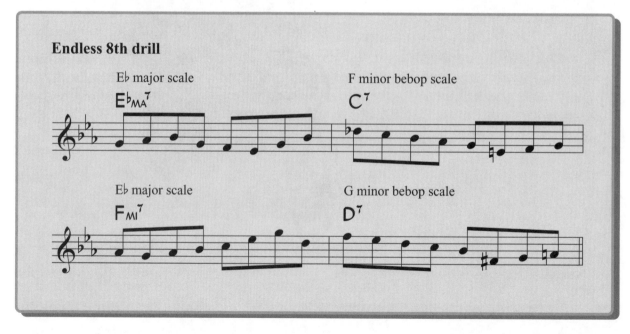

It took a while, but after a few weeks I was shifting from scale to scale with relative ease.

Chapter **14**

A few months later, I looked up from the piano and saw Y. at a nearby table, sporting his familiar scowl. "Listen here," he said to me on the break, "you got that problem fixed—big deal. Now you've got another problem: it's called 'tonic fixation.' Why is it that your first note over a II-V-I in Bb is always Bb? Sure, you don't rest anymore as you make the transition into E minor, but your first note is always E. Is that a musical choice? Are you hearing that note? I don't think so. I think you're just scuffling to make the changes, and the one note that you can count on until your mind fully engages is the tonic. So how about that?"

What could I say? He had me again. The next day I began working on the **continuous scale drill**. It's actually a variation on the endless 8th drill. The only difference is that now I played up and down the full range of the piano over my left-hand chords in a scalar fashion, simply merging into the new scale at the appropriate time:

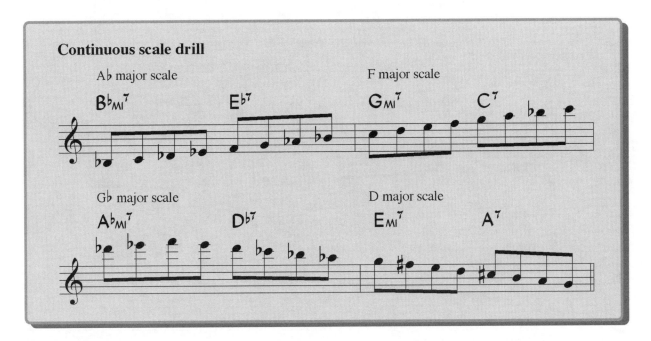

I tried to use the correct fingering for each scale. Sometimes, though, it was impossible to maintain that fingering right at the seam from one scale to the next. In one tune, for example, I was climbing up an Ab major scale, looking ahead to the D major scale in the next measure. When I reached the barline, however, I faced a transition from Eb to E that forced me to synthesize a makeshift fingering until I could re-establish the correct fingering on G:

Chapter **14**

A few weeks later, Y. was back on my case. "Sounds like you've been practicing. But what's all this small interval stuff? Are you really hearing nothing but half steps and whole steps, or is it just that you're not willing to stretch your hand out and grab larger intervals? See, I don't think you're playing what you hear. I think you're just playing what your hand is willing to execute."

Zass was really getting on my nerves, but there was no denying that his suspicions were well founded. The next day I adjusted my exercise again. I still played endless eighths and I still climbed straight up and down the keyboard but now with almost all large intervals. Although it was difficult and didn't sound particularly musical, I could tell that my hand was beginning to relate to the keyboard with much greater control. Again, I practiced it very slowly, and after a few sessions it began to come more naturally. Here's a short example. (For much more on the **large interval drill**, read "Get Big!," page 59.)

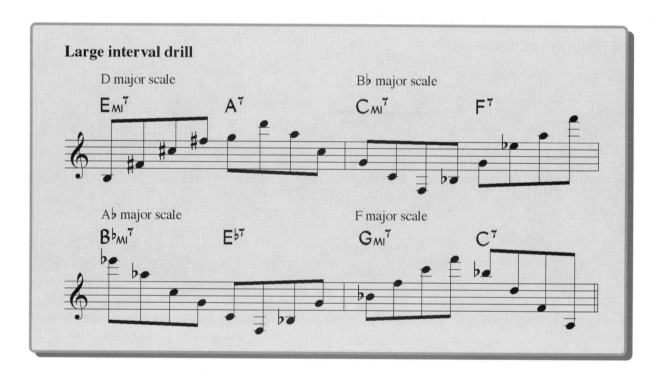

It wasn't long before I saw Y. Zass again. "Y.Z.," I chuckled, "can't you find someone else to harass?"

"Oh, don't you worry, I make the rounds," he shot back. "O.K., I hear smooth transitions from scale to scale, and you're not using the tonic as a security blanket any longer. And you're grabbing huge chunks of the keyboard at a time instead of playing so small. But every time the scale changes your idea changes. What's that about? There you are, playing a hip shape in D melodic minor; then the scale changes to Bb diminished and, just like that, you're on to a different idea altogether. Now, I can believe that the change in harmony might sometimes cause you to hear a new idea—but every time?! I don't think so. I think you're changing your idea because you can't keep it going in the new scale. If you really had it together, you'd be able to stick with an idea as long as it still interested you, regardless of the change in the underlying harmony."

How can someone so disagreeable be so smart? I set to work on the **idea-bending drill**. Over the first II-V, I improvised a short idea (3-4 notes). Then I proceeded to play that idea over every II-V: the same rhythm, the same shape, and the same spot on the keyboard. All I did was bend the notes to fit into each new scale. At first I approached this task in a very regimented way. If my original idea was this:

I characterized it as "C-A-F-G." I bent those notes so that the new version always consisted of whatever type of C, A, F, and G occurred in the new scale:

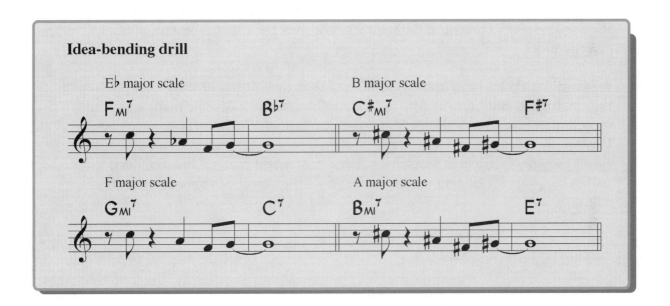

By focusing on the actual spelling of the note names, I was guaranteed of staying in one place on the keyboard, but it led to a couple of problems. For one thing, I found that I was playing different notes for enharmonically-spelled II-V's:

Changing the notes in this way made no musical sense. It was just a bookkeeping quirk. I also found that the idea didn't sound very good in some keys, because the wrong notes were being stressed:

Chapter **14**

So I relaxed the requirements somewhat. I still retained the idea's rhythm, shape, and general location on the keyboard as I went from key to key. But I didn't worry about the actual spelling of the notes, and I went for the best sound, even if it meant breaking the pattern a little.

I worked with the random II-V chart until I could confidently play one idea through the shifting keys. Then I practiced the same exercise over the changes to several of my favorite tunes.

Y. Zass still sticks his head in the club from time to time. Often he listens for a while, then stalks out, muttering angrily to himself. On other occasions he manages to come up with new (and usually dead-on) insights into just what's wrong with my playing. Most of my colleagues still keep their distance from this cantankerous old fellow, and even I can only take him in small doses. But I must admit that Y. Zass occupies a soft spot in my heart for helping me to conquer my scale transitions once and for all.

Chapter **15**

You're Repeating Yourself (hopefully)

> Treat this whole chapter as a practice box. Don't just read it—do it!

There's something irresistible about a real melody. If you can convince the listener that he's hearing a melody when you improvise, he'll stay riveted to every note. Well, you can—and it's not really that difficult. The one element that is common to almost all good melodies is:

Repetition

Repetition. Repetition and more repetition. I'm referring specifically to the repetition of ideas (motifs, as they are often called). Sometimes the idea is repeated exactly as it occurred the first time, as in the tune "Do Nothing Till You Hear From Me":

More often, the motif occurs higher or lower than it did originally. The notes are different but the rhythm and the shape of the line remain intact, as in "It Could Happen To You":

I'll call this type of repetition "pitch-shifting" (The term "transposing" is not appropriate because we associate it with a change of key.) With the exception of a few bebop heads (like "Donna Lee" and "Anthropology"), it's very difficult to name a melody that doesn't feature a healthy amount of repetition. Here are the names of a few melodies (jazz and otherwise) that illustrate my point:

Happy Birthday
O Christmas Tree
Winter Wonderland
Eleanor Rigby
Embraceable You
My Foolish Heart
As Time Goes By
I Remember You
Straight No Chaser

Chapter **15**

What I'm describing here is a process often called motivic development: the spinning out of ideas through the use of repetition, pitch-shifting, and extension. Pick a melody from any genre and see if it doesn't use motivic development as its primary structural element. It wouldn't be too far off the mark to define melody as a set of notes organized through the use of motivic development.

So that's it: if you want your improvising to sound like a melody, you need to use a lot of repetition. Ironically, many musicians avoid using repetition for fear of sounding repetitious, i.e., boring. You bore a listener if you try to elicit the same emotional reaction from him two or three times in a row, but that's not what you're doing when you repeat an idea. When you first introduce an idea, it's new. The listener waits with open anticipation to hear how the idea spins itself out. But when you repeat the idea, his reaction is very different. Now he can gain a certain sense of control, by connecting what he's hearing to what went before. You could draw a parallel between his dual reactions with the effect of a V–I progression. In both cases there is a tension/release mechanism at work.

Simply put, improvising is playing what you hear. What you hear is based in large part on the music you've heard. You've heard thousands of melodies in your lifetime; i.e., you've heard thousands of examples of motivic development. It's a good bet, then, that you naturally hear a lot of repetition and pitch-shifting. Yet, if you're like a lot of developing musicians, you don't use much of it in your improvising. Why not? The answer may be very simple: in order to use repetition in your improvising, you must be able to remember what you just played! When you reach a specific juncture in your solo where the choice is between repeating your last idea or playing something new, the first option must be at least as easy for you as the second or you'll never take it. So, presuming that motivic development is a large part of what you naturally hear, the only thing you need to do is develop your "melodic memory." Here are some exercises to help you with that. I call them "repetition games." Practice them over a simple vamp, such as a II–V.

Simple form

1. Play a short idea (between two and five notes).
2. After a short rest, repeat it exactly (the same notes and rhythm, including what beat it begins on).
3. Play the idea a third time and add on an extension (between two and five notes). Don't pause in between. The extension must sound like an outgrowth of the old idea.
4. The extension is your new idea. You've already played it once. Now repeat it (just the extension—the first idea is gone), then repeat it again with a new extension, and so on.

The form is basically this: play each idea three times—first, as an extension of the previous idea; second, just by itself; and third, as a feeder into the next idea. Here's a diagram:

Idea #: 1 1 1-2 2 2-3 3 3-4 4 4-5 5 5 etc.

Play this example:

Your ideas should be short at first, but you can eventually make them as long or short as you want. The rests between the ideas can be of various lengths. Don't rush through them. If you don't use enough space between your ideas you'll feel as if you're on an "idea treadmill" and you'll panic. So take your time.

Once you're confident that you can begin each repetition of an idea on the same beat, then experiment with moving the idea around within the measure. Play this example:

Now try it using your own ideas.

Chapter 15

Notice how Thelonious Monk uses this device in "Straight No Chaser":

Pitch-shifting form

This exercise is identical to the simple form, except that you'll move your idea up or down in pitch at one point. When you do, you'll need to keep the same shape and rhythm but play it higher or lower within the scale. For example, you could move this idea (in Bb major):

to any of these six other locations within the scale.

Here's the exercise:

1. Play an idea.
2. After a rest, repeat it exactly.
3. After another rest, pitch-shift it within the scale.
4. After another rest, play it again at the new location and extend it into the next idea.

```
                        1   1-2   2              3   3-4   4
Here's the diagram:  1     1                                         4   4-5 etc.
                             2   2-3   3
```

In other words, each idea occurs four times: 1) as an extension of the old idea, 2) simply repeated, 3) moved to a new location, and 4) repeated with an extension. Play this example:

Now try the pitch-shifting form using your own ideas.

Chapter 15

Free form

Here you'll be using the same operations as on the previous exercises (idea formation, repetition, pitch-shifting, and extension), but you'll operate more freely. Here's the exercise:

1. Play an idea.
2. Repeat it or pitch-shift it as often as you like, then extend it to the next idea.

Here's a diagram of how it might look:

This form is less regimented than the previous one, but you must still play in control. Don't insert any filler material. Every note must be a member of a distinct idea, repetition, or shift. Play this example:

For clarity's sake this example follows the preceding diagram, but you can come up with a different scheme. Try the free form now, using your own ideas.

Actual improvising

Picture a kitten engaged in the repetitive activity of chasing a ball from point to point. Bored with that, he tosses the ball up in the air. Then he rolls it down the stairs. It goes under a couch, and when he runs underneath to retrieve it, he finds an old rag. The ball is now history, and the kitten's full attention is on the rag. But then, quite suddenly—he stops. He just stops, as if someone pushed his "stop play" button. He begins to stroll across the floor, simply enjoying the here and now state of being a kitten. He walks by a pencil and then a jellybean with scarcely a sideways glance. Eventually he encounters a ball of yarn that sparks his interest and the cycle begins again.

I want you to become kitten-like in your improvising. Don't play with each and every idea as if it merited equal attention. Stroll until you find something that grabs you, then play with it (repeat, shift, etc.) until it leads you either to another idea or back to strolling. It's through this process that you find the motifs that you want to develop. Here's the simple diagram:

Stroll....free form....stroll....free form....stroll....free form

Here's an example. Play it and look for the ideas amidst the strolling.

Now try it with your own ideas.

Chapter **15**

When you feel comfortable with this last exercise over a II-V vamp, practice it over the chord progression of a standard tune. This will be more of a challenge for several reasons, not the least of which is that you'll have to bend your ideas to match the changing harmony.

What's the point?

These exercises are designed to help you on several levels:

1. To encourage you to conceive of your improvising as a series of ideas, not just notes.

2. To emphasize the importance of repetition and motivic development. This is what will make your improvising sound like a melody.

3. Above all, to stress the value of listening to what you play. Some great improvisers use very little repetition, but they all listen carefully to what they're playing. As a composer, what you write should be somehow connected to what you just wrote. Improvising is composing in real time. What you play must be influenced by what you just played. This can only happen if you specifically remember what you just played, and that can only happen if you're listening to yourself intently.

Disappearing Eighth Notes

Here's a concept that might help you improvise with better flow. Play an endless eighth-note line, using eight notes in every measure. Imagine those eighth notes as a line of seagulls flying in a straight line just over the waves. Now imagine the gulls dipping down into the waves and disappearing for a while, then reappearing, then dipping down again. This is how you should experience the rests between your phrases. In other words, the eighth notes never stop: they just go underwater for a while and then come back up.

If you're a piano player, you can think of it like this: you improvise with a steady stream of eighth notes, keeping your fingers moving continuously. But every once in a while someone grabs your wrist and lifts your hand two inches off the keyboard so that your fingers wriggle harmlessly in mid-air. Then he lowers your hand again until your fingers re-connect with the keyboard and the sound resumes.

One reason why a musician may improvise with shaky time is that he can't get up to speed immediately after a pause. It's as if his sound is a big boulder that he brought to a stop and now has to get rolling again. This is why it's helpful to think of endless eighth notes. You no longer have to get an eighth-note line going after a rest. You just have to merge with the one that was there all along.

This way of thinking will probably have an effect on the way you shape your lines. Specifically, many of them will start and end softly (when the notes are just above the waterline) and get louder in the middle. It will certainly affect the way you hear your own rests. They'll become more energized because you'll already hear the "engine" turning which is going to generate your next line. How's that for a concept—energized rests!

Try singing some eighth-note lines this way first. When you think you've got the right sound, then apply it to your instrument.

Chapter **17**

Get Small!

Here is something for you to explore that will strengthen your control over rhythm and dynamics. Pick a tune or chord progression on which you can already improvise quite well. Now select a very limited range on your instrument—for example, the major third from C to E. It could even be smaller than that (but not much larger). Now improvise while staying exclusively within that range. Imagine that you're playing a solo on the bandstand with a strange new instrument whose entire range is limited to that major third, and you need to play the best, most creative solo of your life. Now pick another equally small range and repeat the exercise. Now again, somewhere else.

A jazz musician must confront the challenge of being able to play throughout the range of his instrument. He doesn't want to be limited to one area. He wants to be flexible. (Read "Get Big!" on page 59). Since he practices this way, he often takes the same attitude on the bandstand. So his solos are often all over the place: high, then low, then high again. Basically, he is using range as a primary variable to make the solo interesting.

See what happens when you deny yourself that particular form of variation. Don't be surprised if you naturally find other means to vary your improvising, such as rhythm and dynamics. Through this exercise you can strengthen your control over these elements. Then you'll continue to use them even after you widen your range again. Your sound will be much more expressive and interesting.

Chapter **18**

Get Big!

Here's an exercise you can do to improve your range and flexibility. I introduced it earlier as the large interval drill in "The Uninvited Fan" (page 46). Very slowly, play straight up and down the range of the piano (no zig-zagging) in the key of Eb major. Keep your hand stretched out at all times and play almost exclusively large intervals (4ths, 5ths, 6ths, etc.). Play a constant stream of swing eighth notes with no rests or breaks. (A break occurs when you lift your hand and reset it as you go up the keyboard rather than smoothly tucking your thumb under.) Use a 1234 1234 1234 fingering except when you have to make adjustments at either end of the line. As soon as you enter each 1234 hand position (after playing the thumb on the way up and after playing the fourth finger on the way down), immediately stretch your hand out fully. Make sure that you use different notes in each octave. Don't settle for a simple arpeggio. Play this example:

Large interval drill

Now try the exercise, improvising your own pitches.

Some of the intervals in this example may be too large for your hand. Just use smaller ones but keep your hand stretched out. Extend the exercise up to the top octave on the piano before you turn around. As in the example, don't try to synchronize the change in the line's direction with the beginning of a measure. Simply turn around when you reach the top of the keyboard and the bottom end of your intended range. If you play the exercise in the right hand alone you can go as far down the keyboard as you want. If you're playing it over a chord progression just go down until you reach your left hand, then come back up.

Chapter **18**

Here again is the exercise in short form:

1. Large intervals
2. Straight up and down (no zig-zagging)
3. Swing eighths throughout
4. No rests or breaks
5. 1234 1234 1234 fingering (except for adjustments at either end)
6. Stretch out your hand after you enter each hand position (after the thumb on the way up, after the fourth finger on the way down).
7. Use different notes in each octave (no simple arpeggios).

Do this exercise slowly. If you feel either pain or panic as you practice it, you'll come to associate those feelings with this type of hand behavior and that means you'll never incorporate it into your improvising. You need to play it so slowly that you can convince yourself it actually feels good to use your hand in this stretched-out way! This exercise is all about flow. If you miss a note, don't stop to fix it. Just merge back into the right scale as you continue up or down the keyboard.

Practice this exercise in the right hand alone at first. Then, when it feels comfortable, try it over a II-V vamp (Fmi7 Bb7, four beats per chord). Try it in some other keys (right hand alone at first, then with the chords).

Let me explain what this exercise is all about. Have you ever heard the expression, "A bad general tends to fight his last war?" Well, a bad piano player tends to play his last solo. As an improviser you try to play what you hear in your head. What you hear is largely a product of all the music that you've heard. And what music have you heard the most? You! You've heard your own playing more than anything else. It's easy to get in a rut in which you keep coming back to the same old sounds you've always played. Now consider this: it's quite probable that you originally selected many of those sounds based not purely on what you heard but on what your hand was capable of playing (as we discussed in "The Censor In The Brain"). Your head is full of sounds that were created by a hand of limited abilities. Now, when you play what you hear, you're playing those sounds!

So here's a way out of that rut. Consider this question: what are the specific behaviors that are peculiar to an advanced pianist's hands? What does he do that you don't? Well, there are probably many things, but I want to suggest three of them.

1. An advanced pianist keeps his hands extended to cover big chunks of the keyboard. It's always easier to quickly contract the hand to play an occasional small shape than it is to expand it suddenly.
2. He is also comfortable both tucking the thumb under his hand when he needs to continue up the keyboard and crossing over his thumb with the fourth (or third) finger on his way down.

3. He has the ability to stretch out and play large intervals between his 3rd and 4th fingers. A less advanced pianist uses a 3-4 fingering only for small intervals, as in a scale.

What if you were comfortable with these techniques? Then your hand would be willing to execute many more of the ideas that your ear suggested. Your melodic impulses would develop more purely along the lines of what you heard rather than what your hand was willing to play (you would effectively anaesthetize the censor in your brain).

Embrace these three techniques at a very slow speed. As you become comfortable with them, you'll incorporate them into your basic way of playing. On the surface it appears to be a purely mechanical exercise (and one which admittedly doesn't sound very musical). But it really goes much deeper than that. It puts you in a position where the only limitations on your improvisational ability are ear-based and not hand-based. The more you hear the better you'll immediately play.

After you become comfortable with this exercise over a II-V vamp, test your wings a little bit. Simply improvise freely over the same vamp. Now that you're just playing, feel free to break most or all of the rules of the exercise. You can use some small intervals, zig-zag, vary your rhythms and fingering, include rests, arpeggios, etc. But don't just go back to your old way of playing. Keep your hand stretched out, using all your fingers (including the 3-4 stretch), and move smoothly up and down the keyboard through the use of tuck-unders and cross-overs. It should feel almost as if your right hand is three feet wide, as if everything that you want to play is underneath your hand (or if it isn't, you can easily get to it by tucking under or crossing over). Finally, try applying this technique as you improvise slowly over tunes.

Chapter **19**

Over the Barline

> Treat this whole chapter as a practice box. Don't just read it—do it!

Play these lines on the piano:

Both of these lines begin with a technique called rhythmic displacement in which a repeating pattern continually shifts its relationship to the beat or measure. In Ex. 1 the pattern consists of three ascending eighth notes. In Ex. 2 it's a group of four eighth-note triplets (actually three notes and a rest).

Rhythmic displacement is a great way to add tension and release to your improvising, and you can also use it as you comp. Most rhythm section players love this device. You'll be able to lock up with them more effectively if you understand their rhythmic games.

Tap your foot. Now sing or say this rhythm (you can use straight 8ths or swing 8ths):

Do it again, counting like so:

It's pretty easy so far, right? Now try it again, counting with these new numbers:

Now, still tapping your foot, count it again but accent every "1":

Practice this until it's easy. Then, with the foot going, play these three lines on the piano.

Do you see what's going on here? You're playing eighth notes in groups of three at a time, using three different techniques.

1. playing a pattern of three different pitches
2. playing two eighth notes and a rest
3. accenting every third eighth note

It takes three measures before the pattern completes its cycle and begins again on the downbeat. Let's examine what you can do with each of these techniques.

Pitch Grouping

Play this sequence just in the right hand at first, then with chords underneath:

I only presented three measures of the pattern but you should extend it up the keyboard over the II-V vamp. Then play it back down.

Chapter 19

Here are several other patterns that group eighth notes in threes. Practice them all.

As with the first pattern, practice these first without the left-hand chords, then with them. Practice the patterns up and down the keyboard. Then write some patterns of your own.

These patterns are great for improvising but only if they're well integrated. In other words, you need to be able to get in and out of them smoothly. Here's an exercise:

1. Improvise freely over the Gmi7 C7 vamp.
2. Without pausing, segue into any of the above patterns.
3. Again without pausing, segue back to free improvising.

Here's an example:

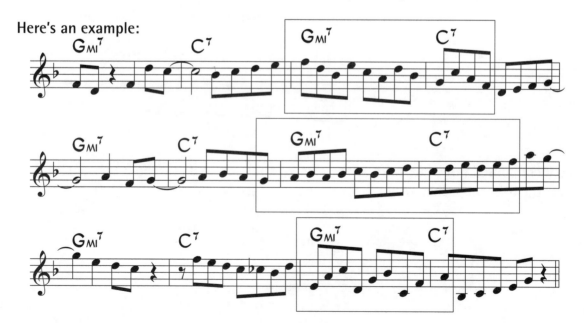

Chapter **19**

Rest Grouping

Here again is the basic pattern:

As long as you maintain this rhythm, your eighth notes will be grouped in threes no matter what pitches you play. I recommend that you explore four types of pitch shapes as you play the rhythm:

1. A pitch shape that is synchronized with the rhythmic grouping. Here are two examples:

2. A simple scale:

3. A shape that conflicts with the rhythmic grouping. Here are several examples:

Grouping pitches in threes (yes, this does conflict with the rhythmic threes due to the rests)

Grouping pitches in fours

Chapter **19**

Grouping pitches in fives

4. Random pitch shapes (Simply improvise and avoid repeating pitch patterns.)

After you've practiced these variations, integrate them with free improvising.

Accent Grouping

Here again is the basic pattern:

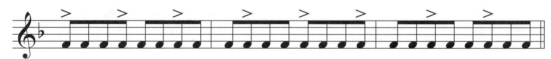

Once again, you're free to experiment with pitch shapes because the three-group will be preserved by the accents alone. Here are examples of each type.

1. Synchronized with accent pattern

2. Scale

3. Conflicting with accent pattern (This example groups the pitches in twos.)

4. Random pitches

After you've practiced these variations, integrate them with free improvising as before.

Tricks for mastering accent groupings

Of the three grouping techniques, accenting is certainly the most difficult for most musicians. There are a few special tricks that you can use to get through some of the more difficult patterns.

1. Play the line while counting the rhythmic grouping out loud and simply accent the note every time you say "1." This is a useful trick for all the shape types (synchronized, scale, conflicting, and random).

Chapter **19**

2. Write out a few measures of the pattern, including the accents; then simply read it. In other words, rely purely on your reading ability to play the pattern correctly until you can internalize it and play by feel. This trick also works well for all the shape types.

3. This trick involves the use of what I call combination patterns. Imagine that you wrote out a few measures of the patterns, as in trick #2, and then erased all the notes except those with accents.

Original pattern

Combination pattern

As you can see, the accented notes form their own regular pattern. Once you've identified it you can use it to place the accents correctly without having to read the music at all. This trick works for the scale shape and it's indispensable for the conflicting pitch shape.

4. Here's a trick that is specifically designed for rest-grouping patterns. Let's say you're trying to learn this pattern:

If it causes you trouble, then first learn this pattern:

Now simply hold the note A down with your left hand and play the rhythm again with your right hand. Only the F and G will sound. Your third finger will just thud silently on the depressed A. After a few beats you'll hear the correct rhythm and you won't need to mute the A anymore. (You'll just omit it.)

Holding down the A's...

results in:

Other Rhythmic Groupings

This entire chapter has focused on one particular pattern: grouping eighth notes in threes. But there are several other groupings worth exploring. Here are some patterns that result from grouping eighth notes in fives:

Pitch grouping

Pitch grouping

Rest grouping (4 notes + a rest)—scale shape

Accent grouping—the pitches grouped in fours conflict with the accents grouped in fives.

Chapter 19

Accent grouping–random pitches

Here are some nice patterns that result from grouping eighth-note triplets in fours:
Pitch grouping

Pitch grouping

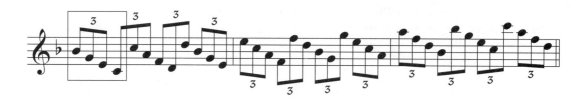

Rest grouping (3 notes + a rest)—the pitches grouped in fours conflict with the rest grouping.

Accent grouping—scale shape

Accent grouping–synchronized pitch shape

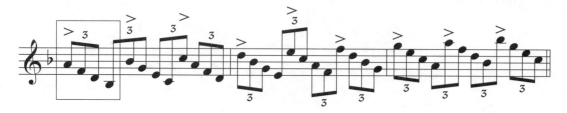

Here are some patterns that result from grouping eighth-note triplets in fives:

Pitch grouping

Rest grouping (4 notes + a rest)—random pitches

Accent grouping—the pitches grouped in twos conflict with the accents grouped in fives.

Remember: as soon as you learn to play a particular pattern, practice integrating it with free improvising. Only when you can make the transition smoothly will that pattern begin to show up in your solos.

After you have familiarized yourself with several of the available rhythmic groupings, you can begin to integrate them with each other. This will create a fascinating sense of randomness in your rhythmic groups. Here is an excerpt of a solo over Tadd Dameron's "Lady Bird" that illustrates this randomness by mixing pitch groupings, mostly in twos, threes, and fours.

Chapter 19

Not only do these rhythms add interest to your improvised line, but they can also be used for playing chords, whether during your solo or someone else's.

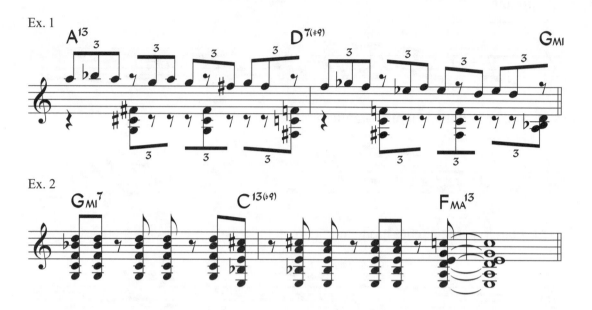

Working on these exercises can have a deepening effect on your basic sense of time. As you sensitize yourself to each subdivision in the measure, you'll be less likely to rush through rests. You'll be less tethered to the first beat of each measure. You won't drag eighth-note triplets when you first enter after a rest. Also, your dynamic control—specifically, your ability to shape a line by varying the volume of the individual notes—will be enhanced by the accent-grouping exercises.

Use a metronome, take it slow, and be patient!

Chapter **20**

Notes That Work

You're an aspiring jazz student. Recently you learned how to select good scales for improvising over chords. It fascinates you how the two sets of structures fit together. You've really had fun working on your improvising in this way, and you feel as if you've been making great progress. Then you go out to see a great band at your local jazz club, and on the break you talk to the piano player.

"Oh, you're studying jazz, huh?" he says. "What are you working on?" You tell him that you've been working with scales over chords, and a pained expression comes over his face. "Wow, I'd watch out for that, man. I mean, do you really want to sound like you're playing scales all the time?"

"Well, uh..."

"Listen," he says, "Let me tell you something. You need to be working on chord-tone outlines. It's all about chord-tones and upper and lower neighbors. That's what the real cats are doing. That's how I got it together. Scales are a dead end."

"Gee, thanks," you mumble and walk away confused.

A month later you've made the switch. You're logging three hours a day, improvising over chord changes by outlining them and elaborating them with neighbors. And it's working! You're beginning to make some real strides. But then you take a lesson from a local legend.

"Chord-tones? Scales?" he says, scratching his head. "What do you think this is? Nuclear physics? Calculus? Why don't you just go to the source, man? No one learns to play worth a dime except by imitating the masters. You learn this music by modeling your playing on those who have gone before. Show them some respect, man. I'm talking about transcribing licks and solos and learning them in twelve keys. That's the only way you build a vocabulary. You can't get a sound together using that analytical stuff."

Two months later, after you've learned several solos and are starting to see the results show up on your gigs, you meet a touring, big-name musician who tells you, "Hey, man, transcribing is highly overrated. It makes everyone sound the same because they're all transcribing the same basic language. Improvising is all about intuition. Just base your improvising on the melody, and play off of that by using your ear. Or make up new melodies, but just focus on playing directly what you hear."

A year later you've made all the rounds, including macrobiotics, reading scriptures, taking conga lessons, and listening to jazz musicians who have the same blood type as you. And by the way, how are you playing, and are you enjoying it?

Each of those great musicians found something that worked for them and stuck with it

Chapter 20

until it bore fruit. Each of them gave you a great idea for developing your improvising, and each spoke logically and convincingly. And who are you to argue? These guys have paid their dues. Yet each of them steered you wrong when he told you that the other approaches were useless.

As you work through the maze of strategies for improving your playing, you will almost certainly encounter several gurus along your path—even a teacher who mistakenly bases a whole curriculum on only one method because it worked for him. Don't be oblivious to their advice. They all have something valuable to offer. But keep your head on straight and don't succumb to discouragement. Pick an approach that works for you and stick with it. As long as you're working hard at what you're doing, you'll get results. Work with that approach until you have a sense of having gone through it and come out the other side. At this point you'll be a bit bored and you'll be ready for something new. Then move on.

I don't mean to imply that you should just use one approach at a time. You may want to try to develop your improvising along several lines simultaneously. That's fine. Too often, though, an aspiring musician gives up on an approach way too soon, before he really gives it a chance to work. He gives up either because someone steers him in a different direction or because he doesn't quickly get the results he was hoping for. Remember, some things take a little time. If your improvising doesn't show immediate improvement, that doesn't necessarily mean you're on the wrong track.

For example, the use of scales for improvisation is a potentially very powerful approach, but at first most players find it especially difficult to get a good sound with it. A musician who tells you that it's an invalid approach probably tried it earlier in his career but gave up on it after a couple of weeks because it was too hard. For you, it might just be the key to the whole thing. If you continually flit from one approach to the next, you'll likely be so busy searching for the right thing to work on that you'll get very little real work done at all.

We'll soon look in detail at these improvisational strategies. First, though, I want to stress that none of these approaches will work unless you listen to a lot of music. Think of it as nutrition. You have to eat a variety of different foods several times a day. Your body rejects what it can't use. Much of the nutritious food will eventually be converted into energy, but it may take a while. Similarly, you have to listen to a variety of music, not just jazz played on your instrument. Listen to singers, pianists, horn players, etc., and listen to jazz, pop, rock, classical—whatever. You won't use it all in your improvising, but take it all in. It will take a while before it will manifest itself in your playing. The Bill Evans album that you listen to today may not affect your style for three years. Listening is a long-range investment.

There's no wrong way to listen. If you want to sit and listen to a CD with all your attention, fine. If you want to put it on as background music while you work, that's great too. Or go to sleep to it. Just because you're not consciously focused on the music doesn't mean that you're not taking it in. In fact, it may well be that your subconscious mind will only begin to absorb the music when your conscious mind is preoccupied with something else—and it's from your subconscious mind that the music will flow.

Scales over chords

1. Learn your scales up and down through the range of your instrument. Pay attention to fingering, accuracy, articulation, tempo, and tone. Learn to play them without looking at the keyboard. When you have them well under control, work up your speed. Spend some time improvising freely with each scale (no chords). It's important that you learn each scale as an improvisational territory in which you can jump around with large intervals, not just as a smooth run up and down your instrument. For a list of scales worth your attention, see Common Scales, Major Scale Modes, and Melodic Minor Modes in the appendix (pp. 310-313).

2. You need to learn the theoretical connections between scales and chords. You'll find a thorough treatment of this material in the next section of this book (page 105).

3. You need to be able to manifest that theoretical information on your instrument. Let's break this task down into two parts.

    a. Improvising in one scale over a vamp (such as a II-V-I). Here you need to work on the specifics of improvising: good time and flow, coherent ideas, good tone, right notes, etc. Explore the large intervals within that scale, and find out what the juiciest notes are within it.
    b. Making the transition from one scale to the next. You should use both the random II-V-I charts in the appendix (pp. 303-306) and actual tunes. Focus on the seams between the scales. You need to be able to play as smoothly at those transition points as you do within each scale, as "The Uninvited Fan" (page 44) makes clear.

4. Learn the sound of each scale/chord combination. You play the notes you play because you hear them, not because they fit within the appropriate scale. But you find those notes more efficiently because you recognize which scale the notes belong to.

Imagine that you're sitting at an electronic keyboard, improvising over a G7 chord and wearing a very odd looking cap. It's equipped with electrodes that can read your mind. A cable runs from the top of the cap into the back of your keyboard. You know that there are many different scales that can be used over a G7, but right now you are only concerned with playing what you hear. The electrodes scan your brain and send the data to the keyboard. Instantaneously the notes of an Ab melodic minor scale light up. However, the computer doesn't do all the work for you. You still have to select the specific notes from that scale to play the line in your head accurately, but your chances are better now that the field is smaller. The next time you encounter the G7, the notes of a G auxiliary diminished scale light up, so you choose from that set.

Chapter 20

Here's an exercise to help develop your ability to discriminate between the various chord/scale combinations. While playing a simple G7 (root, 3rd, and 7th) sing each scale and sample improvisation. Then play both on your instrument. Finally, improvise freely with the scale over the G7. For right now, concentrate on the sound of these scales, not the theory. Later you can learn more about their structures—they're in the appendix on page 310.

All of these scales are equally valid choices for G7. You need to work with each one until you can make good music with it and remember its sound over the chord. Then when you hear a line over a G7 the notes of that scale will light up. This takes a while. Just because you make some ugly sounds at first doesn't mean that the scale approach is not valid. Don't give up on it. It hardly seems fair, but simply staying within the scale is no guarantee that you'll sound good. You have to learn the personality of each note and treat it accordingly. None of the other approaches to improvising compares in complexity to the scale approach, but there are many great sounds that you won't find as easily using any other strategy.

Chord tones and neighbors

Here the basic idea is to use the notes of the chords (the roots, 3rds, 5ths, and 7ths) as the basis for your improvising. It's a much simpler method to understand than scale theory and you can get some good sounds from it quickly. At first you may play something like this:

Although it sounds boring to arpeggiate the chords, it's a good first step. Then you can make it more interesting by using larger intervals, starting on something other than the root and varying your rhythms:

The metaphor of the lighted keys applies here as well. When the chord is Gmi7, every G, Bb, D, and F on the keyboard should light up for you. The chord is not a structure that starts on G and fits within one octave. It's a series of notes that you can play in any order through the full range of your instrument.

> Now practice improvising over the above chord progression using only the four tones of each chord.

Chapter 20

There are certainly more layers of complexity to this approach, but before you confront them you should spend some time improvising over several tunes with simple chord tones. If your time feel is solid and your shapes are interesting you can get a surprisingly good sound with this simple technique.

There is a particular melodic resolution that you should know about. It's a way of getting a smooth line as you go from chord to chord. Sometimes I describe this resolution as "melodic glue" because it's so effective in bonding one chord's line to the next. Specifically, it involves resolving the 7th of a chord down a scale step to the 3rd of the next chord:

This will work as long as the root movement is a descending 5th, such as G to C or C to F. The D7 in the previous progression would typically resolve down a 5th to Gmi7, providing another opportunity for the 7-3 resolution:

In fact, it can help to ground a line more firmly in the harmony by playing the 3rd of each chord first, whether or not you achieve it with a 7-3 resolution or whether the root movement is down a 5th.

Add that resolution to your repertoire. Practice improvising over the above chord progression and over tunes using just chord tones and 7-3 resolutions.

Chapter 20

Like scale tones, each chord tone has its own personality. But you won't encounter tense individuals here: just a bunch of safe, stable ones. At first you might enjoy this friendly terrain, but eventually you'll probably want more tension and release in your line. This is where upper and lower neighboring tones come in. They can transform an initially saccharine, singsong line into something that sounds remarkably like bebop. Here's a pure chord-tone line.

Here's the same line enhanced with upper (N) and lower (n) neighbors.

A lower neighbor is always a half step below its target note. In the above example, lower neighbors include the F# resolving up to G in the second measure, the B-C, F#-G, and G#-A pairs in the third measure, and the G#-A and Eb-E pairs in the last measure.

An upper neighbor is either a half step or whole step above its target. In general, choose the note that fits into the prevailing local key. If this results in a whole step, however, you can often flat it to a half step. You can also insert a half-step passing tone between the whole-step neighbor and its target. In the above example, the upper neighbors include G-Gb-F in the first measure, Ab-G (with the F# lower neighbor in between) in the second measure, and Bb-A in the last measure.

Pick a short chord progression like the one above and practice improvising with just chord tones until you've got the sound you want. Next add in as many 7-3 resolutions as you can. Then pick a specific upper or lower neighbor, such as the lower neighbor to the root of each chord, and include that in your playing:

Chapter 20

Isolate each of the upper and lower neighbors in this way. This is important for two reasons: first, for theoretical control. You need to know exactly what you're playing and how it relates to the chord rather than just throwing in a lot of half-step resolutions and hoping that they're the right ones. Second and most important, for ear-training. For example, if you concentrate for twenty minutes on the upper neighbor to the 3rd and nothing else you'll begin to develop a very specific sense of how that resolution sounds. Then when you hear that sound while you're improvising you'll know where to find it. Remember: ultimately you won't play a note because it's a chord tone. You'll play it because you hear it, but you'll find it more efficiently because you recognize what chord tone or neighbor it is.

After you've isolated each upper and lower neighbor, do the same with each upper-lower pair. For example, use only the upper and lower neighbors to the 5th of each chord.

Notice the various ways in which I presented these pairs. In the first measure, I used an upper-lower-5th combination. In the second measure I reversed the order (lower-upper-5th). In the third measure I played 5th-upper-5th-lower-5th. In the last measure I played lower-5th-upper-5th.

Think of these neighboring tones as seasoning. The basic flavor of the musical steak is to be found in the chord tones themselves. The stronger your control over these notes, the better the taste. But once that's in place, the chromatic spices (the neighbors) will give the meal a much more interesting and sophisticated flavor.

Licks

Learning licks will enable you to play what you hear spontaneously without struggling for the right notes or fumbling for the right fingering. Some musicians are uncomfortable with the concept of using licks because they fear it will inhibit their spontaneity. But used correctly licks can enhance your improvising and make it smoother. The premise is not to deliberately insert them into your solos but to use them to express something you're already hearing. And what you're hearing will be right under your fingers!

Think of the process as "improvising by mosaic." Each lick is a fairly short piece of music that you've practiced until it feels like a single unit. You've worked out the notes and

Chapter 20

the fingering, and you play the whole shape. Then you simply lay down these licks—or tiles—one after another to create your design. Of course, this will be a much more powerful tool if you learn each lick in twelve keys.

You can mine your own melodic content and create your own licks. Stick a tape in your tape recorder. Find a short progression to play at a medium slow tempo. It could be as simple as a II-V or it could be an eight-bar section of a tune. Play it (or perhaps have someone else play it) with the tape rolling, vamping over and over. When you're ready, start scatting over the chords. Tape at least two or three minutes of your singing. Rewind the tape and listen to what you sang (this may be painful). After you've become quite familiar with what you sang, write down several excerpts. In particular, transcribe patterns that you especially liked but also patterns that you sang repeatedly. These little pieces of melody represent who you really are musically. When you first try this exercise you may decide that you really don't like anything that you sang. My advice is to not let that stop you. Just find patterns that you hate the least and proceed.

Where else can you find licks? You can transcribe licks directly from recordings. Simply extract a few choice morsels from any one of your favorite recorded solos and write them down. You can get licks from a teacher or a peer. Just stop him and ask, "What did you just play?" There are several print sources: Jerry Coker's *Patterns For Jazz* and Nicolas Slonimsky's *Thesaurus of Scales and Melodic Patterns* are both fine books.

Once you've found a lick that you like, how should you process it? First, work out the best possible fingering and practice it until it sounds and feels like a single unit, not a bunch of separate notes. Analyze the shape of the lick (What intervals are you playing? What scale degrees are you using?) Now learn the lick in twelve keys with good fingering. Practice playing it in all the keys with little or no hesitation in between. You can use the random note chart (page 301 in the appendix), or you can play the lick through the cycle of 5ths, chromatically, etc.

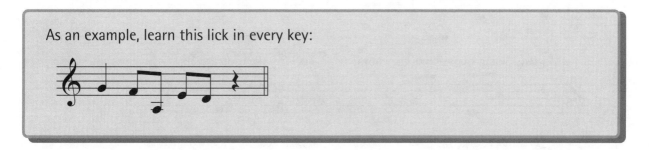

As an example, learn this lick in every key:

The next step is to decide how the lick can best be used over chords. Here are a few good connections for this lick:

Chapter 20

For a II-V, start on the 5th degree of the scale:

Here's how all those connections work for the various C chords:

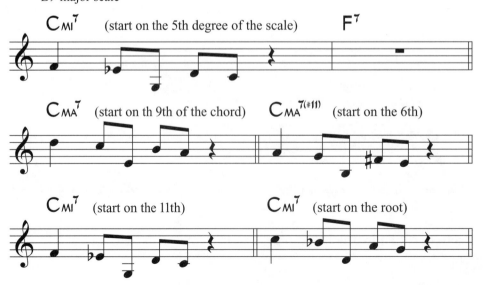

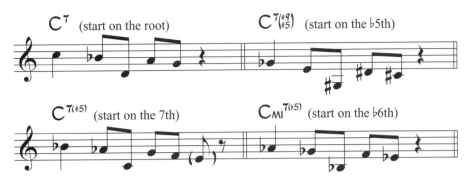

I found these connections using a combination of theory and my ear. If you have a minimal command of theory, just use your ear when you look for connections. It's essentially trial and error.

It's pretty stunning how versatile one lick can be, isn't it? It's as if you first learned the word "mean" as a synonym for "cruel" and then discovered that it can also stand for "signify" and "average." Just as that word functions differently in each context, the lick sounds different over each chord. You may have only learned one lick but you've learned many different sounds. For this reason you'll find that you can begin to sound good after learning only a very few licks.

Once you have the connections down, practice playing the lick over every chord in a tune. Here are the first eight measures of "It Could Happen To You" with the lick placed appropriately.

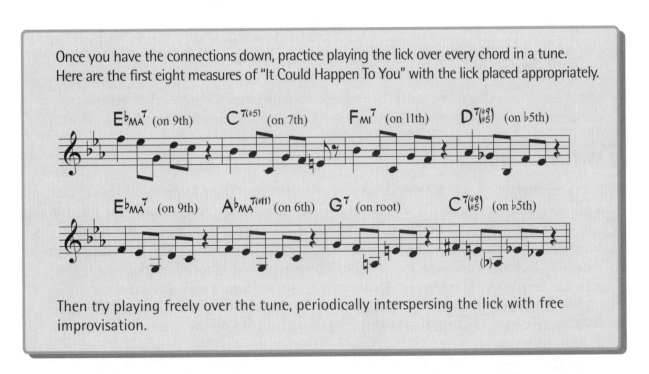

Then try playing freely over the tune, periodically interspersing the lick with free improvisation.

At this point it's safe to say that you've made this lick a part of your vocabulary. Don't be surprised if it shows up spontaneously in your soloing. On the one hand this may seem like a lot of work to process one tiny lick. But again, remember that you're learning a little piece of music that will prove to be very versatile. Also, this process can be a lot of fun. Once you've processed three or four licks you'll find that you can do it much faster and with less struggle.

Chapter **20**

If we can liken the process so far to learning vocabulary, the natural next step is grammar. How can you go smoothly from one lick to the next? Let's say that you've thoroughly processed these two licks:

You could combine these licks into a longer one:

You might want to throw in a passing tone:

Or you might try reversing the order of the licks:

This is just a way of gaining some flexibility with your licks. You may never actually use these particular pairings in a solo but it's still useful to practice possible combinations.

Written-out solos

If you're listening to, say, a Miles Davis solo and thinking, "Oh, I'd love to be able to play a solo like that," sometimes it pays to take the most direct approach: transcribe the solo and learn to play it. It's a simple matter of modeling yourself after one of the masters. Some musicians say you shouldn't write the solo down as you transcribe it—just transfer it directly to your instrument, memorizing it as you go. The rationale is that you'll train your ear better. Try it both ways. However you learn it, learn it well. Work out the fingering and play it smoothly. Try to get it up to speed so that you can play it along with the recording. As daunting as this may seem, try learning the solo (or at least part of it) in several keys.

It's also a good idea to analyze the solo to see what structural information you can glean from it. What scales did the soloist use and how did he use them? How and when does he outline the chord tones? Does the solo feature any recurring licks or is there a short excerpt that you'd like to process as a lick of your own? What role does rhythm play in the solo? If you can extract a general concept or two from the solo you can then practice applying those concepts to your improvising.

You might wonder if there is a hazard of sounding just like the musician you transcribed and not developing a style of your own. There is a small short-term risk of that, but my advice is to forge ahead with energy if this approach works well for you. If you particularly like Sonny Rollins, for example, transcribe eight or ten of his solos. Imitate his notes, articulation, tone, everything. Keep doing it as long as it feels productive, then move on. You'll eventually shed Rollins' influence like an old skin. But even if you don't, it's only a temporary problem because you'll also transcribe Coltrane, Coleman Hawkins, Lester Young, Joe Lovano, and others. Your particular mix of influences will be different than anyone else's and you'll be influenced by different elements. Just remember that learning a transcribed solo is a means to an end and not the end itself. The end is simply to make good music. Let others decide whether your version of good is unusual enough to be thought of as original.

> Here's a great idea: transcribe your own solo. Scat over a chord progression for several choruses, on tape. Then transcribe the entire solo and learn to play it. For better or worse, this solo is a representation of the music you naturally hear. If you were to treat this solo as seriously as a Sonny Rollins solo (work out the fingering, get it up to speed, etc.) you'd learn to play what you hear more competently. This, after all, is the essence of heartfelt improvisation.

Melody paraphrase

Of all the methods for developing improvisational ability, this is the one that seems to be taken the most lightly; but I recommend that you spend some serious time with it.

> Pick a tune and learn to play the melody. In fact, memorize it. Play it several times, exactly as written. Next, play it with a more relaxed rhythm, with a few anticipations and delays. This won't sound like typical improvising yet but just a naturally phrased version of the melody. Do this a few times, varying your rhythms each time. Next, insert an occasional passing tone or ornament. Still think of it as the melody but with a few (not too many) twists. Try this a few times, adding more and more of your notes to the original melody. Next, try replacing some of the melody (instead of merely adding to it) with improvised phrases. Start conservatively, but take more liberties each time around. Don't think of this as improvising yet. You're still just playing the melody. Finally, try improvising freely over the chord progression while hearing the melody firmly in your head the entire time. Practice jumping smoothly back and forth between the melody and improvisation. Of course, you can use the other concrete improvisational approaches (scales, chord tones, etc.) to guide you as you depart from the melody. But in its purest form, this approach is one in which the only structural element is the melody itself; during your departures from it, simply play by ear.

Chapter **20**

Imagine the melody as a life raft. At first you safely navigate around the lake, occasionally dragging a hand or foot in the water. Then you jump into the lake but keep a hold on the raft. You begin to make short swims away from the raft, always keeping it in sight. Eventually you swim all the way to shore, leaving the raft bobbing in the lake, secure in knowing that you can swim back to get it later.

I'm not one who believes that a good solo will necessarily retain particular elements of the original melody. As you spontaneously compose a new melody it can be terribly distracting to try to incorporate some of the composer's actual motifs. Nevertheless, it's vital that you always know where you are in the tune and in the melody as you improvise. By slowly "morphing" from the written melody to free improvisation and back again, you can develop your improvising and your sense of form in a very natural way.

Directly playing what you hear

No matter how much listening you've done, you won't be able to improvise well over a particular tune until you have imprinted its various sounds on your mind. I'm speaking of the melody, yes, but also the roots, the chords, the modes or scales, etc. This imprinting process is something that happens naturally as you hear and play the tune over and over, but you can also develop it in an accelerated fashion by playing and singing the isolated elements. Read "Marinade For Your Ears" (page 90) to see how this is done.

If you've listened to a lot of jazz and you're hearing the various layers of a tune, you won't need to go get an improvised line. It will come and get you! It's like singing in the shower. The improvised line will simply form on its own. And this line is the best thing you could possibly play. Not only will it adhere largely to the theoretical rules, but it will also contain the one element that the theory can't provide you with: you. Theory will only show you the options, not which ones you prefer. But this "shower line" already reflects those preferences. Just trust it and play it.

Think of it as scatting on your instrument. A good scat singer doesn't consciously think when he or she scats. It's just a matter of "pullin' it back and lettin' it go." In that sense, improvising is as passive as taking dictation. You simply type out the line that comes to you without consciously editing it.

But first you need to learn to type. You've got some great sounds in your head now, but which buttons should you press on your instrument to make those sounds come out? Playing what you hear may be difficult at first, but the learning process is easy to explain. To learn how to play what you hear, pick something that you hear—and play it. Choose a melody that you can sing accurately from memory and practice playing it in every key. As your accuracy improves you'll also get better at transferring to your instrument the sounds that you hear in your head when you improvise.

Chapter 20

When you first pick out a melody by ear, you should use what I call the "dumb" approach. Just start playing it without taking into account any theoretical information, including what key you're in. Simply navigate from one note to the next by trying to hear the interval and then respond in real time. You'll probably miss several notes at first, especially when the intervals are large. Just do the best you can. If you miss a note just fix it and go on. Or don't fix it—just play the tune in real time as if you were performing it. Both approaches have merit. Don't practice the tune to perfection. Just go through it once or twice, then move on to the next key.

Eventually you should shift to the "smart" approach in which you examine the tune for clues that will enable you to get the right notes with minimal guesswork. Find the answers to these questions:

1. What scale degree does the melody start on?
2. Does the general key of the tune change? How does the new key relate to the original key?
3. Where are the non-diatonic notes (the notes not in the key) and what altered scale degrees do they represent?
4. Where are the large intervals and what scale degrees do they represent?

There are a surprising number of standard melodies that are diatonic except for a very few chromatic notes. If you know what key you're playing the tune in and you know where the non-diatonic notes are, your guesswork will be limited to the seven notes of the key. And if you can navigate the larger intervals by knowing what scale degrees they represent, then you may very well be able to play the entire melody error-free.

Let's see how you can apply the smart approach to the melody "It Could Happen To You." First, learn the melody on your instrument and practice singing it from memory. Then find the answer to the first question: what scale degree does the melody start on? The first melody note is C, and the key is F major—so the melody starts on the 5th scale degree. If you play this melody in Ab, you should begin on Eb.

Next, does the general key change? The answer is no: it's in F major throughout, despite the presence of some non-diatonic chords.

Where are the non-diatonic notes? There are two on the first line: Eb and B. These are the b7 and the #4, respectively. The same two chromatic tones occur on the 5th line. Otherwise, every note in the melody is in the key of F major.

Finally, where are the large intervals? It's up to you to decide exactly what large means, but let's use the term now to mean any interval larger than a 5th. In that case, there are two of them and they're back to back: from the C at the end of the 7th line down to the C at the beginning of the last line, then back up to Bb. The fifth scale degree goes down an octave to the fifth scale degree, then back up a minor 7th to the fourth scale degree.

Chapter **20**

It Could Happen To You

Burke/Van Heusen

Now play the tune in F without the music. Start on C and just play it by ear, but be ready for the b7 and #4 chromatic notes as well as the large intervals near the end. Then play the melody in Ab. But before you begin, find the starting note (Eb), the b7 and #4 notes (Gb and D), and the "5-5-4" large intervals (Eb down to Eb up to Db). Now play it in several other keys, armed in each case with the same relevant information.

This smart approach may seem almost like cheating at first. It enables you to get the right notes without even hearing them. That's why I recommend that you start with the dumb approach. You need to practice picking out each note purely from an intervallic standpoint, without any crutches to get you through the difficult areas. But you also need to learn to distinguish between diatonic and chromatic tones and you need to become sensitized to the scale degrees that you're playing. Then, when you hear a line of improvisation in your head, you'll be able to transfer that line to your instrument. You can navigate interval by interval or you can recognize the scale degrees of the notes.

Chapter **21**

Marinade for Your Ears

> Treat this whole chapter as a practice box. Don't just read it—do it!

I've already stressed the importance of hearing the various layers of a tune accurately and now I want to show you those layers. To really get them inside you, you need to sing them. Don't worry if you don't have a great voice; just sing the pitches as well in tune as you can. Although I've warned against singing while you play, in this exercise you should sing along with the piano at first, then on your own.

I've selected Cole Porter's "Everything I Love" as our vehicle. Almost any tune would do, especially from the repertoire known collectively as the Great American Songbook (Rodgers and Hart, Jerome Kern, Harold Arlen, Cole Porter, Irving Berlin, Johnny Mercer, etc.). You'll find a wealth of such tunes in Sher Music's *The Standards Real Book*.

First, learn to sing the melody from memory. Take it four bars at a time, fine tuning each line before you move on to the next. It would be a great idea to learn the lyrics as well, but at this point it's fine if you just sing the melody with a syllable like "la."

Next sing the roots of the chords. Again, take the time to get each note in tune.

Next sing the two inner lines, known in choruses as the tenor and alto parts. Play through them and identify which chord part I've written for each chord. In both cases you'll see that I'm using exclusively 3rds and 7ths (except in bar 9) and that the lines move smoothly from note to note.

Next up are the arpeggios. In order to maintain the harmonic rhythm of the progression, I wrote the four-beat chords ascending and descending and the 2-beat chords just ascending. You may prefer to sing them all up and down. Sing these very slowly and zero in on each pitch.

The modes are certainly the most difficult. Take them in small doses and get them right. I use the term "modes" loosely here to mean improvising scales sung from the roots of the chords. In some cases that results in standard modes while in others it yields melodic minor modes, harmonic minor modes, and diminished scales. As you know, there are several possible scales or modes for each chord. I simply selected one that I thought worked well, but feel free to replace it if you prefer.

Beyond these six items (melody, roots, tenor and alto parts, arpeggios, and modes), there are several other workouts you could try. Some are fun, others difficult but worthwhile. Try the sample walking bass line and sample solo. You've already sung the mixed 3rds and 7ths in the tenor and alto parts, but now sing the unmixed 3rds, 5ths, and 7ths. These will be more difficult because you'll have to jump around in parallel with the root movement.

Everything I Love

Cole Porter

Chapter **21**

Tenor part

Alto part

Chapter 21

Arpeggios

Modes

Chapter 21

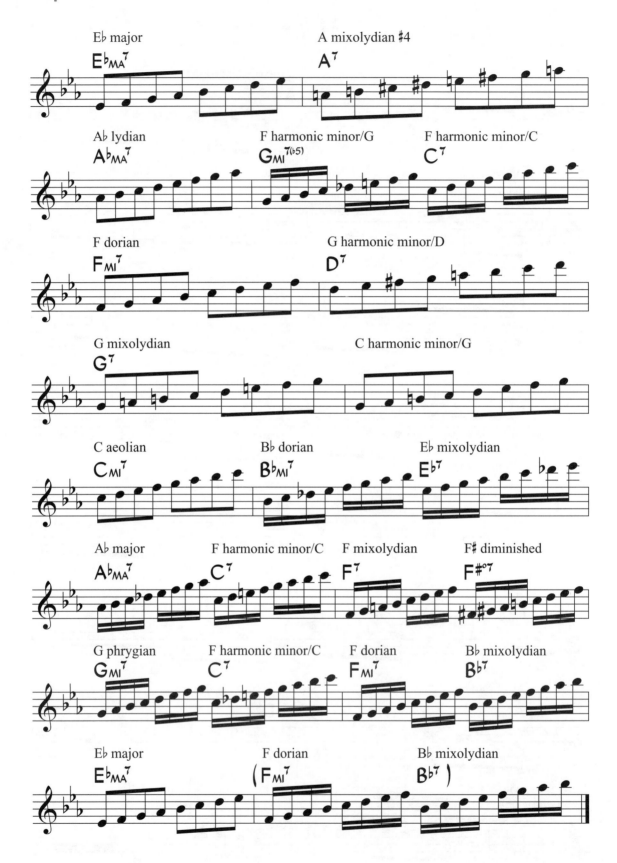

Sample bass line

I composed this bass line using the roots of the chords and connecting material (scales, passing tones and neighboring tones). You can try to compose your own, but first transcribe a few bass lines and get some guidance from a good bass player.

Chapter **21**

Sample solo

3rds

Chapter 21

5ths

7ths

Chapter 21

If you can sing all these layers, it's safe to say that you've marinated your ears in the sound of the tune. If you're still looking for more punishment, here are some suggestions:

1. Scat over the changes, limiting yourself to the four basic chord tones.

2. Scat over the changes, limiting yourself to the notes of each mode.

3. Sing several of these layers with "theory syllables" instead of "la." There are four basic types. I'll use the melody to illustrate them.

   a. Scale degrees in the key of Eb major

   b. Chord tones

   c. Intervals from one melody note to the next

d. Note names in other keys

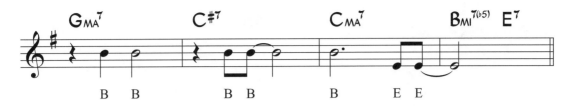

You could apply these syllables to other elements such as the roots.

Scale #:	1	#4	4	3	6
Chord #:	R	R	R	R	R
Interval:		tritone	half	half	5th
New key:	G	C♯	C	B	E

Obviously, it would be silly to sing the roots with chord-tone syllables ("root-root-root," etc.), but the other approaches could be useful.

I'm primarily concerned that you sensitize your ear to the various layers that comprise a tune. You can accomplish that by just using "la." The point of these new syllables is to connect your ear to your brain, i.e., to apply theoretical labels to the sounds that you've trained yourself to hear. Ultimately, theory is a useless tool to a jazz musician if he can't make the connections between theoretical structures and real aural experiences. But if you use these exercises to learn what a perfect 5th sounds like, or what the 3rd of a minor 7th chord sounds like, or what the 4th degree of a harmonic minor scale sounds like, then theory will take on a more authentic reality for you in your musical endeavors.

Here is a chart that shows all the layers that you can sing as well as my recommendations for which syllables to use.

Chapter **21**

Ear-training Exercises for Tunes

Practice these exercises:
1. with just the piano
2. with piano and voice
3. with just the voice
4. with the piano on the roots and the voice on the task

	"La"	Scale degree	Chord tone	Interval	Note-name (various keys)
Melody	*	*	*	*	*
Root	*	*		*	*
Inner Voice #1	*		*		
Inner voice #2	*		*		
Arpeggio	*				*
Sample bass line	*				
Written solo	*				
Mode	*				*
3rd	*				
5th	*				
7th	*				
Chord-tone scatting	*		*		*
Mode scatting	*				*

* especially relevant

Part V *Theory Demystified*

This section contains very specific information on how scales work with chords and how chords work with each other. You'll learn about the blues (scales, phrasing, and chord progressions), diminished and pentatonic scales, and even new piano fingering. Theory is useful only to the extent that you manifest it as real music. So learn to play the tunes you've analyzed and explore the various pathways on the piano or your own instrument.

Chapter **22**

Harmonic Astronomy

What is theory for?

Jazz is best learned aurally. You imitate, transcribe, and play with musicians who are better than you, and you take it all in by ear and process it. What role does theory play in this scenario? Strictly speaking, theory is simply an after-the-fact description of the sounds that you can learn directly by ear, so is it really of any use?

Think of theory as scaffolding, as a structural foundation around which your ear can develop. It presents you with several pathways from which to choose, not with ironclad rules. It can introduce you to sounds earlier than through the use of a purely ear-based approach.

I've occasionally heard a young musician express distrust of theoretical knowledge, fearing that it will destroy the mystery and the magic of music for him. No one who has learned his theory feels this way. Read what Bill Evans had to say about this on page 285.

Questions

"How do chords fit together?"
"Which scales work over chords for improvising?"
"What's the best way to memorize a tune?"
"What's the best way to transpose a tune?"

I hear these four questions all the time, and I'd like to answer them by using a celestial metaphor. But first let me strongly recommend that you sit at a piano as you navigate this chapter. You won't need any advanced piano skills, just a knowledge of basic chords. It will make the going easier if you can see and hear the structures on the piano as you go.

The Planets

Look at the diagram on the next page. You're looking down on a solar system. In the center of the system you'll find the sun, CMa7. It's the I chord in the key of C major, and it's surrounded on all sides by planets (the medium-sized disks). Starting at "twelve-o-clock" and going clockwise, the planets are Dmi7 (II), Emi7 (III), FMa7 (IV), G7 (V), Ami7 (VI), and Bmi7(b5) (VII).

Play these chords (both the sun and the six planets) on the piano. You'll need only white notes. These are the seventh chords that fit within the C major scale.

C major "cosmic"

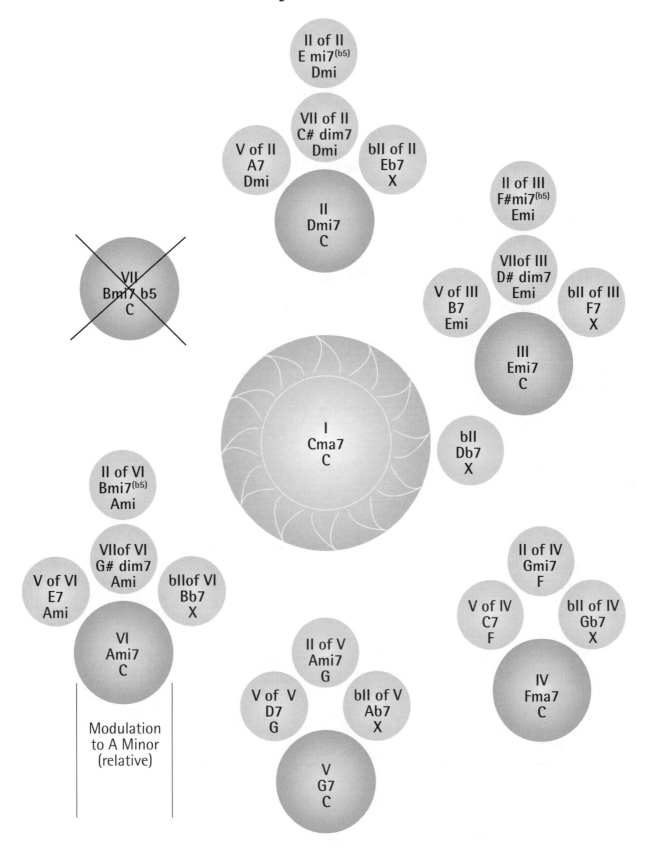

Chapter 22

Just as in a real solar system in which the planets are pulled toward the sun, the planetary chords will want to resolve to the I chord (i.e. the tune will probably end on a CMa7).

Notice that the VII chord (Bmi7(b5)) is crossed out on the diagram. Now look just below it and you'll see another Bmi7(b5) functioning as II of VI. Minor 7(b5) chords almost always function as II chords, so it's safe to discount the VII chord altogether.

The Moons

Every planet except the VII is surrounded by a system of moons. These moons behave just like real ones: they gravitate toward their respective planets. Notice that in each case one moon is farther from its planet than the other moons (for example, II of II, Emi7(b5)). This moon will also gravitate to its planet but will crash into one of the closer moons first (such as V of II, A7).

The Moons of the Minor Planets (II, III, and VI)

Play the four moons surrounding the II chord (Dmi7). Notice that you'll need some black notes in every case. In other words, none of these chords fits within the C major scale. Then play the following chord progressions:

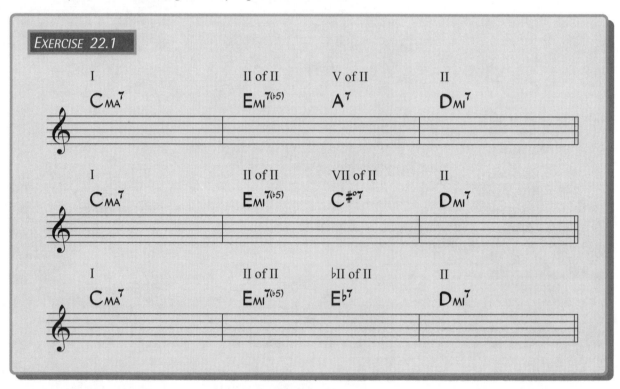

Did you experience the resolution as each close moon proceeded to the Dmi7? There is a good explanation for this. All three chords contain the same tritone interval (C#-G). This is a tense interval that demands resolution. The C# resolves up a half step to the root of the Dmi7, while the G resolves down a whole step to the third of the Dmi7 (F).

EXERCISE 22.2

Play the A7, C#dim7, and Eb7 chords again and find the C#-G tritones within them. Play the C#-G tritone and resolve it to D-F.

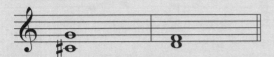

Now play the progressions in Exercise 22.1 again and listen for that resolution.

Now play this D minor bebop scale (we'll discuss its theoretical structure soon):

D minor bebop: D E F G A Bb C C# D

Two of the close moons, A7 and C#dim7, fit neatly into this D minor scale; so does the distant moon Emi7(b5). The Eb7 doesn't (hence the "X"—more on that later as well). Confirm these relationships on the piano.

Now examine the moon systems surrounding the III planet (Emi7) and the VI planet (Ami7). They are of the exact same type; in other words, all three minor planets are surrounded by four-moon systems.

Explore the III and VI systems on the piano by playing progressions similar to those in Exercise 22.1, arranging the chords in a sun/distant moon/close moon/planet sequence. Here's an example:

EXERCISE 22.3

In all of these systems the distant moons are optional. The first four measures of "It Could Happen To You" can be written with or without them.

Chapter **22**

It Could Happen To You - without distant moons

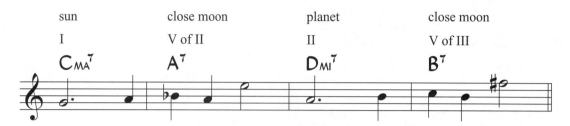

It Could Happen To You - with distant moons

The Modulation Tunnel

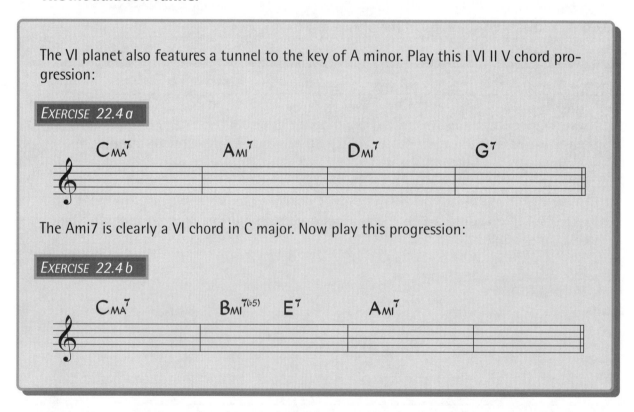

The VI planet also features a tunnel to the key of A minor. Play this I VI II V chord progression:

EXERCISE 22.4 a

The Ami7 is clearly a VI chord in C major. Now play this progression:

EXERCISE 22.4 b

Now that you've preceded the Ami7 with a II of VI and V of VI, you may hear it more as a I chord in the new key of A minor, the relative minor key of C major. It's very common for a tune to modulate from a major key to its relative minor, so it's very possible that you'll hear the note A as more stable than C.

The Moons of the Major Planets (IV and V)

Now examine the moons that revolve around the IV planet (FMa7). There are only two nearby moons: C7 (V of IV) and Gb7 (bII of IV). There is no VII of IV. This chord would be Emi7(b5). Just as the VII planet is crossed out because it doesn't exist in a major key, so also the VII moon of a major planet doesn't exist. The C7 fits into the key of F major, but the Gb7 doesn't (hence the X).

Again we have a single distant moon, the Gmi7 (II of IV), and again it will crash into a nearby moon on its way to the FMa7 planet (resulting in the progressions Gmi7 C7 FMa7 and Gmi7 Gb7 FMa7). Notice that this chord is a minor 7, not a minor 7(b5) chord (as it was for the minor planets).

The V planet (G7) is essentially a major planet like the IV, so it has the same three-moon system. Notice that the II of V is Ami7, the exact same chord as the VI planet. Depending on the actual context, we might experience the chord either as a VI or a II of V. If the chord functions as a VI, we hear it in the key of C major. If it functions as a II of V, we hear it in the key of G major.

Finally, examine the sun (CMa7). Because it's a major chord, you should consider it to have the same three-moon system as the IV and the V. I chose not to write in the II (Dmi7) and the V (G7) as moons, because they've already appeared as planets, but you will find the bII chord (Db7). The relevant chord progressions here would be Dmi7 G7 CMa7 and Dmi7 Db7 CMa7.

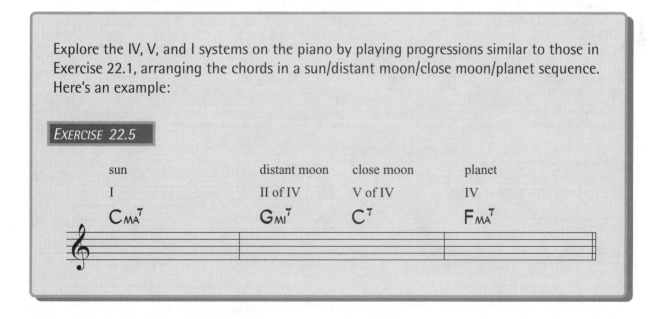

Explore the IV, V, and I systems on the piano by playing progressions similar to those in Exercise 22.1, arranging the chords in a sun/distant moon/close moon/planet sequence. Here's an example:

EXERCISE 22.5

sun	distant moon	close moon	planet
I	II of IV	V of IV	IV
C ᴍᴀ⁷	G ᴍɪ⁷	C⁷	F ᴍᴀ⁷

Chapter 22

Now explore the entire C major cosmic. Begin with the sun, CMa7. From there you may go to any planet or moon. Also, from any planet you may go to any other planet or moon. If you go to a distant moon (such as II of II), proceed next to a close moon of the same planet (such as V of II). From any close moon, proceed either to the planet or to another chord built on the same root as that planet (a moon of another planet). For example, A7 (V of II) must either go to Dmi7 (II) or to D7 (V of V). B7 (V of III) must either go to Emi7 (III), E7 (V of VI), or Emi7(b5) (II of II). Here's a sample exploration. Play through it, then make up your own progressions.

EXERCISE 22.6

You may have noticed one deviation from the rules in my sample exploration: the D7 (V of V) on line 5 proceeded to Dmi7 (II) before it resolved to G7 (V). This specific delayed resolution is very common.

Analyzing a tune in a major key

Now you're ready to analyze the chord progression to the tune "I Should Care" (page 114). Write in the Roman-numeral functions for each chord and the corresponding key centers. Afterwards, refer to the appendix on page 314 to check your answers.

You should have only three difficulties:

1. Fmi7 Bb7 does not appear on the C major cosmic. It may look like a II-V in Ebb, but it's actually functioning in a different way (refer to "New Pathways Home," page 135).
2. Bmi7(b5) E7 appears on the C major cosmic as a II of VI and V of VI, but the first time they appear in this tune they go to Gmi7 (II of IV) instead of VI (Ami7). Surprise!
3. How about the two Ami7's in bars 14 and 15? We've already discussed how ambiguous this chord can be. Is it a VI in C? Is it a I in A minor? Or is it a II of V? The first Ami7 is probably a VI or a I, but a strong case could be made for calling the second one a II of V. The next chord (D7) is a V of V.

You'll find that you can analyze many tunes with these cosmic charts, particularly ones that belong to the so-called Great American Songbook. I've included a blank cosmic on page 308 in the appendix. I recommend that you make eleven copies and fill them out in each of the other eleven keys. Then look through a fake book (such as the *Standards Real Book* or the *All-Jazz Real Book*, both by Sher Music) and analyze several tunes. Don't get discouraged if there are some tunes that don't behave as the cosmics predict that they should. Almost every tune will feature a few surprises. You'll find almost nothing but surprises in the compositions of Wayne Shorter, Herbie Hancock, and other more modern composers. Many of these compositions can be viewed in part as reactions against the traditional use of harmony, so it should be no surprise that a cosmic analysis of them will reveal very little.

One more qualification: many tunes, even older ones, will simply modulate to a new key. If you try to make sense of those chords with the original cosmic, you'll run into trouble. Cole Porter's "I Love You" starts in F major but modulates to A major in bar 12. Jerome Kern's "All The Things You Are" modulates from Ab major to C major to Eb major to G major to E major and finally back to Ab major! In such cases, simply refer to the cosmic that represents each new key.

One of the most fundamental problems that any artist in any discipline must confront is the conflict between unity and variety. When a composer writes a piece of music, he wants it to be unified, but he also wants it to be interesting. A tune with one chord (CMa7) has a tremendous amount of unity but no variety. A tune using all six planets

Chapter 22

I Should Care

Sammy Cahn
Axel Stordahl
Paul Weston

(fine)

(CMa7, Dmi7, Emi7, FMa7, G7, and Ami7) would still have a lot of unity, and it would have much more variety, but perhaps not enough. So what is a composer to do? Should he randomly insert some extra chords that are not in the key of C? Stick a BbMa7 in here, an Abm7(b5) there? This will undoubtedly increase the variety in the tune but at the cost of unity. The tune will not make as much sense.

Composers have resolved this problem in the same way from before Bach's time. The solution is to insert chords that, while not in the key of C, will lead back into the key of C (to one of the chords that fit into C)—in other words, moons! Now the tune has more variety but just as much unity. Since the solution is so elegant, composers of almost every style have used it with great regularity. It shows up in classical, folk, rock, country, and jazz.

Improvising Scales

Now I want to be more specific about the scales themselves. When I say that the CMa7 chord is a I chord in C major, it means that you can improvise using the notes of the C major scale. But it would be better for you to think in terms of the C major bebop scale, which includes an additional #5 scale degree.

> C major scale = C D E F G A B C
> C major bebop scale = C D E F G G# A B C

The additional G# is a tension tone, typically used as a half-step connector between G and A. It's not a note that you would camp out on for any length of time.

> Play both the C major and the C major bebop scale on the piano to hear how they sound. Then play them again and sing along. Then try singing them without the piano. Finally, improvise with a C major bebop scale over a CMa7 and over a II-V-I in C major (Dmi7 G7 CMa7)

When I say that E7 (V of VI) is in the key of A minor, it means that you can improvise using the notes of an A harmonic minor scale. But it would be better for you to think in terms of the A minor bebop scale, which includes an additional b7 scale degree.

> A harmonic minor scale = A B C D E F G# A
> A minor bebop scale = A B C D E F G G# A

The additional G natural is a perfectly good note. It sounds good over the Bmi7b5 (II of VI) and over the E7 (V of VI).

> Play both the A harmonic minor and the A minor bebop scale on the piano, then try singing them without the piano. Finally, improvise with an A minor bebop scale over Ami and over a II-V-I in A mi (Bmi7(b5) E7 Ami).

Chapter **22**

Remember the earlier discussion of Ami7 (is it a VI in C major or a I in A minor)? If you decide that it's a VI chord in C major, you'll improvise with the notes of the C major bebop scale. If you decide that it's a I in A minor, you'll improvise with the notes of an A minor bebop scale. The two scales have exactly the same notes! Consequently, the discussion of whether the chord is a VI or a I becomes purely academic.

You must be wondering what scales to use for the bII chords; as you can see, they're all marked with "X"s. These chords are not in a key, strictly speaking. Nevertheless, there is a perfectly good scale to use for improvising. For every bII chord, use a melodic minor scale on the 5th of the chord. For Db7 (bII) use an Ab melodic minor scale. For Eb7 (bII of II) use Bb melodic minor. For F7 (bII of III), use C melodic minor—and so on. I'm using the term "melodic minor" here in the jazz sense, as a major scale with a b3 both ascending and descending. Don't flat the 6th and 7th degrees on the way down as in classical music theory.

C melodic minor scale = C D Eb F G A B C

Play this scale on the piano and sing it. Then play it over an F7 and improvise with it.

The Minor Cosmic

Wait a minute, there's something missing: what if the tune is in a minor key? In order to prepare for such a situation, you need to know what a minor cosmic looks like. Let me warn you in advance, it's a much messier system than the major cosmic. There are strange occurrences on the "solar," "planetary" and "lunar" levels, and some of the scale choices are from Mars!

Take a few minutes here to examine the C minor cosmic on page 117. Find the surprises, then read on.

Earlier in this chapter I introduced the C minor bebop scale. Now here's a new scale of my own concoction:

C composite minor = C D Eb F G Ab A Bb B C

With the addition of the A natural to the minor bebop scale, every member of the chromatic scale from G up to C is included. You can view this scale as the combination of the C minor bebop scale with the C melodic minor scale. A tune that is in the key of C minor may have some chords with Ab's, some with A's, some with Bb's and some with B's. Here's a very common example:

Cmi Cmi(Ma7) Cmi7 Cmi6

Chapter **22**

C minor "cosmic"

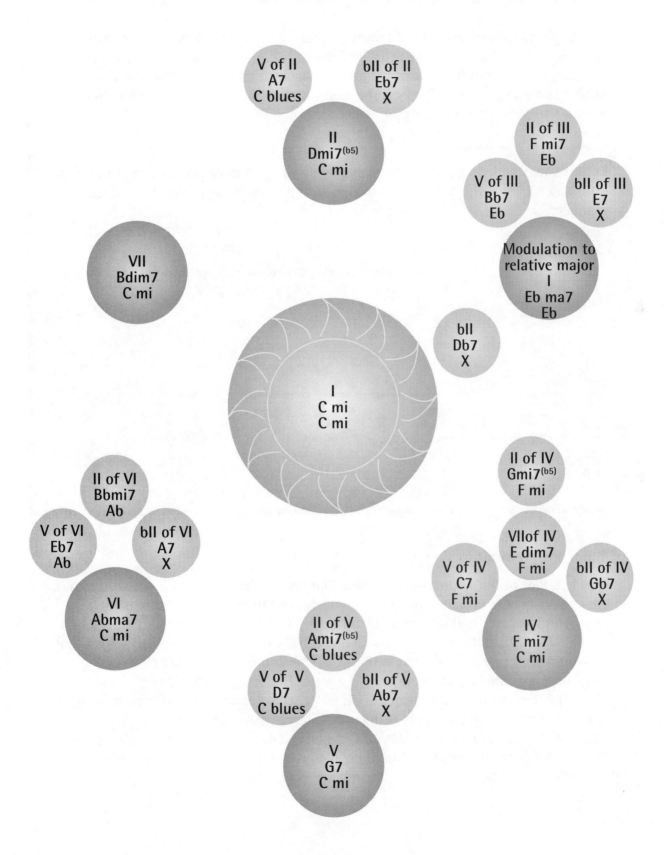

Chapter 22

I've listed Cmi (C minor triad) as the I chord (the sun) on the C minor cosmic, but all of the chords in the above progression may be considered as I chords. This tendency to use all the chromatic possibilities is just one of the messy aspects of the minor key.

Let's begin by looking at the normal aspects of the cosmic. The IV planet is Fmi7 and is in the key of C minor. Improvise with the C minor bebop scale. The moon system surrounding the IV chord is just what we would expect with a minor planet. The VI planet is AbMa7 and is in the key of C minor. The moon system surrounding the VI chord is just what we would expect with a major planet.

Explore the IV and VI systems on the piano by playing progessions similar to those in Exercise 22.1, using the sun/distant moon/close moon/planet sequence. Here are some Examples:

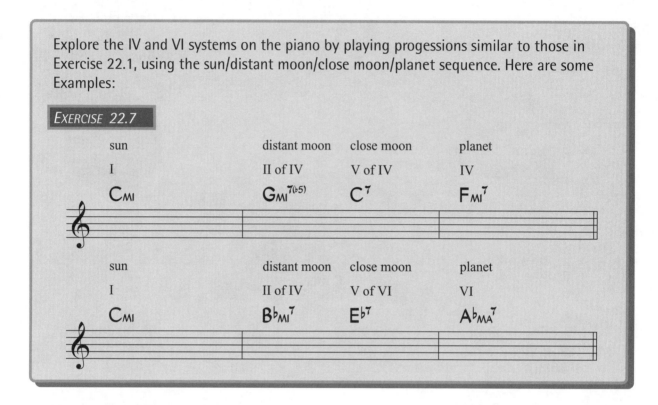

EXERCISE 22.7

sun		distant moon	close moon	planet
I		II of IV	V of IV	IV
Cₘₗ		Gₘₗ⁷⁽ᵇ⁵⁾	C⁷	Fₘₗ⁷

sun		distant moon	close moon	planet
I		II of IV	V of VI	VI
Cₘₗ		Bᵇₘₗ⁷	Eᵇ⁷	Aᵇₘₐ⁷

Minor cosmic oddities

Now let's look at the surprises. First, notice that the VII chord (Bdim7) is not crossed out. We've already observed diminished 7th chords functioning as VII's of minor planets. Consistency requires that we also allow for Bdim7 (VII) to resolve to Cmi (I). Now look at the III planet (EbMa7). It's a major planet and it has exactly the three-moon system that we would expect. What's odd here is that you'll never hear the EbMa7 as a III chord. You'll hear it as the I chord in the key of Eb major (the relative major key of C minor). This is the reverse side of the phenomenon we observed earlier when we saw how easy it was to modulate from C major to its relative minor key (A minor). Here, though, the situation is more extreme. In the key of C major, you might or might not hear the move to the Ami7 chord as a change of key (it could just be the VI). But in the key of C minor, an EbMa7 always signals a move to the relative major key.

All of the other oddities on the C minor cosmic seem to have one source: an aversion to the note E natural. The most distinctive note in the key of C minor is Eb. It's the note that gives the key its minor sound. There are certain chords and scales which we would expect to see on a minor cosmic, based on the way the major cosmic was built, but these items don't appear on the minor cosmic because they have E naturals in them. There's something about the E natural that seems to threaten the integrity of the basic key. Frankly, this is just my opinion (remember—this is jazz theory). I don't really know why these chords and scales are absent in minor tunes—they just are. Let's take them one at a time (and remember, play them on the piano):

1. There is no II of II (Emi7b5). Play this progression:

   | Cmi G7 | Cmi Emi7(b5) A7 | Dmi7(b5) G7 | Cmi |

   Does the Emi7(b5) sound terrible? I don't think so. But I can't think of a single tune in a minor key that has this chord other than Benny Golson's "Whisper Not"—and in that case the tune has already changed keys to D minor.

2. There is no VII of II (C#°7). Replace the A7 in the previous progression with C#°7. Again, it doesn't sound terrible, but it's too far out of the ordinary to warrant inclusion on the cosmic.

3. There is a V of II (A7), despite the fact that there is an E in the chord (it's the 5th, which is omitted in most voicings). Play this progression:

   | Cmi A7 | Dmi7(b5) G7 | Cmi |

   The A7 on the C major cosmic is in the key of D minor. In the progression

   | CMa7 A7 | Dmi7 G7 | CMa7 |

   it sounds fine when you improvise with the D minor bebop scale over the A7 (Use the C major scale for all the other chords.) But now try using the D minor bebop scale for the A7 in the first progression (Use C minor bebop for all the other chords.) Does it sound terrible? I wouldn't go that far; it's just not what I would naturally hear. Now play the same progression again. This time use a C blues scale over the A7.

   C blues scale = C Eb F F# G Bb C

   This colors the A7 in a way that blends it into the C minor key more naturally. For that matter, you could play a C blues scale over the entire progression. You'll find that you can almost get away with "slamming" a C minor bebop scale over the whole progression, but C blues is probably a bit smoother over the A7.

4. There is a V of V (D7), but the G major scale (which was recommended for the D7 on the C major cosmic) sounds quite bad. Treat this in the same way we treated the A7: color it with a C blues scale. This will sound much better. And again, C minor bebop works pretty well too.

Chapter 22

5. There is a II of V, but it's not an Ami7 like it was on the C major cosmic. Why not? Because the 5th of Ami7 is E natural! The 5th is flatted to bend the chord into C minor. Play this progression:

| Cmi Ami7(b5) | D7 G7 | Cmi

On the Ami7(b5), try improvising with C melodic minor (or C blues)

That's about it. Pretty messy, isn't it? Music is very mathematical—except when it isn't.

Now explore the entire minor cosmic chart as you did the major cosmic, proceeding from the sun through distant moons to closer moons to planets.

Analyzing a tune in a minor key

Now analyze "My Funny Valentine" on page 122. The only troublemaker is the Abmi6 chord in bar 15. The notes of this chord are Ab Cb Eb F. With the F down an octave (F Ab Cb Eb) it's simply an Fmi7(b5). Notice that the next chord is a Bb7, which is the V chord that sends you to the relative major key of Eb. Retroactively, we can now view the Fmi7b5 as an altered II chord in that key (Fmi7(b5) instead of Fmi7). Spelled as an Abmi6, we might call it an altered IV chord in Eb. The rest of the tune should be easy. Check your answers in the appendix on page 316.

I've included a blank minor cosmic in the appendix on page 309. Make several copies and fill them out in other keys.

Back to the beginning....

Here are the four questions that began this chapter:

"How do chords fit together?"
"Which scales work over chords for improvising?"
"What's the best way to memorize a tune?"
"What's the best way to transpose a tune?"

While there's much more to it than what we've discussed here, I hope that you have a sense of how to deal with the first two questions. As for the last two? Once you understand the cosmic structure of a tune, you can memorize and transpose it easily. By way of explanation, here's another metaphor:

Chapter **22**

You build a house using a detailed set of blueprints. Within a week a fierce tornado destroys both the house and the plans. While you're not thrilled by these misfortunes, you find that you don't need the blueprints because you now have a detailed under-standing of how the various parts of the house fit together. You can easily rebuild the house on the same site. If you decide not to rebuild the house in tornado country, you can easily rebuild somewhere else. The site may be different, but the essential structure is the same.

It's the same with a tune. Once you understand its structure, you can easily re-create it in the same key or any other. The term "transposing" is a misnomer here, because it suggests that you are moving the tune from one key to another. You don't move the house, plank-by-plank, brick-by-brick, to another site. You don't move the tune, chord-by-chord, phrase-by-phrase, to another key; you simply re-create it.

Chapter 22

My Funny Valentine

Ballad

Rodgers/Hart

(fine)

Cop-out Scales

Play this chord progression:

| EXERCISE 23.1 | | CMa7 | FMa7 | Dmi7 G7 CMa7 |

What key is the FMa7 in? Of course it's in C major, like the rest of the progression. If you improvised with an F major scale, the note Bb wouldn't sound very good, would it?

Now play this progression:

| EXERCISE 23.2 | | CMa7 Gmi7 C7 | FMa7 | Dmi7 | G7 | CMa7

Now what key is the FMa7 in? Is it still in C major? After all, the Gmi7 C7 was inserted simply to lead us to the same IV chord we had before. Or is it in F major? Were the two new chords so effective in leading us to the FMa7 that we now hear it as the I chord?

Here's what I think: it's both. We simultaneously hear the FMa7 as the IV in C and the I in F. Try improvising over the chord with the C major scale, making sure to include the note B. Now try using the F major scale, making sure to include the note Bb (ideally as a passing tone between A and C). Do you have a preference? Does either one sound bad? If you don't like the Bb, does it sound as bad as it did over the FMa7 in example 1?

When I improvise, I simply try to play the sounds that I hear in my head. If scale/chord theory helps me to do that, great. If it contradicts what I hear, I'll go with my ear instead (and later attempt to fine-tune my theoretical views so that they more accurately describe what I hear). To explain what I really hear over the FMa7 in exercise 23.2, I'll need to temporarily profess to having multiple personalities (I've been accused of worse!).

One of my personalities hears the FMa7 as a IV chord in C major and doesn't like the sound of the note Bb. My other personality hears it as a I chord in F major and doesn't like the sound of the note B natural. Neither of my personalities has any problem with the six notes that are common to the key of C and the key of F (C, D, E , F, G, and A). Both my personalities are concerned only with playing what I hear, not with the need to improvise within a recognizable scale.

So here's what happens: my ear gravitates to the path of least resistance, namely those six common notes. Does the note Bb sound terrible to me? No, of course not. After all, one of my personalities loves it. Similarly, I have no big problems with the B natural. But the scale that describes the notes that I naturally hear is neither the C major scale nor the F major scale, precisely: it's the C "hexatonic" scale! Call it the C "cop-out" scale if you want. It's as if I can't figure out whether the chord is a IV in C or a I in F so I use the six safe notes. But--and this is important--it's not my mind that's copping out, it's my ear.

Chapter **23**

It's really a simple matter of probabilities. Over any chord, all twelve notes of the chromatic scale are valid candidates for improvisation, but your ear will naturally gravitate to some notes more than others. In the case of the FMa7 in example 23.2, most players will first gravitate to the six notes of the C hexatonic scale (C D E F G A). The notes B and Bb are somewhat less likely candidates, and, of course, the least probable notes are the four other outside ones (Db, Eb, Gb, and Ab).

Situations often arise where a chord is being pulled in two different directions, functioning in one way with respect to the preceding progression and in another way with respect to the progression that follows. There's even a name for such an event: "pivot chord." In these situations, you don't need to come up with a traditional scale to describe what you're hearing. If the two scales under consideration differ only by one or two notes, your ear may very well gravitate to the common tones between those scales. Don't force a seven-note scale over a chord in the name of theoretical neatness if your ear only hears five or six. Never forget that in jazz, theory is an after-the-fact discipline that we use to describe music that sounds good to us. If we need to coin a new term or create a new scale in order to do that, then so be it.

Most Consonant Scales

> Treat this whole chapter as a practice box. Don't just read it – do it!

Here's another way of choosing scales to use over chords. Not only will it give you some new uses for the major scale, but it will also generate almost all the uses for the melodic minor, diminished, and whole tone scales. You'll have at least one good solution for each chord that is not in a key, and you'll have alternative sounds for each chord that is in a key.

Most consonant scales for minor 7ths

Consider the chord Cmi7. Build a scale for this chord using these instructions:

> Start on any chord tone. Go up a whole step (W) or to the next chord tone, whichever comes first. Proceed from any non-chord tone up to the next chord tone.

Here's how it looks:

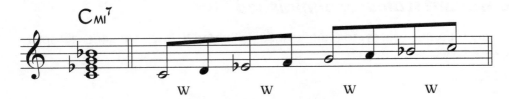

These are the notes of the Bb major scale. Played from C to C, it's called the C dorian mode (see page 312 in the appendix). Sometimes a Bb major scale is used over a Cmi7 because it's functioning as a II chord. You would have to consider the context of the chord in the progression to make that choice. Here we didn't consider a context. We just allowed the shape of the chord itself to dictate the scale by adding whole steps above each chord tone. So it stands to reason that we would get the same result for any chord that had the same shape (any minor 7th chord). Build the scale for Ami7 using the same process.

This is the A dorian mode (the G major scale from A to A). In both cases the result is a major scale built on the 7th of the chord. This is what I refer to as the most consonant scale for the chord.

The most consonant scale for a chord consists of the chord tones and the notes a whole step above the chord tones.

Chapter **24**

Most consonant scales for major 7ths

Let's apply the same process to find the most consonant scale for CMa7.

This is a G major scale from C to C (C Lydian mode). It's a major scale built on the 5th of the chord. Using that relationship, it's easy to figure out that the most consonant scale for EbMa7 is Bb major. For BMa7 it's F# major.

The most consonant scale is a primitively simple structure. When you choose this scale for improvising, you're merely using the chord tones plus other notes that won't clash with the chord tones. In each case the actual shape of the chord itself, not the context of the chord in the progression, determines the scale. For example, the most consonant scale for a major 7th chord is a major scale built on the 5th, regardless of whether the chord is a I or a IV in the key.

Most consonant scales for diminished 7ths

Now let's apply the same process to a diminished 7th chord. (For convenience I'll spell the 7th as an A instead of a Bbb.)

This is a C diminished scale. It may seem almost too nice and neat that the most consonant scale for a diminished 7th chord is a diminished scale built on the root. But in a sense there was no diminished scale until this concept created it. Since this is the scale that matches the shape of a diminished 7th chord, it's only logical to call it a diminished scale. All we're doing here is applying the process that created the diminished scale to all the other chord types as well.

The blanket metaphor

You might find this metaphor useful in understanding most consonant scales. Drape a blanket over your television set. Now drape it over a lamp, a piano, a toaster, yourself, whatever. The blanket will assume an endless number of shapes, but it's just one blanket. Now drape the chord-tone-plus-whole-step scale over a minor 7th chord. It will assume the shape of a dorian mode. Drape it over a major 7th chord and it takes on a lydian shape. Drape it over a diminished 7th chord and it looks like a diminished scale. It's just one blanket—the chord-tone-plus-whole-step (most consonant) scale—but it changes its shape according to the chord underneath. Unlike the real blanket, however, the scale is given a different name for each shape it assumes.

Here's an example to illustrate my point. As we saw, the most consonant scale for CMa7 is the G major scale (C lydian mode).

If you bend the chord into a C dominant 7th by flatting the B, you'll bend the most consonant scale in the same way. This will yield a G melodic minor scale (C lydian dominant, or C mixolydian #4—see page 313 in the appendix), which is precisely the most consonant scale for C7.

It should be clear from this example that the most consonant scale for a chord is purely dependent on the shape of the chord itself.

Building most consonant scales for other chords

The next page is a worksheet. I've supplied you with the tones for each chord type. You should add the whole steps and try to identify the scale. If appropriate, find the traditional name as well as the modal name (as a C mode). For example, the most consonant scale for Cmi7 is Bb major (traditional) or C dorian (modal). After you've finished, check your answers on the following page.

Chapter **24**

Chapter 24

I need to state clearly that the term "most consonant scale" is not to be equated with "best scale." In fact, in most cases the best scale for a chord is the key scale, which may be very different indeed. Later I'll discuss how to choose between key and most consonant scales. But be aware that the most consonant scale represents just one good sound over a chord, and often not the best.

Nevertheless, look at the value of what we've done here. You now have scales to use over all the chords for which the tonal (key) system offers no clear solutions. And you know almost all the possible uses for melodic minor, diminished, and whole tone scales (as well as some new uses for the major scale).

The major 7#5 chord

I say "almost" because there is one use for a melodic minor scale that is not strictly of the most consonant scale type. Look what happens when we add whole steps to the notes of a CMa7(#5):

This is a strange scale indeed, one with no established name. It's tempting to call it a C whole tone scale with an added B, but that would suggest that the B is functioning as a passing tone (which is certainly not the case, as B is the 7th of the chord). Nevertheless, this scale doesn't work very well over the CMa7(#5) chord. The A# doesn't sound good, despite the fact that it's a whole step above a chord tone. Ironically, it works much better if we replace the A# with an A, even though A lies a half step above the G# in the chord. You can't land on the A. You have to finesse the half-step clash by using it as a passing tone between G# and B (the 5th and the 7th). Now, however, the scale is a familiar one: A melodic minor.

Most consonant scales for dominant 7ths and the effect of context

I've emphasized the fact that most consonant scales are shape-based structures, not context-based. While this is true, you have to be especially careful when you use most consonant scales with dominant 7th chords. Notice that I included six dominant chords on the worksheet. The C7 and the C13 share the same most consonant scale (G melodic minor), but the other four each have a different solution. Now examine this chord progression:

This is a II-V-I progression in the key of F minor. The C7 will usually be played with some combination of these alterations: b9, #9, and #5. These notes (Db, Eb, and Ab, respectively) are all members of the F minor scale. Even if you don't actually add these notes to your voicing, the listener will still hear the chord as being colored by the sound of the F minor scale. These alterations will often be included in the written name of the chord (e.g., C7(#5b9)), but even if it's written as a simple C7 you should think of it as an altered chord. This will affect your most consonant scale choice: it's Db melodic minor, not G melodic minor. To generalize: the most consonant scale for a V chord in a minor key is a melodic minor scale on the b2. If you build it from the root of the chord, it's called an altered scale.

Here's a II-V-I progression in the key of F major:

We hear this C7 as being colored by the notes of the F major scale, so it's an essentially unaltered chord. You might add a 9th (D) and/or a 13th (A) to the voicing, but the most consonant scale would be G melodic minor with or without them. The important thing to realize about this chord, however, is that you can exercise tremendous freedom in your choice of extensions. You don't need to alter the chord, but you can, and in various ways. You can play it as a C7(#5b9) with a Db melodic minor scale, as a C9(#5) with a C whole tone scale, as a C13(b9) with a C auxiliary diminished scale, or as a C9sus4 with an F major scale. Of course, you can leave it unaltered and use the G melodic minor scale or the key scale, F major.

Here's a II-bII-I progression in the key of B major:

In a strict sense, the C7 is not in a key. It doesn't fit within the B major scale, and it's not functioning as a V in F. Since there is no key scale, this is a classic case for the use of a most consonant scale. When it functions as a bII chord, a dominant 7th seems to resist most alterations. It can be altered, but the unaltered form is generally a much more natural sound. The most consonant scale, then, would be G melodic minor.

So it appears that you do have to consider a dominant 7th's function before you choose its most consonant scale. The shape still determines the scale, but you won't know the specific shape of the dominant 7th until you consider its relationship to the other chords in the progression.

Chapter 24

Here's a summary of dominant 7th functions starting with the most common. I've included the key scales, suggested alterations, most consonant scales, and sample lines.

V in F major: unaltered (Gmm)
b9 #5 (Dbmm)
9 #5 (C whole tone)
13 b9 (C aux. dim)
9 sus4 (F major)

V in F minor: b9 #5 (Db mm)

bII in B major (but no key): unaltered (Gmm)

bII in B minor (but no key): unaltered (Gmm)

bVII in D major (but no key): unaltered (Gmm)

VII in Db major (but no key): b9 #5 **(Db mm)**
(F minor bebop)

IV in G major (but no key): unaltered (Gmm)

III in Ab major (but no key): b9 #5 **(Db mm)**
(F minor bebop)

Feel free to replace any b9 with a #9 in these voicings. You'll notice that I used the phrase "but no key" to describe all but the first two C7 functions. For example, I described the C7 as a bII in B major (but no key). This means that even though the C7 relates to the key of B major as a bII chord, it's not officially in that key. Don't improvise with a B major scale over the chord.

Most consonant scales vs. key scales

So when should you use most consonant scales? Can you use the most consonant scale for every chord in a tune, regardless of whether it's in a key? You should experiment with all the possibilities and see what you think. I know what works for me, but you'll need to strike your own balance between key scales and most consonant scales.

Here are the chord changes to the tune "The Nearness of You." Improvise over the entire tune using key scales, then go back and use only most consonant scales. Listen and compare them.

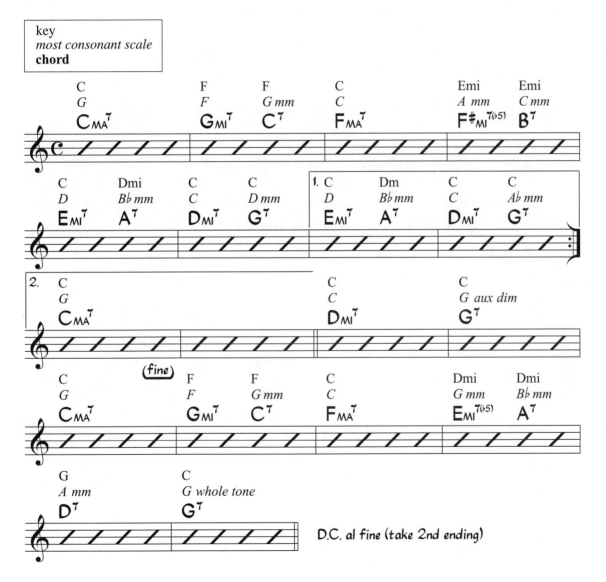

D.C. al fine (take 2nd ending)

Chapter 24

Scales are a useful way of describing what I naturally hear. What I've discovered is that my ear usually gravitates to the key scales in most situations rather than the most consonant scales, with a few notable exceptions:

1. Certainly I hear most consonant scales for chords that are not in a key. The most common example of this is a dominant 7th chord functioning as a bII. I usually consider this chord to be unaltered and use a melodic minor on the 5th.
2. I prefer the most consonant scale to the key scale for a dominant 7th functioning as a V of V. The D7 in the 7th bar of the bridge in "The Nearness of You" is a V of V. I like the G# from the A melodic minor scale over this chord. It's the #11th of the D7, and it's the one note that distinguishes the most consonant scale (A mm) from the key scale (G major).
3. I take full advantage of the various options on a dominant 7th that functions as V in a major key. I especially like the auxiliary diminished scale (with a b9th and regular 13th in the voicing) and the melodic minor on the b2 (with a b9th and #5th), but I also use the whole tone scale (with a regular 9th and #5th).
4. I often use most consonant scales on II-V-I's in minor keys:

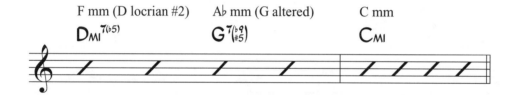

Read more about this in "The Minor II-V-I Progression" (page 211).

5. I'll sometimes hear a lydian mode (a major scale on the 5th) for a major 7th chord functioning as a I chord. It's very common to finish off a tune with a lydian run on the last chord.

New Pathways Home

Credit for the essential ideas in this chapter belongs to the great musician Gary Peacock. I've simply added a little around the edges.

Traditional resolutions: the V-I and the bII-I

Tension-release mechanisms surround us in every part of our lives. You can't move a muscle (literally) without experiencing one. They are to be found in physics, politics, personal relationships, visual art, and certainly in music. The V-I chord progression is by far the most common example of musical tension and release. It plays a prominent role in every style of Western music as well as in music from many other cultures. But did you ever wonder why it works? Why exactly does V resolve to I so convincingly? The answer to this question starts with these two intervals. Play them on the piano:

Listen to how tense the first interval is and how "un-tense" the second one is. The first interval (B-F) is a diminished 5th (known more generically as a tritone). It resolves smoothly to the second interval (C-E), which is a major 3rd. This is precisely the mechanism that causes G7 (V) to resolve smoothly to C (I):

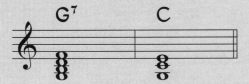

There are many other chords that contain the B-F (or Cb-F) tritone. All of them resolve smoothly to a C chord. Play them on the piano:

The last progression (Db7 to C) is of particular interest because it provides us with a second dominant 7th chord that resolves to C. It's a bII chord, and it resolves to C because it has the same B-F tritone (Cb-F) as the V chord (G7). As this is the tritone that is responsible for the resolution, I'll call it the "resolving tritone."

Chapter 25

Now consider the interval between the roots of these two dominant chords, Db and G. It's another tritone! The G7 and the Db7 are a tritone away from each other. It doesn't matter whether you go up or down a tritone from G. You'll still end up on Db, because a tritone is exactly half an octave. In the G7 the resolving tritone is comprised of the 3rd (B) and the 7th (F). In the Db7 the resolving tritone is comprised of the 7th (B) and the 3rd (F). Not only do these chords share the same resolving tritone, but in both cases that tritone consists of the 3rd and the 7th of the chord.

There is a significant difference between G7 and Db7, however. The notes of G7 fit neatly into a C major scale. In the G7 to C progression, then, you can improvise with the notes of a C major scale. The notes of a Db7 (specifically, the non-tritone notes—the root and the 5th) don't fit into the key of C major. Even though Db7 leads to a C chord, don't improvise with a C major scale. Use the most consonant scale, Ab melodic minor, over the Db7, then use C major over the C chord.

Let's review what we've learned so far about these two dominant 7ths:

> The V chord and bII chord (a tritone away from each other) resolve to I because their 3rds and 7ths form the same resolving tritone. The V chord is in the key, but the bII chord is not. (Improvise with a melodic minor scale built on the 5th of the chord.)

Because both of these chords resolve to I, they can often be used interchangeably. In other words, you can substitute a Db7 for a G7 in a chord progression:

This process is called tritone substitution. It refers specifically to the replacement of one dominant 7th with another one built a tritone away. Notice the smooth root movement in the II-bII-I progression.

You may already be familiar with this well-trodden theoretical information. So now I want to examine some newer ways to resolve to a I chord. This information will have implications for analyzing, composing, reharmonizing, and improvising over chord progressions.

Newer resolutions: the III-I, IV-I, bVII-I, and VII-I

Let's take another look at the resolving tritone:

The notes C and E are the two most stable notes in the C major chord. The B-F tritone is wrapped tightly around those notes. The F resolves down a half step to E, while the B resolves up a half step to C. In other words, the tritone contracts to the root and the 3rd of the chord. But consider what would happen if we wrapped a tritone around the 3rd and the 5th instead. This interval (E-G) is a minor 3rd, smaller than the C-E major 3rd. Consequently the tritone wrap will not be as tight. One of the notes will resolve by a half step, but the other will resolve by a whole step. Because it's a looser fit, there are two different tritones that resolve inward to the 3rd and the 5th:

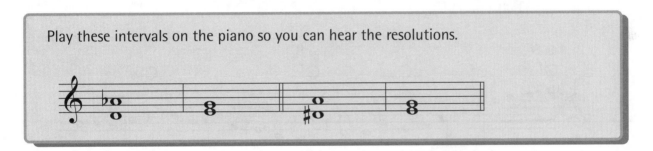

Play these intervals on the piano so you can hear the resolutions.

Now remember two points that we discussed before:

1. The 3rd and the 7th of a dominant 7th form a tritone.
2. Two dominant 7ths a tritone away from each other will share the same 3-7 tritone.

The D-Ab tritone is formed by the 3rd and 7th of Bb7. It's also the 7th and the 3rd of E7, the tritone substitute for Bb7. The D#-A tritone is formed by the 3rd and 7th of B7. It's also the 7th and 3rd of F7, the tritone substitute for B7. So there are four new dominant 7ths that resolve smoothly to C.

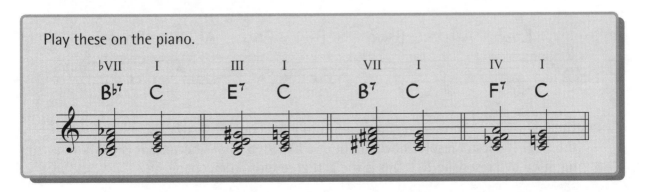

Play these on the piano.

Chapter 25

Altogether, there are now six dominant 7ths that resolve to I: bII, III, IV, V, bVII, and VII. Notice that the last three are a tritone away from the first three. This information has profound implications for substitution. Instead of replacing a G7 (V) with a Db7 (bII), you can now consider a B7 (VII), a Bb7 (bVII), an E7 (III), or an F7 (IV) instead.

Applications of this theory

Here are four ways in which you can use this new substitution theory:

1. As a composer: you can create more interesting chord progressions.
2. As a re-harmonizer: same as above—you're just messing with someone else's chord progression instead of your own. At first you would do this very deliberately with pencil and paper, but eventually you could learn to improvise new chord progressions on the fly.
3. As an improviser: This is a particularly exciting application of the theory. Simply put, it involves improvising over one chord progression as if it were another to achieve a more outside, interesting sound. For example, improvise over a V-I as if it were a bVII-I or a VII-I:

Play the first example with a Bb7 in the first bar. The line matches the chord. Now play it with a G7 instead. Now your two hands don't agree with each other, but each hand is playing a dominant 7th that resolves to C. The conflicting sounds converge in the next measure, creating tension and release. Do the same for the second example. Play the first line with a B7, then with a G7. The note F# is supposedly forbidden over a G7, but it works fine as part of a B7 outline.

4. As an analyzer: you'll be able to make sense of many chord progressions that have previously confused you. For example, here's a section of the tune "My Romance" in Bb:

The Bb7 is a V of IV resolving down a 5th to a IV chord (Eb maj7). But what about the Ab7? It doesn't resolve down a 5th or a half step. That's because it isn't a V or a bII: it's a bVII resolving to I. This is the actual resolution mechanism:

Expanding V's to II-V's

Here's a natural expansion of the theory that yields some more interesting chord progressions. It's standard practice to replace a V chord with a II-V progression:

You can do the same with each of the six dominant 7ths that resolve to I. For example:

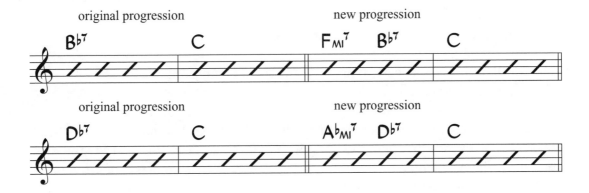

Dominant 7th overview

Now let's examine each of the six dominant 7ths in more detail.

1. **G7 C (V-I):** This is the only dominant 7th that is actually in the key. You can improvise with the C major scale. You also have a lot of freedom with this chord. You can alter it in many ways and use appropriate most consonant scales (b9, #5 with Ab melodic minor; b9, natural 13 with G auxiliary diminished; natural 9, #5 with G whole tone). You can precede the G7 with a Dmi7, but you could also use a Dmi7b5.

2. **Db7 C (bII-I):** The Db7 is not in a key. You can alter it, but it's typically played as an unaltered chord. The appropriate scale is Ab melodic minor. You can precede the Db7 with an Abmi7.

Chapter 25

As soon as we pass beyond the V and the bII chord, it's very important to realize that the remaining four progressions (III–I, IV–I, bVII–I, and VII–I) are much less common. Each of those dominant 7ths also occurs in traditional cosmic harmony but functions in a different way:

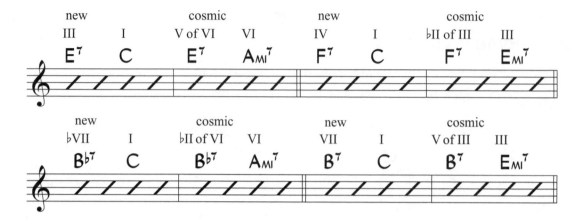

Since your ear is much more familiar with each of these dominant 7ths in its cosmic function, you'll tend to hear it in that way even when it's functioning in the new way. This will affect the way you improvise over the chord, the way you voice it, and how you precede it with another chord.

3. **E7 C (III–I):** This is the least common of the six dominant 7ths that resolve to C, but it's a very common chord as a V of VI. Functioning in that way, it would be in the local key of A minor. Because it is V in a minor key, it should be altered (b9 or #9 and a #5). Improvise with the key scale, A minor bebop, or the most consonant scale (which, due to the alterations, is F melodic minor). If you decide to precede the E7 with a II chord, it should be Bmi7b5, not Bmi7, because the progression is in A minor. All of these considerations are still relevant when the E7 resolves directly to C. You'll just get a more natural sound if you treat the chord as if it were resolving to VI.

4. **F7 C (IV–I):** This should sound familiar to you. It's the old gospel IV chord! It's also part of standard blues harmony. On a C major cosmic, though, the F7 functions as a bII of III. It's not in a key, so improvise with the most consonant scale (which, be cause the chord is unaltered, is C melodic minor). Precede the F7 with a Cmi7 if you like.

5. **Bb7 C (bVII–I):** This is the most common of the four new dominant 7ths that resolve to I. More traditionally, it functions as a bII of VI. It's not in a key, so impro vise with the most consonant scale (which, because the chord is unaltered, is F melodic minor). You can precede the Bb7 with an Fmi7.

6. **B7 C (VII–I):** This chord functions more traditionally as a V of III. It's in the local key of E minor. Because it is V in a minor key, it should be altered (b9 or #9 and a #5). Improvise with the key scale, E minor bebop, or the most consonant scale (which, due to the alterations, is C melodic minor). If you decide to precede the B7 with a II chord, it should be F#mi7b5, not F#mi7, because the progression is in E minor. All of these considerations are still relevant when the B7 resolves to C.

Here, then, are the progressions, scales, and sample improvisations. Play them and make up your own improvisations:

Chapter 25

Other chords using the same resolutions

Here are two other chord progressions in which the same resolving tritones are at work:

The Fmi6 chord has the same D–Ab tritone as Bb7 (bVII) and E7 (III). The tritone contracts to the 3rd and the 5th of the C chord, E and G. Here's an excerpt from "Embraceable You" that features this resolution:

The Cdim7 chord has the same Eb–A tritone as B7 (VII) and F7 (IV). The tritone once again resolves to the 3rd and the 5th of the C chord. Here's an excerpt from "Stella By Starlight" that features this resolution:

Resolutions to a minor chord

From the first page of this chapter I've discussed various ways of resolving to a C major chord. Now it's time to investigate new pathways to a C minor chord. We'll use the same approach, looking for tritones that contract to either the root and 3rd or to the 3rd and 5th of the chord. Now the intervals in the triad are reversed. The minor 3rd is on the bottom, between the root and the 3rd. We'll find two tritones to wrap around that interval. The major 3rd is now on top, between the 3rd and the 5th. Only one tritone will wrap around that interval.

Play these intervals on the piano so you can hear the resolutions:

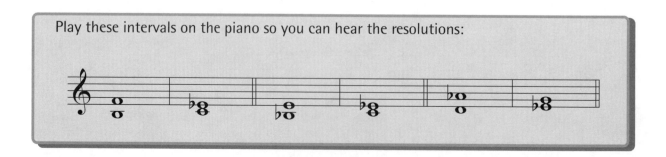

As before, each of these resolving tritones represents the 3rds and 7ths of two dominant 7ths spaced a tritone away from each other. Play these on the piano:

When you compare these six dominant 7ths to the ones that resolve to a C major chord, you'll see that four of them are the same: the two most traditional ones, G7 (V) and Db7 (bII), as well as E7 (III) and Bb7 (bVII). The other two, F7 (IV) and B7 (VII), have been replaced by dominant 7ths a half step higher: Gb7 (bV) and C7 (I). In "Harmonic Astronomy" I discussed the fact that E natural is a problematic note in a C minor environment. The E7 to Cmi progression is a bit odd sounding for that reason. Both Gb7 and C7 include an E in their resolving tritones, so they also don't resolve convincingly to C minor. In the case of the C7 resolving to C minor, there is not even any root movement. For this reason, this is the weakest resolution of all. The other three chords (G7, Db7, and Bb7) resolve strongly to C minor.

Other chords using the same resolutions

There are two other chord progressions in which the same resolving tritones are at work:

The Ebdim7 in the first progression is functioning as a bIIdim of II. It leads to the Dmi7 (II) for two reasons. First, the half-step root movement is strong. Second, although the chord doesn't have the G-Db resolving tritone that is found in the more traditional Eb7 (bII of II), it has another resolving tritone: Gb-C. The Gb resolves down a half step to the 3rd of the Dmi7 chord (F), while the C resolves up a whole step to the root (D).

In the second progression the D7 is a bVII of III. It is followed by VII of III (D#dim7) and then III (Emi7). Both the D7 and the D#dim7 contain the same resolving tritone, F#-C, which contracts to G and B, the 3rd and 5th of Emi7. The D#dim7 actually has another resolving tritone (D#-A) that contracts to E and G, the root and 3rd of Emi7. Of course, D7 is much more commonly a V of V in C. Functioning in this way, it would be in the local key of G major and its most consonant scale would be A melodic minor. Because this is so much more familiar to your ear, you'll probably hear those same scales even when the chord is functioning as a bVII of III.

Chapter 25

Did you notice that these last two examples introduced another major expansion of the entire tritone theory? Up until then I had only spoken about new pathways to a I chord. But bIIdim of II leads to II; bVII of III leads to III. So, speaking in cosmic terms, we've suddenly created several new moons around each planet. Now, instead of just V of x and bII of x, there's also III of x, bVII of x, etc. For example, "Stella By Starlight" features a bVII of V:

You can use a two-step process for analyzing most standard tunes. First, use the cosmic sheets. You'll usually find that at least 90% of the chords function as standard moons or planets. Then go back and deal with the remaining chords. Such a chord will usually contain a tritone that resolves smoothly to the root and the 3rd or the 3rd and the 5th of the next chord. It might be a dominant 7th functioning as a bVII, or a minor 6th chord functioning as a IVmi6, or a diminished 7th functioning as a bIIdim of II. If you can find the tritone in the chord and track its resolution to the next chord, you'll understand how that chord is functioning in the progression.

Analyze the chord progression to Gershwin's "Embraceable You" (page 145), and then check the solutions on page 326 in the appendix. You'll find many traditional moons and planets, as well as some of these new resolving-tritone chords. If you feel that you understand the material in this chapter and in "Harmonic Astronomy" (page 106) go on to the final installment in my presentation of harmonic analysis: "Probable Chord Functions" (page 146).

Chapter 25

Embraceable You

Gershwin-Gershwin

Chapter **26**

Probable Chord Functions

> **Treat this whole chapter as a practice box. Don't just read it—do it!**

It's one thing to carefully analyze a tune in the privacy of your own studio, then methodically improvise over it, play it in twelve keys, and memorize it. It's quite another thing when someone places a new tune in front of you on the bandstand and you're expected to respond immediately as if you've played the tune for years. You don't have time to pull out a blank cosmic sheet or even a pencil, so you need to be able to grasp the essential structure of the tune as you play it. There is a way of doing this so that no one would guess that it's your first time through the tune.

Here's the approach in a nutshell: you view each chord through the lens of prior experience. Each chord type (major 7, minor 7, etc.) can serve several different functions, but those functions can be ordered according to a hierarchy of probabilities, from most probable to least probable. You begin by assuming that the chord is serving its most probable function, and you look for supporting evidence in the surrounding progression. If the evidence is lacking, you proceed to the second most probable function, and so on down the list until you've found a sensible explanation.

So what functions do chords usually play, and what evidence should you look for to support those functions? Read through this chart carefully, then we'll discuss several examples of how to use it:

Probable Functions Chart

Chord type	Probable function (from highest to lowest probability)

Major 7
(and 6th chord)

1. Diatonic (I or IV in major key, VI in minor key)
   Example: GMa7   Ami7 D7   **GMa7**   CMa7
2. Modulation to a new major key
   Example: EbMa7 Bb7 EbMa7 D7 **GMa7** Ami7 D7 GMa7
3. Non-diatonic: bIIMa7, bIIIMa7, or bVIMa7
   Example: GbMa7 Eb7   Abmi7 **GMa7** GbMa7
4. Color unity
   Example: EbMa7 **GMa7** EMa7 CMa7 DMa7

Minor 7

1. Diatonic (II, III, or VI in a major key, IV in a minor key)
   Example: FMa7 **Gmi7** C7 FMa7
2. II of a major planet
   Example: CMa7 **Gmi7** C7 FMa7   Dmi7 G7
3. IV-7 in a major key (borrowed from minor key; often goes to bVII)
   Example: DMa7 **Gmi7** C7 DMa7
4. I in a minor key
   Example: **Gmi7** Ami7(b5) D7 **Gmi7**
5. Color unity
   Example: Emi7 **Gmi7** Fmi7 Abmi7

Dominant 7

1. Diatonic (V in a major key, V in a minor key)
   Example: Cmi Dmi7(b5) **G7** Cmi
2. V or bII of a major or minor planet
   Example: AbMa7 **G7** Cmi7 **B7** Bbmi7 Eb7
3. bVII, VII, III, or IV (alternate tritone resolution)
   Example: AMa7 Dmi7 **G7** AMa7
4. Blues harmony (I, IV, V)
   Example: **G7** C7 **G7** **G7** C7

Minor 7[(b5)]

1. Diatonic (II in a minor key; not VII in a major key)
   Example: Fmi **Gmi7(b5)** C7 Fmi
2. II of a minor planet
   Example: EbMa7 **Gmi7(b5)** C7   Fmi7   **Ami7(b5)** D7
3. VI in a minor key (may be viewed as II of V)
   Example: Bbmi **Gmi7(b5)** Cmi7(b5) F7

(continued next page)

Chapter 26

Chord type	Probable function (from highest to lowest probability)

Diminished 7	1. VII of a minor planet
	   Example: GbMa7 **Gdim7** Abmi7 **Adim7** Bbmi7
	2. bIIdim7 of II in a major key–resolves to II
	   Example: EMa7 **Gdim7** F#mi7 B7
	3. Idim7 in a major key (possibly written as #IVdim7)–resolves to IMa7
	   Example: Ami7 D7 **Gdim7** GMa7
	4. VII in a minor key
	   Example: Abmi **Gdim7** Abmi

Minor(Ma7)	1. I in a minor key
	   Example: Ami7(b5) D7 **Gmi(Ma7)**
	2. IVm(Ma7) in a major key — resolves to I
	   Example: DMa7 Emi7 **Gmi(Ma7)** DMa7

Major 7(#5)	1. IMa7(#5) (resolves to I)
	   Example: Ami7 D7 **GMa7(#5)** GMa7
	2. Color unity
	   Example: EMa7(#5) **GMa7(#5)** EbMa7(#5) CMa7(#5)

Minor 6	1. IVmi6 in a major key (resolves to I due to tritone)
	   Example: DMa7 Emi7 **Gmi6** DMa7
	2. Imi6 in a minor key
	   Example: Ami7(b5) D7 **Gmi6**
	3. IVmi6 in a minor key (diatonic—has the same notes as the IIm7(b5) and resolves to V)
	   Example: Dmi **Gmi6** A7 Dmi

Chapter 26

So there you are, winging a new tune on the bandstand, and you encounter a GMa7 chord. How is it functioning in the tune? What scale should you improvise with? The chart says that a major 7th chord usually functions diatonically, as a I or IV in a major key or as a VI in a minor key. The primary evidence to support each of these functions is to be found in the key signature. If the tune is in G major (one sharp), then of course the GMa7 is a I chord. If there are two sharps in the key signature, the chord is either a IV in D major or a VI in B minor (and you'll know which, because you already know which of those keys the tune is in).

Example 26.1

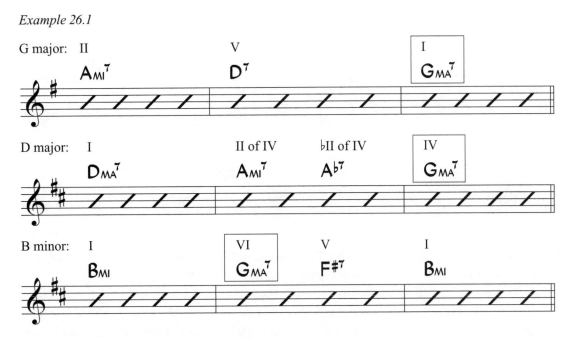

But if the tune has a key signature of three flats (Eb major), the evidence supports none of those most probable functions. The second option on the list is that the GMa7 is a I chord in a new key. The obvious evidence that would support this function is that the chord is accompanied (preceded and/or followed) by other chords that are diatonic in the key of G major (such as a II V I).

Example 26.2

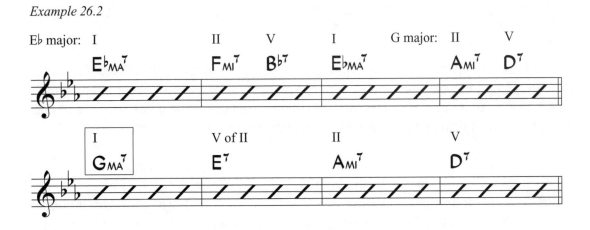

Chapter 26

But you don't find that context in this tune. Could it be a bII, bIII, or bVI chord? If the general key is Gb and you've already ruled out a modulation, then the GMa7 is probably a bIIMa7. Occasionally this chord will occur at the end of a tune to harmonize a tonic melody note more adventurously than a I chord does. Sometimes it simply replaces the more common bII dominant 7 chord (as in this progression: Abmi7 GMa7 GbMa7). In this context, you should improvise using the most consonant scale for the GMa7 (D major scale). In the turnaround BMa7 D7 GMa7 C7, the GMa7 is functioning as a bVIMa7 (again, use the D major scale).

Example 26.3

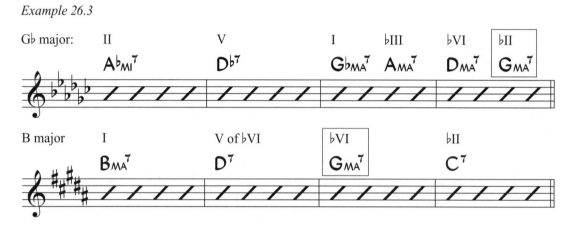

If none of these contexts occur in this tune, go to the final option on the list. "Color unity" is a term I use to describe a progression of several same-type chords (e.g., all major 7ths, all minor 7ths, all dominant 7ths, etc.) that don't bear obvious tonal relationships to each other. Such a progression works because all the chords share the same type or color; for example, BbMa7 BMa7 GMa7 EMa7. Here again, you should improvise with the most consonant scale.

Example 26.4

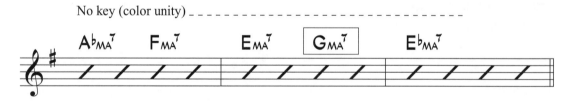

My process, then, is to scroll down through the various functions that the GMa7 can play until I find the one that the evidence supports. This may seem like a tedious process, but with practice it becomes virtually instantaneous. In the great majority of cases, you'll find the logical analysis for a chord within the first two options.

Now let's take the dominant 7th chord as an example. If the tune is in the key of Eb major, what's the most probable dominant 7th you'll encounter? Bb7, of course—the V chord. If you're looking at any other dominant 7th, it's probably a secondary dominant (a V or a bII of a major or minor planet). Here are the traditional cosmic functions for dominant 7ths in Eb major:

Example 26.5

Chapter 26

What if you find a secondary dominant that doesn't go where it's supposed to? The Probable Functions Chart suggests that this chord is either a bVII, VII, III or IV chord (refer to "New Pathways Home," page 135). Again in Eb major:

Example 26.6

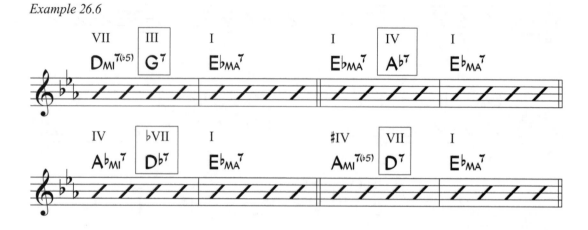

If none of these functions describe the situation, perhaps it's simply because you're looking at a 12-bar blues. Specifically, if you find an Eb7 that shows no tendency to resolve to the IV chord, it's probably just a I chord in the Eb major blues progression. Actually, all the other dominant chords in the blues progression can be easily analyzed using the Probable Functions Chart:

Example 26.7

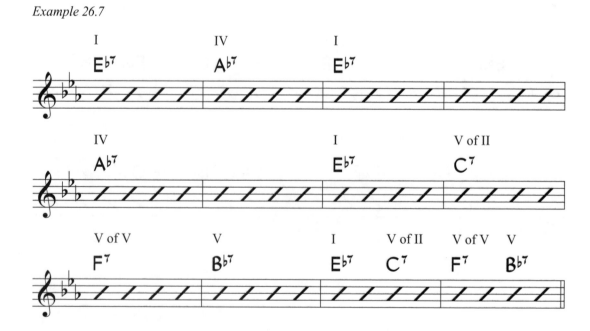

Let's take one more example: Gmi6. Its most probable function is as a IVmi6 in the key of D major. As the "New Pathways Home" chapter explains on page 142, this chord resolves to a I chord for the same reason a bVII chord (C7) does: they both contain the resolving tritone E-Bb. But if the tune is in the key of G minor, then the Gmi6 is simply a I chord. Otherwise, it may be functioning as a IV in D minor. Unlike the IVmi6 in D major, this Gmi6 doesn't resolve to I—it resolves to V. This is because it has exactly the same notes as an Emi7(b5) (the II chord in D minor, which also typically resolves to V). You'll find minor 6th chords functioning this way on a lot of older charts. Ironically, even though the chord symbol is written Gmi6, if you examine the written piano score you'll often find an E in the bass.

Example 26.8

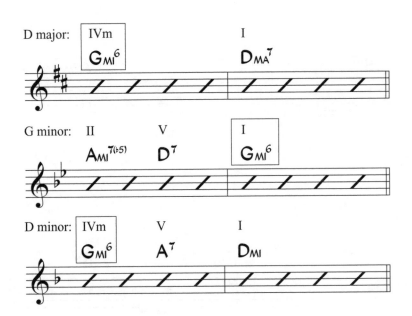

Analyze the following standard tunes. Then see the appendix (pp. 318–325) for the solutions.

Chapter **26**

Everything I Love

Cole Porter

Chapter 26

My Foolish Heart

Washington/Young

Ballad

D.S. al Coda

Chapter **26**

How Long Has This Been Going On?

George and Ira Gershwin

Chapter **26**

D.C. al 2nd ending al fine

Chapter **26**

Since I Fell For You

Buddy Johnson

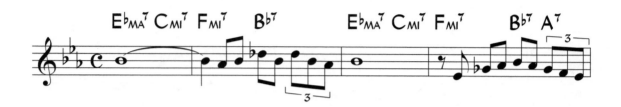

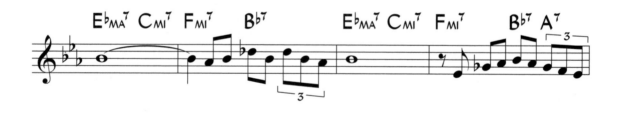

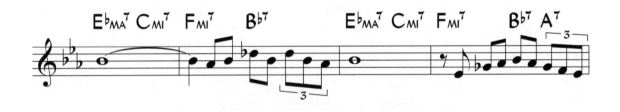

Chapter **27**

Getting the Blues

Although the blues may not be as complex a musical genre as jazz, there's still no way to treat the subject comprehensively in one chapter. I'm just going to try to answer a few specific questions:

1. What is a blues scale?
2. What is a major blues scale?
3. What are the most standard 12-bar blues progressions, and what are some variations?
4. How do you choose blues scales over a standard 12-bar blues progression?
5. How can phrasing contribute to an authentic blues sound?
6. How do you choose blues scales over standard chord progressions?
7. What other scales may be used over the blues?

What is a blues scale?

Here's an F blues scale (sometimes called an F minor blues scale):

There's no preferred view of this scale. You can construct it using any of these definitions:

1. a series of intervals: minor 3rd, whole step, half step, half step, minor 3rd, whole step
2. a series of scale degrees: 1 b3 4 #4 5 b7 1 of a major scale.
3. a minor pentatonic scale plus a tritone (#4)

> Before you read on, play this scale in a few different keys.

What is a major blues scale?

Here's an F major blues scale:

There are also several ways to view this scale:

1. a series of intervals: whole step, half step, half step, minor 3rd, whole step, minor 3rd
2. a series of scale degrees: 1 2 #2 3 5 6 1 of a major scale
3. a pentatonic scale plus a #2
4. the second "mode" of a minor blues scale

The last definition bears a closer look. Here is a D (minor) blues scale:

Play the scale as written. Then play it from F to F. It's an F major blues scale. These two scales bear the same relationship to each other as F major scale and D natural minor.

> **Before you read on, play this scale in a few different keys.**

What are the most standard 12-bar blues progressions, and what are some variations?

Here are the chords for a basic blues in F. You might play this progression in a classic blues band, so I'll call it the **blues blues**. In an even more basic progression, the IV chord in measure #2 is played as a I chord. In some cases the IV chord in bar #10 is played as a V.

This is a basic blues in F that you might play in a jazz group. I'll call it the **jazz blues**.

Of course, jazz musicians are always looking for variations. Here are some standard substitutes and additions that are often made to the **jazz blues**.

Chapter 27

There's a particular reharmonization often referred to as the Parker blues. It's the chord progression to Charlie Parker's tune "Blues for Alice":

Compare this progression to the basic jazz blues progression. They both include a I chord in bar #1, a IV chord in bar #5, and a II chord in bar #9, after which both progressions are essentially the same. But the Parker blues uses II-V progressions down in whole steps (i.e., a cycle-of-5ths progression) to get from the initial I chord to the IV chord in bar #5, and it uses II-V progressions down in half steps to get from that IV to the II in bar #9.

You can mix and match these progressions. For example, you could play the first four measures of the Parker blues and then switch to the reharmonized progression that precedes it.

Here is a basic **minor blues**:

Here's a sample elaboration on the minor blues progression:

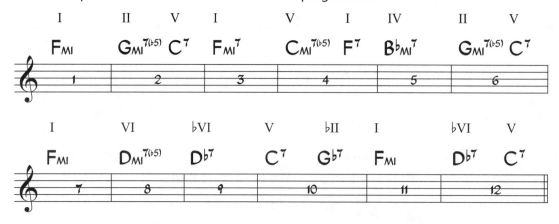

> **Practice playing and improvising over these progressions in several keys.**

How do you choose blues scales over a standard 12-bar blues progression?

1. Improvise over an F major blues progression (i.e., blues-blues, jazz blues, etc.) with the F major blues scale and F blues scale.
2. Improvise over an F minor blues progression with an F blues scale.

There's a little fine print. When using an F major blues scale on a Bb7 (the IV chord), you're likely to find the note A distinctly unpleasant because it lies a half step above the 7th of the chord. That's no reason to reject the whole scale. You just need to avoid that note if it bothers you. Here's a sample solo over an F jazz blues progression using both the F blues and major blues scales:

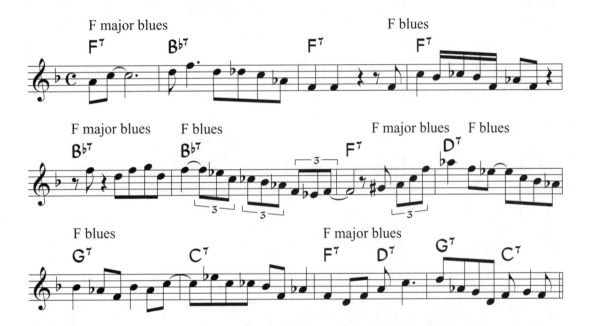

Practice improvising over an F blues progression using a mixture of these two scales.

How can phrasing contribute to an authentic blues sound?

There is a form of phrasing in the blues that has its roots in the early call-and-response tradition. Although there are many permutations, the basic idea is to divide the 12-bar form into three 4-bar segments. You make your essential melodic statement during the first four bars. In the next four bars, you repeat that statement more or less verbatim. In the final four bars you have a choice of either repeating it again or playing something new. A common approach to the last four bars is to begin with a repetition but finish the phrase with new material.

Chapter 27

Many blues melodies are based on this phrasing structure, such as "Sonnymoon for Two":

Sonny Rollins

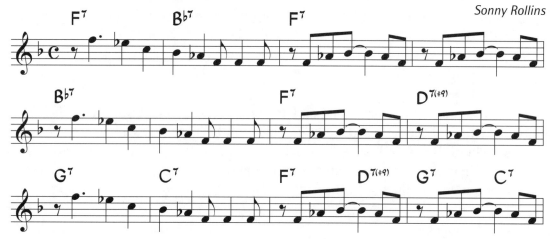

©1954 Son Rol Music Co. used by permission

Following are three different versions of this phrasing format for you to explore. They differ from each other only in the way the initial 4-bar statement is structured:

Version #1: 4-bar motif

> Play a single 4-bar motif. Then repeat it verbatim. Then repeat it again or play new material.

Notice that the motif is actually less than four bars long. Most of the actual melody occurs in the first two bars. Your motif can be longer but you still need time to breathe at the end. Also notice that I use an Ab instead of an A in measure #5 during the Bb7. Here I simply bent the melody to avoid the clash problem that we discussed earlier. Finally, notice that I began to repeat the motif again in bar #9 but opted to end it with a new twist.

This is the simplest version to understand but it may be the most difficult one to do, for one simple reason: you need to be able to remember four bars of music! Keep it simple. Use some long notes, repeated notes, and rests, and stick to a simple structure in your choice of notes. "Sonnymoon," for example, is based on a simple descending F minor pentatonic scale. As you create your motif, think of it as a song with lyrics.

Version #2: 2-bar motif

> Play a 2-bar motif (including breathing room at the end). Repeat it in bars #3-4 but end
> it with new notes. Then, as before, repeat the entire 4-bar structure in bars #5-8, and
> then again (or not) in bars #9-12.

The challenge here is to remember how the motif changes in bars #3-4. You'll need to
return to that new material in bars #7-8, so listen carefully when you first create it.
Notice that I chose to use all new material in bars #9-12. A common variation on this
version is to transpose the motif up a 4th in bars #5-6 in parallel with the root movement then back down in bars #7-8.

Version #3: 1-bar motif

> Play a 1-bar motif (including the rest at the end). Repeat it in bar #2. Repeat it again in
> bar #3 but add a tag that extends into bar #4. Remember the tag, because now you need
> to repeat the entire 4-bar structure in bars #5-8; then again (or not) in bars #9-12.

Chapter **27**

Again, notice that I bent the motif in bars #5-6 to make it work with the Bb7 and that I began the last 4 bars with a repetition but ended it with new material.

If you really want to play the blues authentically you need to listen to a lot of blues. You'll hear these three phrasing versions and many others. Be creative in your phrasing. These versions are just here for you to have fun with and to explore. Use them as general guides, not as strait jackets.

How do you use blues scales over standard chord progressions?

The common denominator between key scales and most consonant scales is that the notes of each chord fit within its scale. For example, the notes of C7 (C E G Bb) are all members of its key scale (F major) and its most consonant scale (G melodic minor). Blues scales operate very differently. A single blues scale is used over a long series of chords, many of which don't fit within the scale.

The basic idea is startlingly simple:

1. For a major-key tune, use both the major and minor blues scales built on the tonic.
2. For a minor-key tune, use the minor blues scale built on the tonic.

That's it. As long as the tune adheres to its general key you can improvise with these scales over the entire progression, including any secondary chords. Using harmonic astronomy terms, you can use these scales as long as the original cosmic harmonic scheme is in force, over planets and moons. Here's a progression in the key of F major:

Not one of these chords fits completely within either an F blues scale or an F major blues scale, but you can improvise with both of those scales over the progression.

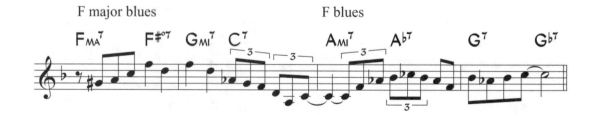

Here's a progression in F minor with an F minor blues scale line:

Naturally, a certain tension results when you use scales such as these that don't match the chord tones in a nice, neat way. This tension needs to be released in a timely manner. You need to play these scales smoothly and with good time. If your line hesitates along the way or pauses on certain notes, it will just sound wrong. And there are certain combinations of scales and chords that are particularly difficult to play convincingly. An F (minor) blues scale causes a lot of tension over an FMaj7 (I) or an Am7 (III), chords that are not intended to sound tense. The F major blues scale matches those chords better and causes much less tension. But I wouldn't rule out the minor blues scales in these situations. It's up to you to explore the various combinations and find your preferences.

Here's an analysis of "Since I Fell For You" showing the key scales, a few most consonant scales (mcs, appearing in italics), the major and minor blues scales and a sample solo comprised almost entirely of those blues scales. Although the local key scales and most consonant scales change often, the general key of this tune is Eb major throughout. Consequently, only the Eb blues scale and Eb major blues scale are used. I've limited this solo to the blues scales for demonstrational purposes only. It's usually a better idea to intersperse a few other scales with them to create a more varied sound.

Chapter 27

mcs = *most consonant scale*

mi = *minor bebop scale*

mm = *melodic minor scale*

Since I Fell For You
(sample blues solo)

Slow $\frac{12}{8}$ Feel

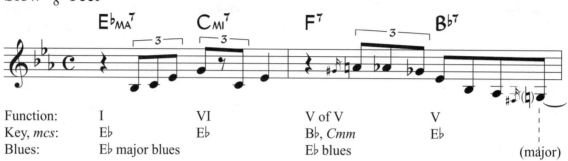

Function:	I	VI	V of V	V
Key, *mcs*:	Eb	Eb	Bb, *Cmm*	Eb
Blues:	Eb major blues		Eb blues	(major)

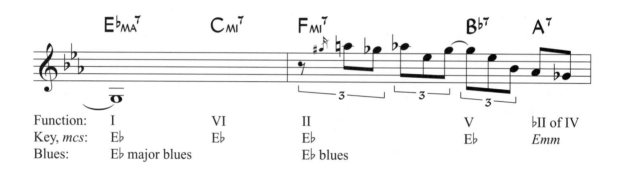

Function:	I	VI	II	V	bII of IV
Key, *mcs*:	Eb	Eb	Eb	Eb	*Emm*
Blues:	Eb major blues		Eb blues		

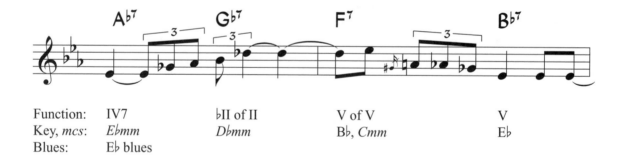

Function:	IV7	bII of II	V of V	V
Key, *mcs*:	*Ebmm*	*Dbmm*	Bb, *Cmm*	Eb
Blues:	Eb blues			

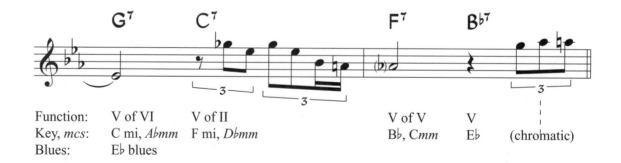

Function:	V of VI	V of II	V of V	V
Key, *mcs*:	C mi, *Abmm*	F mi, *Dbmm*	Bb, *Cmm*	Eb	(chromatic)
Blues:	Eb blues			

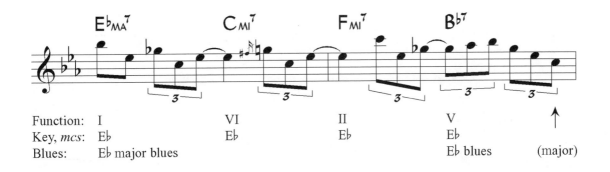

Function:	I	VI	II	V	↑
Key, *mcs*:	E♭	E♭	E♭	E♭	
Blues:	E♭ major blues			E♭ blues	(major)

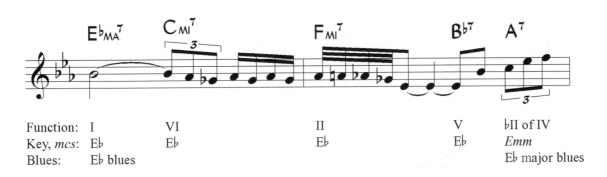

Function:	I	VI	II	V	♭II of IV
Key, *mcs*:	E♭	E♭	E♭	E♭	*Emm*
Blues:	E♭ blues				E♭ major blues

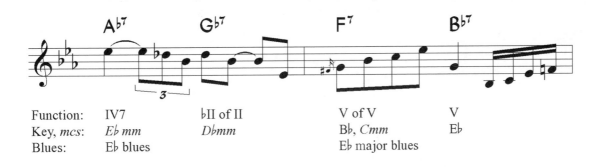

Function:	IV7	♭II of II	V of V	V
Key, *mcs*:	*E♭ mm*	*D♭mm*	B♭, *Cmm*	E♭
Blues:	E♭ blues		E♭ major blues	

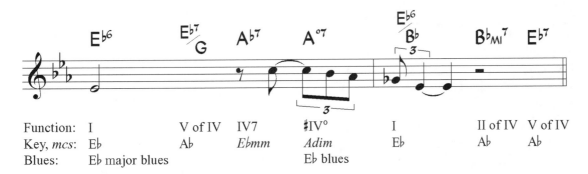

Function:	I	V of IV	IV7	#IV°	I	II of IV	V of IV
Key, *mcs*:	E♭	A♭	*E♭mm*	*Adim*	E♭	A♭	A♭
Blues:	E♭ major blues			E♭ blues			

Chapter **27**

Function:	IV7	♭VII7
Key, *mcs*:	E♭mm	A♭mm
Blues:	E♭ blues	

E♭ major blues

Function:	I7		II of IV	V of IV
Key, *mcs*:	B♭mm		A♭	A♭
Blues:	E♭ major blues			E♭ blues

Function:	IV7	♭VII7
Key, *mcs*:	E♭mm	A♭mm
Blues:	E♭ blues	

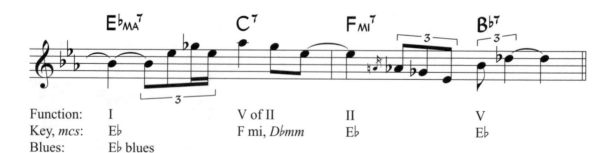

Function:	I	V of II	II	V
Key, *mcs*:	E♭	F mi, *D♭mm*	E♭	E♭
Blues:	E♭ blues			

Practice improvising over this tune using a mixture of the Eb blues and Eb major blues scales. Use the chord chart on page 160.

Chapter 27

What happens to blues scales when a tune changes keys? I'm referring here to a true modulation, not a secondary dominant situation. Simply switch to the blues scales that are appropriate to the new key. When a tune modulates from F major to A major, as in Cole Porter's "I Love You," use A major blues and/or A blues scales. You may find that you don't hear blues lines as readily in the new key as in the original key, opting for key scales instead. Or you may find that using the key scale at the onset of the modulation helps establish the new key firmly enough that the new blues scales can then follow.

Here's an exercise that underlines the difference between the use of blues scales and other scale types. Play a random series of dominant 7th chords starting with an F7 and changing every two beats. Choose any order you like but return to F7 every four measures. Improvise over the entire progression with F blues and F major blues.

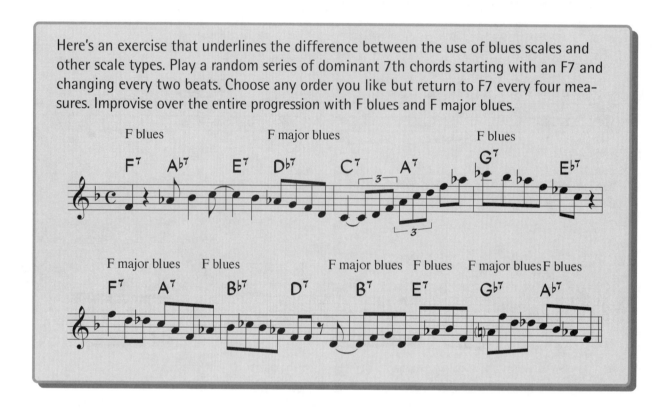

Imagine improvising over this chord progression with most consonant scales, such as mixolydian #4 or auxiliary diminished. You'd be forced to switch scales on every chord. Only the blues and major blues scales allow you to overlay a single sound over such an active chord progression. You can switch back and forth between the two scales as often as you like, but don't combine the notes into a single "major-minor" blues scale. That results in a virtually chromatic scale that obscures the two original flavors. It's like saying, "Well, I like ice cream and I like potatoes, so let's mix them together."

What other scales may be used over the blues?

Here's an extensive but not exhaustive list of possible scales for each chord in a jazz blues. The scale in bold type corresponds to the notes in the solo. I wouldn't recommend packing one twelve-bar chorus this full of notes or scales. I've done it here for demonstration purposes only.

* I chose a G minor bebop scale here because the D7 is V/II. The local key is G minor.

> Practice improvising over the F blues progression using these scales. Don't necessarily stay with one plan throughout—feel free to mix and match.

Chapter 28

Pentatonics—A Double Dose

Simply put, a pentatonic scale is any scale made up of five notes. Pentatonic scales have existed in music for thousands of years. They play a prominent role in the music of most Eastern cultures.

Here's a pelog scale, from Java:

This Japanese pentatonic is known as a hira-joshi:

Here's an in-sen scale, also from Japan:

Construction of the pentatonic scale

Within the twelve tones of a chromatic scale there is almost an endless number of pentatonic permutations. Nevertheless, in Western music the term "C pentatonic scale" is almost always used to indicate one particular set of notes:

The most straightforward definition of this scale is expressed in terms of degrees of the major scale: 1 2 3 5 6 (1). Notice what degrees are omitted: 4 and 7. These are the notes that form the only tritone in the major scale and are responsible for defining its tonality. You could say that a C pentatonic scale is "a C major scale without a G7." This scale is sometimes referred to as a major pentatonic to distinguish it from the minor pentatonic scale.

Before you continue, play the pentatonic scale in a few keys.

You've heard this scale before, of course. It's a fundamental sound in music as wide-ranging as Irish folk, bluegrass, and jazz. Here are the opening bars of two well-known standards that begin with pentatonic scales:

Construction of the minor pentatonic scale

Here's a C minor pentatonic scale:

Of course, you could view this scale as a set of scale degrees: 1 b3 4 5 b7 (1). But it's also the fifth mode of an Eb major pentatonic scale.

These two scales bear the same minor 3rd relationship to each other as several other scale types:

C natural minor	=	Eb major
C minor bebop	=	Eb major bebop
C (minor) blues	=	Eb major blues
C minor pentatonic	=	Eb (major) pentatonic

Before you continue, play the minor pentatonic scale in a few keys.

Chapter **28**

Modal and tonal chord progressions

The "double dose" reference in the title of this chapter could be applied to the simple fact that there are two primary pentatonic scales, major and minor. Instead, I'm referring to the two ways in which pentatonics are used over two very different types of chord progressions, modal and tonal. A modal progression is hardly a "progress-ion" at all: it involves staying on one chord or a very short vamp for a long time. A tonal progression is one in which there is tension and release of the type featured in most standard tunes: an evolving chord progression that includes V-I's (and probably II-V-I's).

In order to better understand the theory of pentatonic usage, you'll want to try out the various scale/chord combinations on the piano. This will be easier if you know how to finger the pentatonics. A five-tone scale would appear to suggest division into a 3-group and a 2-group. It's fine to do it that way, at least at first, but for an alternative view read "Performing 2-groupotomies on Scales" (page 203).

I've chosen the tune "Softly, As In A Morning Sunrise" as the vehicle for discussing both uses of pentatonic scales. The A section of the tune can be thought of as a modal progression, and the B section (the bridge) is tonal.

Softly As In A Morning Sunrise

Hammerstein/Romberg

Chapter 28

Use of Pentatonic Scales with Modal Progressions

First, let's modify the chord progression in the A section of "Softly." Think of it now as sixteen measures of a C minor chord. The Fmi7 (IV) simply represents a contrast to the I chord. Other lead sheets for the same tune use a Dmi7(b5) G7 (II V) instead, but through the use of pentatonic scales and new voicings, you'll replace those chords with a more interesting form of tension and release.

Here are some modal voicings for the C minor chord. They're derived from the most consonant scale, C dorian mode. Play them on the piano:

The procedure here is to comp with a mixture of these voicings. The cumulative effect is to produce the sound of the C dorian mode, which implies a Cmi7 chord rather than stating it overtly:

The voicings built on Eb and Bb both contain the Eb-A tritone. The other five voicings are true "fourth-stacks" (two perfect fourths). You may decide to avoid the tritone voicings at first, especially the one built on Bb, but ultimately they're all valid sounds. The voicings built on D and A are not intended to serve as C minor voicings by themselves. Use them in conjunction with the others as I did above.

Before you continue, practice comping with these voicings with your left hand until you can do it comfortably and accurately without looking at the keyboard.

Here again is a C minor pentatonic scale:

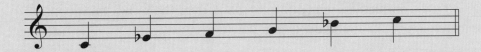

Notice that this scale also fits completely within a C dorian mode. Now practice improvising with the notes of this scale while comping with the modal voicings.

Chapter **28**

Here's an altered pentatonic that you might enjoy trying as well.

The only difference is an A instead of the Bb. It still fits into the C dorian mode so you can still comp with the same voicings. This pentatonic produces more of a Cmi6 sound instead of Cmi7.

Here are some nice two-handed voicings that you could use either to comp behind someone else or to use in your own solo. Although there are Bb's in some of these voicings, the highest notes connect to produce the Cmi6 altered pentatonic.

Practice improvising with both of these pentatonic scales over the left-hand modal voicings and intersperse some of the two-handed voicings.

Now you've got a basic foundation in the use of pentatonics over a modal progression. If you're playing smoothly and with solid time and creating interesting shapes with the scales, you've probably already got a pretty good sound going. The beauty of a modal progression, however, lies in the freedom it affords you to take side trips. I'll refer to the sound you're currently playing as the "home sound." Now I'll show you how you can leave this sound to create tension and return to it to create release.

Outside-inside use of pentatonics over modal progressions

Here's the basic idea: start by improvising with the home sound, then smoothly segue into some other pentatonic and then back again. The more radically different the new pentatonic is from the home pentatonic, the clearer the effect will be. The B pentatonic is very different from the C minor pentatonic and the Cmi6 pentatonic.

The Bb pentatonic scale differs from the C minor pentatonic only by one note (D instead of Eb). In fact, the entire scale fits within the C dorian mode. Although it would sound fine, it wouldn't be very effective as a tension-producing device.

The F pentatonic scale also fits into C dorian, and it only differs from the Cmi6 pentatonic by one note (D instead of Eb). Again, it wouldn't produce much tension. Most of the other pentatonics would work quite well. In fact, you can pass through several outside pentatonics before you return home.

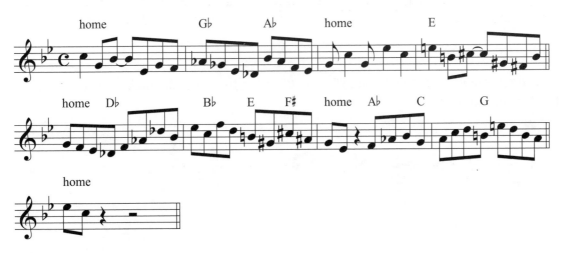

182

Chapter 28

Notice how this technique is used in the melody to "Mr. Clean":

Weldon Irving

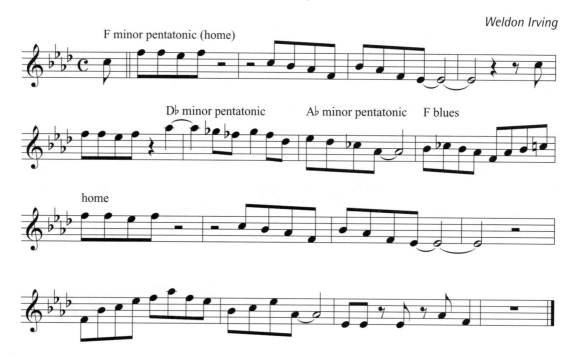

2

These side trips out of the home scale result in significant melodic tension. This will only be effective if the release comes smoothly and in a timely fashion. If you stumble getting out or back in again, it will just sound wrong. Obviously, you need to know your pentatonic scales very well if you are to make smooth transitions.

What happens to your left hand during all these outside-inside games in the right hand? It can go outside the home sound as well. You can shift to the seven modal voicings of another dorian mode such as Eb dorian:

Or you can simply use random fourth stacks and tritone/fourth stacks that are outside the C dorian mode:

It all sounds pretty random, doesn't it? Well, it's about to get even more so. The left hand can go out while the right hand stays in and vice-versa. If both hands do go out at the same time, they don't need to agree with each other tonally. For example, if the improvised line goes out by shifting up a half step, the voicings can go down a whole step. It all comes down to this: the harder you hit your head against the wall, the better it feels when you stop. It's a tension-release mechanism. The tension can be as great as you want it to be, providing that you can resolve it smoothly.

Here are four permutations — play each one:

In-in: both hands stay within the home sound.

Out-in: the voicings go out and back in while the improvising stays in.

In-out: the voicings stay in while the improvising goes out and back in.

Out-out: the voicings and improvising go out and back in at the same time.

Chapter **28**

Now try improvising within each of these formats. For these tension-release mechanisms to work, it's vital that you never lose a sense of the home key. You have to truly experience the "in" as "in" and the "out" as "out." If you just start stringing pentatonics together without hearing the tonality accurately, you won't make good choices. So begin your explorations conservatively. Play a lot of the in-in sound at first, gradually expanding your ability to go out in either hand without losing a sense of the key.

Use of Pentatonic Scales with Tonal Progressions

The reason that you can take such freedoms when improvising over a modal progression is that the basic key is so firmly established. The listener is willing to hear all sorts of tension because he always knows what the release will be, if not when it will be. But when the chord progression is tonal there is no one scale that stands as the home sound. Certainly the music is in a key, but several other local key scales or most consonant scales will be interspersed throughout. Consequently, the outside-inside games are less workable. The listener has enough to do to follow the chord progression without having to fight through a set of pentatonics that don't agree with the harmony. You can get plenty of variety in your improvising without going out, because the inside pentatonics will usually change from chord to chord.

Very simply, pentatonics in a tonal progression work as subsets of the more complete key and most consonant scales. If the music is in the key of C major, consider the pentatonics that fit within that key. If you've opted for the most consonant scale for a Bb7 (F melodic minor), then look for pentatonics within that scale. Let's begin by examining which scales contain pentatonics:

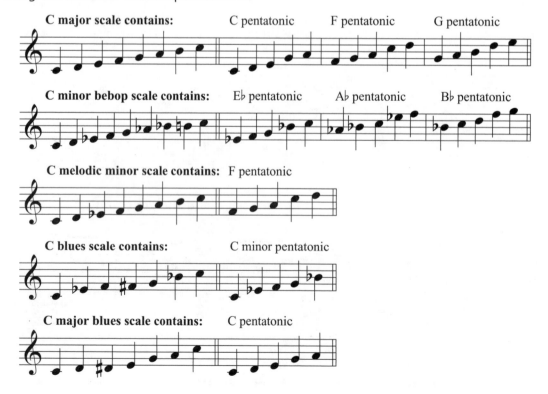

In general terms, then:

Pentatonics occur on I, IV, and V of a major scale.
Pentatonics occur on III, VI, and bVII of a minor bebop scale.
A pentatonic occurs on IV of a melodic minor scale.
A minor pentatonic occurs on I of a blues scale.
A pentatonic occurs on I of a major blues scale.
Pentatonics do not occur in diminished or whole tone scales.

I'm going to streamline this list for you. First of all, you won't need the minor bebop scale as you look for pentatonics. The pentatonics generated by that scale will either be duplicated by another appropriate scale or will not work due to complications still to be discussed. And we can set aside the blues and major blues scales for this discussion. If you've read "Getting the Blues" (page 162), you know how to use those scales, and the pentatonics within them will happen as a matter of course. So the only structures that you'll need to generate pentatonics are the major and melodic minor scales.

It's almost this simple: wherever a major scale is appropriate, use pentatonics on I, IV, and V of that scale. Wherever a melodic minor scale is appropriate, use the pentatonic on IV of that scale. The only complication is that there are situations in which some of the major-scale pentatonics don't work.

Play and improvise with each of these pentatonics over a CMa7

Do you hear that F pentatonic doesn't work very well? If you were to improvise with a C major scale over this chord, you would finesse the note F — i.e., you'd resolve it to E. But there is no E in an F pentatonic scale. The next available note underneath the F is D. Notice how much less convincing the F pentatonic line sounds than the C major line:

The F is a tense note because it lies just a half step above a chord tone (the 3rd, E). In the G pentatonic there are no such half-step problems. In the C pentatonic, the C lies a half step above the 7th (B), but it is stabilized because it's also a member of the chord (the root).

Chapter 28

When a pentatonic scale contains a non-chord tone that lies a half step above a chord tone, that scale will not work for that chord.

Here's another example of the same problem:

The key scale (F major) generates F, Bb, and C pentatonics (I, IV, and V). Both F and Bb pentatonics contain the note F, which clashes with the E in the chord. Neither of those scales sounds very good over the chord for that reason. The lone survivor is C pentatonic.

As you know, a most consonant scale is built by placing whole steps above chord tones. Every note in a most consonant scale is therefore a safe note, requiring no finesse of the type that I mentioned above. Do you see what this implies for pentatonics? That's right: the pentatonics that are generated by most consonant scales will always work! The pentatonics won't include any half-step clashes because the scale that generated them doesn't include any. Only when you're using a key scale to generate pentatonics must you be on the lookout for clashes.

But wait a minute: a melodic minor scale is used only as a most consonant scale, so the pentatonic built on IV of that scale will always work. A major scale is used both as a most consonant scale and a key scale. When it's being used as a most consonant scale, the pentatonics (built on I, IV, and V) will all work. When it's being used as a key scale you may find clashes, but not if the key scale and the most consonant scale are one and the same. For example, you might choose an F major scale over a Gmi7 because the chord is functioning as II in that key, as in a II-V-I progression. You can check for clashes but you won't find any because F major scale also happens to be the most consonant scale for Gmi7.

You can summarize the previous discussion with this rule:

Pentatonics are generated by major scales (on I, IV, and V) and melodic minor scales (on IV). Specific pentatonics may not work if the generating scale is a major scale functioning solely as the key but not also as the most consonant scale. In that instance, check for clashes.

Pentatonics with minor 7th chords

Let's see how this rule applies to finding pentatonics for Cmi7. This chord can function as a II in Bb major, a III in Ab major, a VI in Eb major, a I in C minor, or a IV in G minor. As I mentioned earlier, we don't need minor key scales (minor bebop) to find pentatonics. If the chord is in a minor key, simply use the most consonant scale instead to find the pentatonics. The most consonant scale for Cmi7 is Bb major.

There are actually three reasons why we might use a Bb major scale as our pentatonic generator: 1) the Cmi7 is functioning as II in Bb major: 2) the Cmi7 is functioning as I in C minor or IV in G minor, so we use the most consonant scale instead; or 3) the Cmi7 is not in a key, so we use the most consonant scale.

Our only reason for using either the Ab or Eb major scale as a pentatonic generator for Cmi7 is that it's the current key scale. This is where you might run into clashes. Try these scales out over Cmi7:

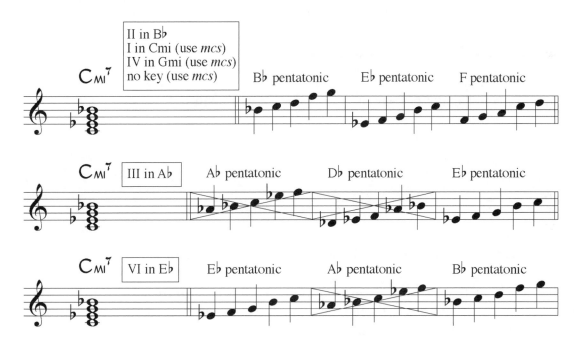

As predicted, all three of the scales from Bb major work fine. When the chord is III in Ab major, neither the Ab nor the Db pentatonic works due to half-step clashes (Ab over G and/or Db over C). When the chord is VI in Eb major, the Ab pentatonic fails once again.

Pentatonics with major 7th chords

A similar analysis can be carried out for a CMa7 chord. The most consonant scale is G major. The chord can function either as a I in C major, IV in G major, or VI in E minor (in which case the most consonant scale, G major, becomes the generator). We saw previously that the C major scale generates C, F, and G pentatonics (I, IV, and V) but that only C and G survive. The G major scale generates G, C, and D pentatonics, which all survive.

Chapter **28**

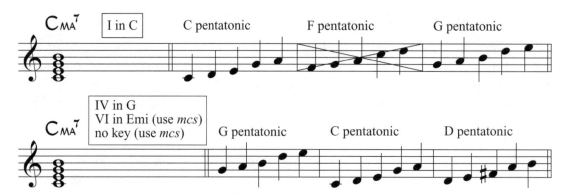

Earlier I said that the pentatonics generated by a most consonant scale will always work. This is true, but only to the extent that the most consonant scale itself works. If you're improvising over a CMa7 chord that is functioning as a I in C major, and if you hear that key scale rather than the most consonant scale (G major), then you should select your pentatonics from C major (C and G pentatonics). If the G major scale sounds odd to you over the chord in this context, then so will the D pentatonic scale that it generates.

Pentatonics with dominant 7th chords

Now let's see how to use pentatonics over dominant 7ths. Traditionally, a C7 functions either as a V in F major or F minor, or as a bII tritone substitute in B major or B minor:

In "New Pathways Home" (page 135) you learned that dominant 7ths can function in other ways but also that those functions can be compared to one of these simpler ones. When a C7 functions as a bII chord, you should improvise with the most consonant scale (G melodic minor). When a C7 functions as V in F minor, it's in the key of F minor but you should use the most consonant scale instead to generate pentatonics. Be careful here, though: this C7 should be thought of as an altered chord (b9#5), so the appropriate most consonant scale is Db melodic minor.

When a C7 functions as V in F major, you can use that scale to generate pentatonics. But F major is only the key scale, not the most consonant scale, so watch out for half-step clashes. And remember that you've got a lot of freedom with a V chord in a major key. You can alter it and use the Db melodic minor scale to generate pentatonics. (You can also use other most consonant scales such as C auxiliary diminished or C whole tone, but these will not generate any pentatonics.)

Examine these C7 pentatonics carefully:

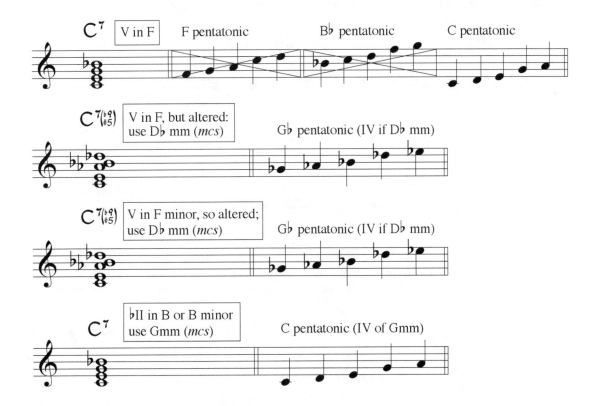

Only C and Gb pentatonics survive! The C pentatonic appears both as the lone survivor from the F major scale and as IV of G melodic minor. The Gb pentatonic occurs whenever you alter the chord. Add these possibilities together and you get a very simple rule:

> For an unaltered dominant 7th, build the pentatonic on the root.
> For an altered dominant 7th, build the pentatonic a tritone away from the root.

Whether you choose to play an unaltered dominant 7th because it's V in a major key or because it's a bII chord, the only pentatonic that works is built on the root. Whether you choose to alter a dominant 7th because it's V in a minor key or simply because you want that color, the only pentatonic that works is built on the tritone.

Pentatonics with a tonal chord progression

Now let's examine the pentatonics for an actual tonal progression. Refer back to the bridge of "Softly, As In A Morning Sunrise." Here's the complete key/most consonant scale (MCS)/pentatonic analysis.

Chapter 28

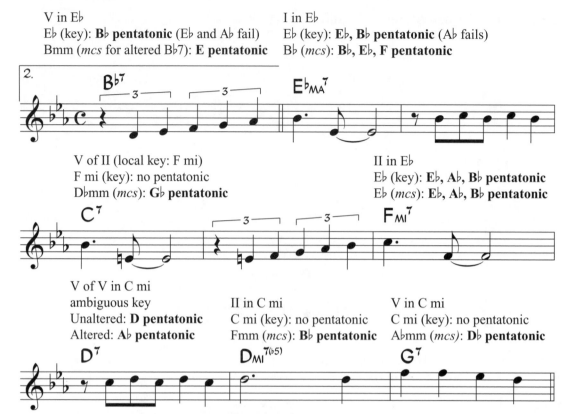

V in Eb
Eb (key): **Bb pentatonic** (Eb and Ab fail)
Bmm (*mcs* for altered Bb7): **E pentatonic**

I in Eb
Eb (key): **Eb, Bb pentatonic** (Ab fails)
Bb (*mcs*): **Bb, Eb, F pentatonic**

V of II (local key: F mi)
F mi (key): no pentatonic
Dbmm (*mcs*): **Gb pentatonic**

II in Eb
Eb (key): **Eb, Ab, Bb pentatonic**
Eb (*mcs*): **Eb, Ab, Bb pentatonic**

V of V in C mi
ambiguous key
Unaltered: **D pentatonic**
Altered: **Ab pentatonic**

II in C mi
C mi (key): no pentatonic
Fmm (*mcs*): **Bb pentatonic**

V in C mi
C mi (key): no pentatonic
Abmm (*mcs*): **Db pentatonic**

Notice: 1. The dominant 7ths get either a pentatonic on the root, the tritone, or both.
2. None of the pentatonics for Fmi7 fail, because the key scale is the same as the most consonant scale.

Why minor bebop scales fail as pentatonic generators

I said earlier that minor bebop scales wouldn't be necessary for generating pentatonics. Don't take my word for it—here's the proof. Look at the last two chords of the bridge: Dmi7(b5) and G7. Both chords are in the key of C minor. According to the table near the beginning of this section, the C minor bebop scale generates three pentatonics (Eb, Ab, and Bb). Because C minor bebop is only the key and not the most consonant scale, you must check for half-step clashes. Both Eb and Ab pentatonics contain the note Eb, which is a non-chord tone for Dmi7(b5) and lies a half step above the root D. Consequently, both these scale fail, leaving only Bb pentatonic, the scale we already generated using F melodic minor.

All three of the pentatonics from C minor bebop contain the note C, which is a non-chord tone for G7 and lies a half step above the 3rd (B), so all three fail. The most consonant scale for this G7 (Ab melodic minor) yields a Db pentatonic.

If you used a C minor bebop scale to generate pentatonics for Cmi7, you'd reject Ab pentatonic because of the Ab-G clash. This leaves Eb and Bb pentatonics, two of the three scales we generate using the most consonant scale (Bb major). And if you applied C minor bebop to a IV chord (Fmi7), all three of the pentatonics (Eb, Ab, and Bb) would work, but you can generate them just as easily using the most consonant scale (Eb major). So you really lose nothing by limiting your pentatonic generators to major and melodic minor scales, and it keeps things simple (or at least simpler).

Which pentatonic generator should you use, the key or the most consonant scale?

You already know that you should use the most consonant scale for a chord that is not in a key, such as a bII chord. You know to do the same for a chord that is in a minor key, because the minor bebop scale yields no new results. But how do you handle a chord that is in a major key? I recommend that you use the key instead of the most consonant scale, at first. Pentatonics are a somewhat exotic sound to begin with. It asks a lot of the listener when you base your pentatonic choices on a scale that is not as grounded in the tonality as the key scale. Once you've gained control over the more basic sound, however, go back and find some fresh new pentatonics from the most consonant scales.

Examine the chart on the next page. It's a summary of pentatonic choices for various chord types. After you've analyzed a tune for key scales and most consonant scales, you can simply find the function of each chord on the chart and transpose the surviving pentatonics to match it. For example, an AbMa7 functioning as a VI in C minor would derive pentatonics from its most consonant scale, Eb major. The survivors would be Eb, Ab, and Bb pentatonics.

I'll conclude this chapter with a complete solo over "Softly." In the A sections, look for random outside-inside pentatonics and voicings. During the tonal bridge section, look for pentatonics that are subsets of the keys or most consonant scales.

Chapter 28

Pentatonic Scale Choices

Pentatonics are generated from a major scale on I, IV, and V.
Pentatonics are generated from a melodic minor scale (mm) on IV.

For a chord in a major key, generate pentatonics from the key or the most consonant scale (mcs). For a chord in a minor key or in no key, generate pentatonics from the mcs.

A pentatonic must be excluded if it includes a non-chord tone that lies a half step above a chord tone. Check for this only when generating pentatonics from a major scale that is not the mcs.

Chord	Function	Key	Pentatonic generator	Subset pentatonics	Surviving pentatonics
Cma7	I	C major	C major	C F G	C G
	IV	G major	G major	G C D	G C D
	VI	E minor	G major (mcs)	G C D	G C D
	none	none	G major (mcs)	G C D	G C D
Cmi7	II	Bb major	Bb major	Bb Eb F	Bb Eb F
	III	Ab major	Ab major	Ab Db Eb	Eb
	VI	Eb major	Eb major	Eb Ab Bb	Eb Bb
	I	C minor	Bb major (mcs)	Bb Eb F	Bb Eb F
	IV	G minor	Bb major (mcs)	Bb Eb F	Bb Eb F
	none	none	Bb major (mcs)	Bb Eb F	Bb Eb F
C7	V	F major	F major	F Bb C	C
	V	F major	G mm (mcs)	C	Bb
	V	F major	Db mm (mcs)	Gb	Gb
	V	F mi	Db mm (mcs)	Gb	Gb
	bII	none	G mm (mcs)	C	C
	III	none	Db mm (mcs)	Gb	Gb
	IV	none	G mm (mcs)	C	C
	bVii	none	G mm (mcs)	C	C
	VII	none	Db mm (mcs)	Gb	Gb
	none	none	G mm (mcs)	C	C
	none	none	Db mm (mcs)	Gb	Gb
Cmi7(b5)	II	Bb minor	Eb mm (mcs)	Ab	Ab
	VI	Eb minor	Eb mm (mcs)	Ab	Ab
	none	none	Eb mm (mcs)	Ab	Ab
Cdim7	VII	Db minor	none	none	none
	bII of II	none	none	none	none
	Io	none	none	none	none
	none	none	none	none	none
Cmi6	I	C minor	C mm (mcs)	F	F
	IV	G minor	C mm (mcs)	F	F
	none	none	C mm (mcs)	F	F

Pentatonic Solo on "Softly As In A morning Sunrise"

194

Chapter 28

Chapter **29**

Diminished Opportunities

Treat this whole chapter as a practice box. Don't just read it—do it!

The diminished scale is a motherlode of great sounds that you can incorporate into your improvising. It's been a staple of the jazz vocabulary for over fifty years. In this chapter I want to introduce you to two forms of the scale and show you how to use them. Here's a C diminished scale:

As I've shown underneath the staff, the diminished scale is a series of alternating whole steps (W) and half steps (H). There's no particular convention regarding the spelling of the notes. I would suggest that you repeat only one letter name (as I did with Ab and A natural) and that you avoid using awkward names like E sharp or B double flat.

Before you continue, you should write, play, and sing a few diminished scales.

An interesting pattern emerges if you look at this scale written for two octaves:

Look at the segment of this scale between the two Eb's. The interval structure is W H W H W H W H — just as it is from C to C. By definition, then, these are the notes of an Eb diminished scale. Now look at the segment from Gb to Gb or from A to A. It's the same alternating sequence of whole steps and half steps. As soon as you can play the C diminished scale you can also play the Eb, Gb, and A diminished scales because they all have exactly the same notes. Notice that those four notes are separated by minor 3rds. Played together, they form a Cdim7 chord.

Now look at the segment of the C diminished scale from D to D. The interval structure is backwards: H W H W H W H W. This structure has its own name: it's an auxiliary diminished scale. There are actually four auxiliary diminished scales embedded in the C diminished scale: D, F, Ab, and B. These four notes are also separated by minor 3rds. Together they form a Ddim7 chord.

Before you continue, you should write, play, and sing a few auxiliary diminished scales.

Chapter 29

Let's think about what you've learned so far:

1. The interval structure of a diminished scale is W H W H W H W H.
2. The interval structure of an auxiliary diminished scale is H W H W H W H W.
3. A diminished scale has eight distinct notes. You can begin the scale on any one of those notes. In four cases, the resulting structure will be a diminished scale. In the other four cases, the resulting structure will be an auxiliary diminished scale. Both the four diminished scales and the four auxiliary diminished scales are separated by minor 3rds.

You can think about these scales in many different ways. In fact, the more flexible your perspective, the more creative you'll be with them. Here are three new ways to look at a C diminished scale:

1. a Cdim7 chord with a whole step following each chord tone (i.e., the most consonant scale):

2. a Cdim7 chord with a half step preceding each chord tone:

3. the combined chord tones of a Cdim7 and a Ddim7:

It's very easy to remember how these scales work with chords:

Use a diminished scale on the root of a diminished 7th chord:

Use an auxiliary diminished scale on the root of a dominant 7th chord:

I don't want to give the impression that you can always use these scales. Depending on the context, a scale of a different type (major, melodic minor, etc.) might be more appropriate, especially for dominant 7ths. But when a diminished or auxiliary diminished scale works with a chord, it works according to these rules.

Here's some math that you may have already figured out. As we discussed, the C diminished scale pattern actually represents four specific diminished scales (C, Eb, Gb, and A). Each diminished scale pattern will behave the same way. The G diminished scale pattern represents the G, Bb, Db, and E diminished scales, and the D diminished scale pattern represents the D, F, Ab, and B diminished scales. But there are only twelve diminished scales altogether. So as soon as you've learned the C, G, and D diminished scale patterns, you've learned all twelve. Not only that, but you've also learned all twelve auxiliary diminished scales.

Chapter 29

Before you proceed any further you should learn all three of these scale patterns. Make sure you can begin and end on any note, not just C, G, and D. Practice improvising with them over diminished and dominant chords. You can use the random note chart in the appendix (page 301) to practice this.

You can incorporate these scales into your improvisation over standard chord progressions. The first eight bars of "It Could Happen To You" include four dominant 7ths (C7, D7, G7, and C7 again). Play this example of auxiliary diminished scales:

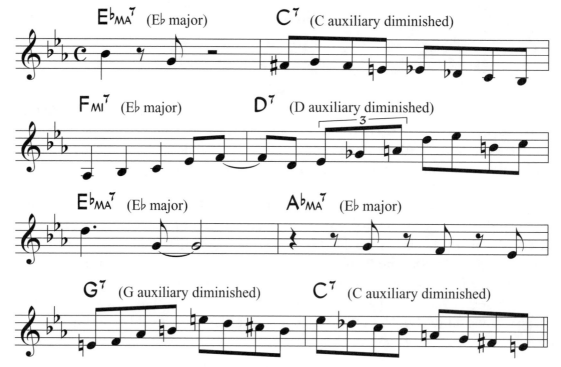

Practice improvising over these chords with auxiliary diminished scales.

Diminished scale patterns

In the above solo I improvised freely, simply jumping around within the scales (as in the fourth bar) or playing them as runs (as in the eighth bar). There is another way of approaching these scales that is very popular among jazz musicians: patterns. I'm speaking specifically about the transposing of small shapes up or down in certain intervals to create longer lines.

Pick any shape that fits within a C diminished scale:

Now carefully transpose that shape up in minor thirds four times. Your last version should be exactly an octave higher than the first.

Play this pattern. Notice that it fits entirely within the C diminished scale—not just the first shape, but the whole pattern. Play the pattern over a Cdim7 chord, then play it over a B7. The C diminished scale has the same notes as the B auxiliary diminished scale, which works for a B7.

You will find that one shape can yield a tremendous variety of great patterns. For example, transpose the previous shape up in tritones instead of minor 3rds. Your third version will be an octave higher than your first. Then transpose it up in major 6ths (diminished 7ths).

Now transpose the shape down in minor 3rds, tritones, and major 6ths:

Now rearrange the four notes of the original shape:

Chapter 29

Each of these new shapes can be put through the same ascending and descending transpositions as the old one:

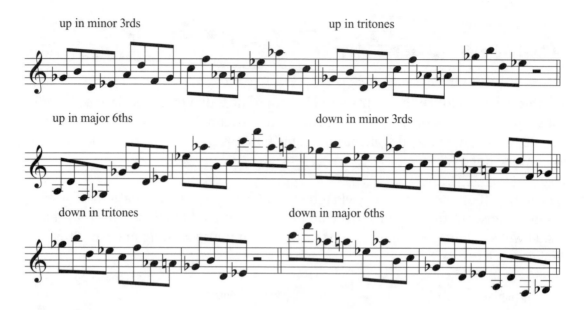

Another very effective permutation is to change the rhythmic subdivision:

Here are a few sample shapes from the C diminished scale that you might experiment with:

Pick any of these shapes or make up your own and practice transposing it up or down in minor 3rds, tritones, and major 6ths. Rearrange the order of the notes. Change the rhythmic subdivision (triplets to eighths or vice-versa). You'll like some permutations much more than others. It would be a good idea to keep track of your favorites in a notebook.

So far I've written every pattern as it appears in the C diminished scale. To have full flexibility in your improvising, you need to practice the licks in all keys. But remember: one you can play a pattern in C diminished, G diminished, and D diminished, you've got it in all twelve keys.

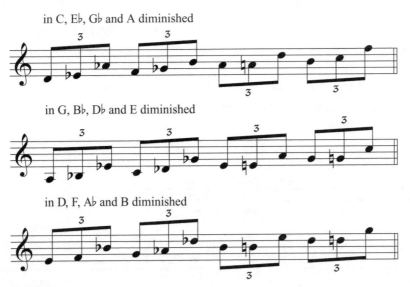

For Pianists

Here are the fingerings for the diminished scales. There are two good ones for the C and D patterns but only one for the G pattern. Try them out.

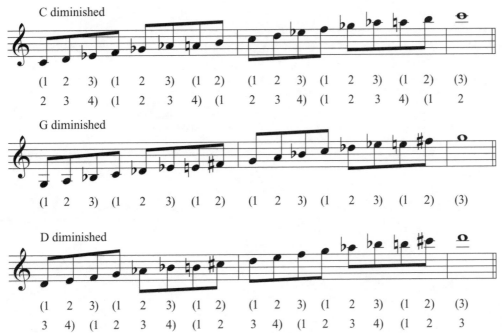

If you find it more comfortable, you can change the 2-group fingerings from (1 2) to (1 3).

Chapter 29

Here's some very important voicing information. Many of the voicings that you use—both left-hand and two-handed—fit within the diminished scale. Just as you can transpose a shape up or down in minor thirds, you can do the same with these voicings without leaving the scale:

While soloing over a Cdim7 chord for a full measure, you can play all four of these voicings in your left hand because they all fit within the C diminished scale.

If you are comping on an F7 for a full measure, you might start with the voicing that I've written on beat #1. You can actually play all four voicings, however, because they all fit within the F auxiliary diminished scale.

Performing "2-groupotomies" on Scales

> Treat this whole chapter as a practice box. Don't just read it—do it!

Pentatonic scale fingering

Many pianists use this fingering for the C pentatonic scale. Try it out:

Notice what happens from G up to C: 1 (thumb) 2 (index finger) 1 (thumb). At fast speeds it's difficult to get the thumb under to C that quickly. You'll either slow down, land too heavily on the C, or both. At first glance there seems to be no alternative. How else can you split up a 5-note scale, other than into a 3-group and a 2-group?

There's a clever solution to the 2-group problem. Don't think of the pentatonic scale as a 5-note structure. Think of it as a 10-note, two-octave structure, and use this fingering:

Now there's no 2-group. Instead, there's a 3-group, a 4-group, and another 3-group. Your thumb will now have more time to get to the next note. Almost every pentatonic scale will be easier to play if you adopt this type of fingering (two 3-groups and one 4-group). Here are the one-octave and the two-octave fingerings for all twelve pentatonics:

Chapter 30

Scale type: **1-Octave Pentatonics**   one 2-group, one 3-group

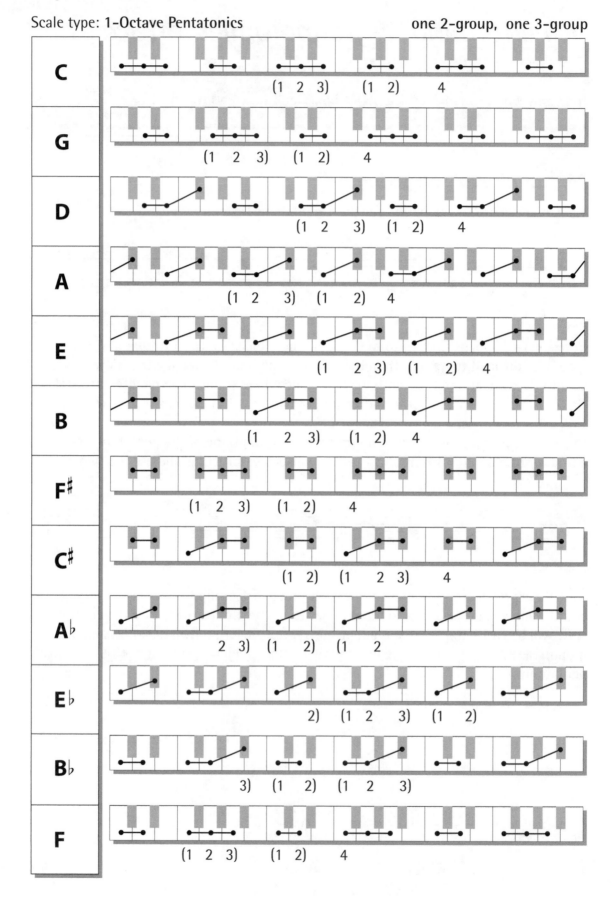

Scale type: **2-Octave Pentatonics**   two 3-groups, one 4-group

Chapter 30

Using the two-octave fingerings, play these scales through a range of four octaves up and down. Notice that in each case there are two possible starting fingers. You could start the Eb pentatonic scale on 4 and use the 4 123 123 1234 fingering or you could start it on 2 and use the 23 1234 123 12 fingering. Practice it both ways.

I'd be surprised if you like all twelve of these new fingerings at first. In particular, E and Ab pentatonics may be more awkward than with the one-octave fingering.

One-octave fingerings:

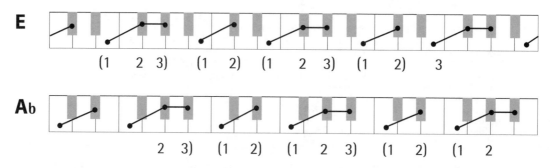

Both of the new fingerings require you to put your thumb on a black note at one point; the one-octave fingerings don't. It never hurts to have more than one fingering for a scale. You'll have more flexibility. True, you may never use the new Ab fingering when you run the scale for several octaves. But what if you wanted to play just the segment of the scale that runs from Bb up two octaves to Ab? Now compare the two fingerings.

One-octave fingering:

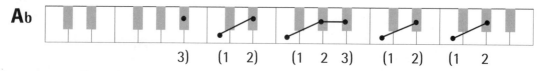

Two-octave fingering:

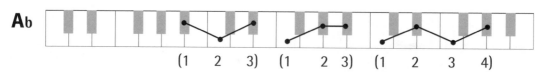

The new fingering is better here. It only becomes more awkward when you have to tuck the thumb under from Ab to Bb. The same is true for E pentatonic. Using the new fingering, play it from G# up to F#, starting with the thumb on G# (123 123 1234). That's an improvement over the old version (3 12 123 12 12).

Of course, we're talking about a very specific issue here: how to finger a scale when you run it up and down the keyboard. When you improvise freely within the scale, playing the notes in a more zigzag way, these fingerings become irrelevant. Instead, you need to improvise your fingering along with the notes.

Blues scale fingering

Now let's take a look at the blues scales. Most of these 6-note scales can be fingered using two 3-groups, which allows for high-speed playing. In some cases you'll need to start with an unexpected finger in order to do this. If you start a G blues scale with the thumb you'll apparently be forced into a 4-group and a dreaded 2-group. One solution is to finger the scale 23 123 12. Now you've got two 3-groups. Still another option is to think of the scale as a 12-note, two-octave structure, which can then be played using three four-groups. This allows you to start with the thumb and still avoid a two-group.

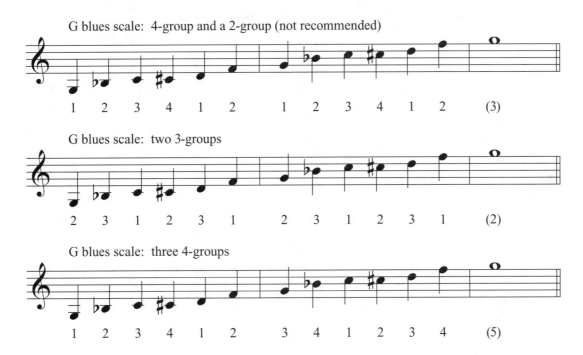

Almost every blues scale can be played with a one-octave (two 3-group) fingering, a two-octave (three 4-group) fingering, or both. The Ab blues scale is the only one for which a one-octave (4-group and 2-group) fingering seems the most comfortable. Here are the fingerings that I recommend for all twelve blues scales.

Chapter 30

Scale type: **Blues**

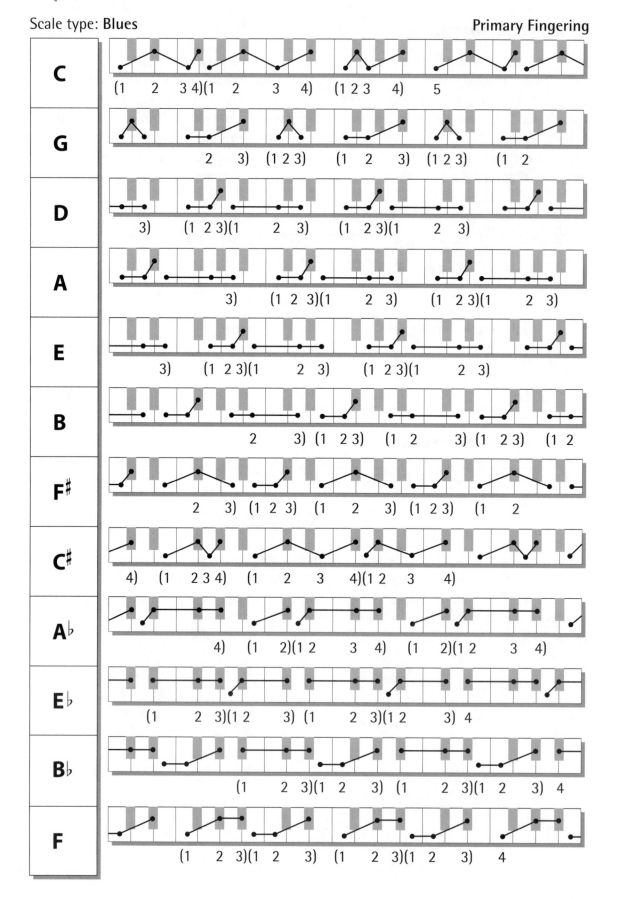

Scale type: Blues

Alternate Fingering

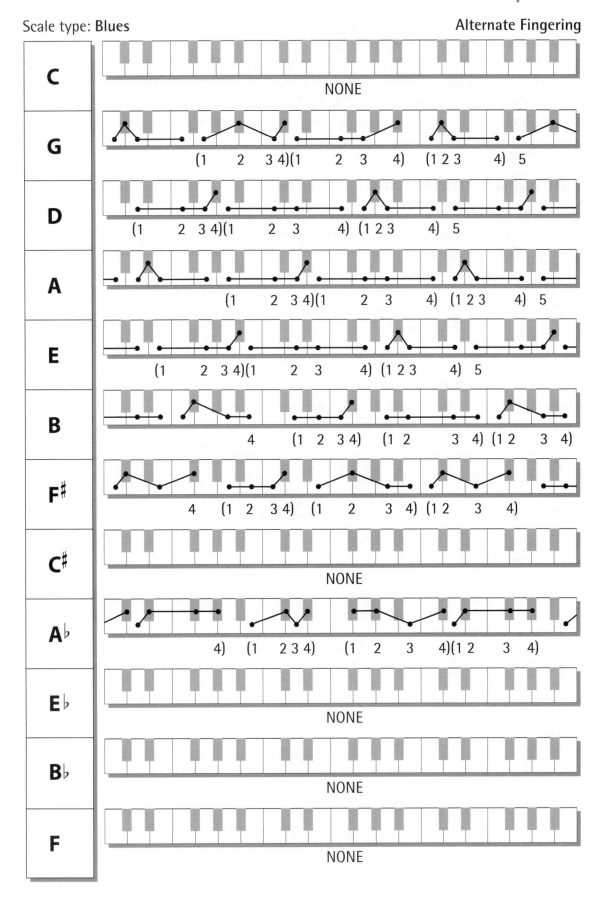

Chapter **30**

The two-octave fingering for Ab blues forces you to place your thumb on a black note (Gb); the one-octave fingering doesn't. Yet even in this case it might be worthwhile to know both fingerings. Play a segment of the Ab blues scale going from Gb up almost two octaves to Eb, using the two-octave fingering. (From Gb, it would be 1234 1234 1234.) Now try the same segment using the one-octave fingering (34 12 1234 12 12). The two-octave fingering only becomes more awkward when you have to tuck the thumb under from Eb to Gb.

Fingering for other scales

There are other scale types that appear to require 2-groups. In some of these cases it's possible to use an alternative fingering, in some cases not. You may be accustomed to playing a D diminished scale with this fingering:

This is not a particularly awkward fingering, despite the 2-group. The thumb still has enough time to get under to D. Yet consider this alternative:

Now you've got two 4-groups (instead of two 3-groups and a 2-group). This is an improvement, especially if you start the scale on F or B.

In the case of the C whole tone scale, you're stuck with a 2-group and a 4-group.

Chapter **31**

The Minor II-V-I Progression

The most common chord progression in jazz is the II-V-I. Duke Ellington's "Satin Doll" and John Coltrane's "Moment's Notice" are very different tunes, yet they both consist almost entirely of II-V-I's. Thelonious Monk used II-V-I's effectively in "Ruby My Dear" and "Ask Me Now," as did Cole Porter in "I Love You." There are thousands of such examples.

But the term II-V-I really describes two progressions, one in a major key and one in a minor key. Most jazz students learn very early about the major II-V-I, how to play it, and how to improvise over it. In this chapter, however, I'd like to shine the spotlight on the minor II-V-I. Here are the chords for a II-V-I in the key of C minor:

What's the best approach for improvising over this progression? First of all, that's a loaded question. You learned in "Notes That Work" (page 73) that there are many different answers. But let's limit this discussion to one approach, that of using scales over chords. Even here there are many choices. I'll list them all together, then go back and discuss each one.

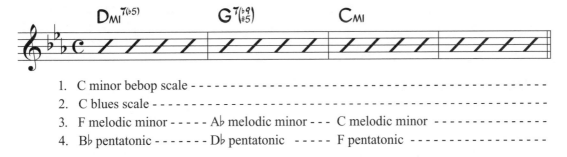

1. C minor bebop scale -
2. C blues scale -
3. F melodic minor - - - - - Ab melodic minor - - - C melodic minor - - - - - - - - - - - - - - -
4. Bb pentatonic - - - - - - - Db pentatonic - - - - - F pentatonic - - - - - - - - - - - - - - - - - -

The minor bebop approach

Now let's examine the first plan. I think that the C minor bebop scale represents the most fundamental sound over this progression, the one to which most musicians naturally gravitate. Here are the notes in a C minor bebop scale:

C minor bebop scale: C D Eb F G Ab Bb B C

I introduced you to this scale in "Harmonic Astronomy" (page 106). It's a C harmonic minor scale with an additional b7 (Bb). Use it over all three chords and see what you think. Run the scale from D to D over the Dmi7(b5), from G to G over the G7(#5b9), and from C to C over the Cmi chord. Then just improvise over the progression. You'll find that you gravitate to different scale tones on each chord. Over the Dmi7(b5), the chord tones are nice, but so are G and Bb. The note Eb works well too, but more as a passing tone between D and F. The note B may sound the least smooth to you, but play with it and see if you can find ways to make it work. Over the G7(#5b9), most of the notes sound great. Now C is the note that works only as a passing tone. Over the Cmi chord, watch out for the Ab. There's tension there that demands resolution. The B natural is an interesting note. You can land on it to good effect, unless there's a Bb in the chord.

Why do I think that this is such a fundamental sound over the progression? The notes of a Dmi7(b5) are D F Ab C. The notes of a G7(#5b9) are G B Eb F Ab. Often this chord will have a #9 (Bb) instead of a b9. The notes of a Cmi chord are C Eb G, but it's often expanded to a 7th chord with an addition Bb or B. Add all these notes together and you get a C minor bebop scale. It's the only scale that contains all the notes of all three chords. In some circles this scale has been denigrated in favor of other options, but I think that's wrong. It may very well describe what you naturally hear over the progression.

> **Improvise over the II–V–I in C minor using the C minor bebop scale.**

The blues approach

Let's move on to the second scale option, the C blues scale. Here are the notes:

   C blues scale: C Eb F F# G Bb C

You might think of this scale as 1 b3 4 #4 5 b7 1 of a major scale or perhaps as a series of intervals (minor 3rd–whole step–half step–half step–minor 3rd–whole step). This is almost as fundamental a sound over the minor II–V–I as the minor bebop scale. Many musicians would use it as their first choice. Here's a sample:

There are a lot of troublemaker notes in this scale: Eb and F# over the Dmi7(b5), C and F# over the G7(#5b9), and F# over the Cmi chord. The tension that these notes produce is of an unusual type, however, one that doesn't necessarily require resolution in the traditional sense. There are some sounds here that would be considered unacceptable in any other context, but when they occur in a blues environment they seem to work well.

> Improvise over the II–V–I in C minor using the C blues scale.

The melodic minor approach

The third plan is a bit trickier because you must use a different scale for each chord. Play the three melodic minor scales up and down for at least two octaves. Here are the notes:

    F melodic minor: F G Ab Bb C D E F
    Ab melodic minor: Ab Bb Cb Db Eb F G Ab
    C melodic minor: C D Eb F G A B C

You can think of the melodic minor scale as a major scale with a b3. (Classical musicians learn the melodic minor scale as a more complex structure that has two different note sets depending on whether it's ascending or descending, but in jazz the major scale b3 definition applies in both directions.)

Now "modalize" these scales: play the F melodic minor from D to D (the root of the Dmi7(b5), the Ab melodic minor from G to G (for the G7(#5b9)), and the C melodic minor from C to C as you did before. These new structures have names (refer to Melodic Minor Modes in the appendix on page 313):

    D locrian #2 (F melodic minor from D to D): D E F G Ab Bb C D
    G altered (Ab melodic minor from G to G): G Ab Bb Cb Db Eb F G
    C melodic minor: C D Eb F G A B C

It can be very instructive to compare these note sets to the more fundamental C minor bebop scale, just to see which notes are lost and which are gained:

Chapter **31**

C minor bebop scale from D to D

D locrian #2 (F melodic minor from D to D)

C minor bebop scale from G to G

G altered (A♭ melodic minor from G to G)

C minor bebop scale

C melodic minor scale

As you can see, I've circled the differences. Notice the new notes in the melodic minor scales:

Dmi7(b5): the new note is E (the 9th)
G7(#5b9): the new note is Db (the b5th)
Cmi: the new note is A (the 6th)

These new color notes are responsible for the unique flavor of the melodic minor scales. Without them, there's nothing to distinguish your note choice from the more basic C minor bebop scale. Here are some sample sounds:

This is a great sound. Bill Evans is just one musician who used melodic minor scales to great effect. You may need to work with the new notes for a while before they become natural to you, but it's well worth the effort.

Improvise over the II-V-I in C minor using the three melodic minor scales.

Chapter **31**

The pentatonic approach

Now we move on to the final scale option: the pentatonics. These scales are derived directly from the melodic minor scales that we just examined. The notes of the Bb pentatonic scale are all found in the F melodic minor scale, the Db pentatonic notes are in Ab melodic minor, and the F pentatonic notes are in C melodic minor. In a sense, you're still using the melodic minor solutions but omitting two notes. Here are the notes in each scale:

Bb pentatonic: Bb C D F G Bb
Db pentatonic: Db Eb F Ab Bb Db
F pentatonic: F G A C D F

Because these scales are subsets of the melodic minors, you might think that the effect would be much the same, but it's not true. Over the Dmi7(b5) we lose the color note (E), as well as the b5th (Ab). Over the G7(#5b9), we still have the color note (Db), but we lose the two most fundamental members of the chord, the root (G) and the 3rd (B). Over the Cmi chord we also retain the color note (A), but we lose both the 3rd (Eb) and the major 7th (B). It should come as no surprise, then, that the pentatonics yield a very different sound from the melodic minor scales.

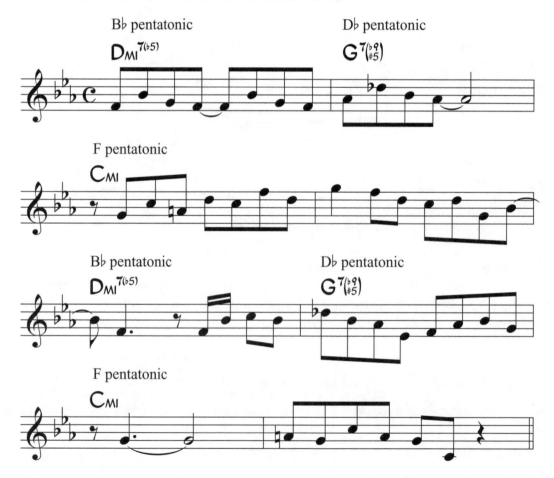

This is clearly the most exotic of the four plans, but sometimes that might be just what you're looking for. As with the previous options, you should explore these sounds at length, exposing your ears to them until they become more a part of you.

Improvise over the II–V–I in C minor using the three pentatonic scales.

Adding chromaticism

All the musical examples in this chapter have been carefully written to stay entirely within the prescribed scales. This was for clarity's sake only. A mature improviser will enhance these scales (especially the minor bebop and melodic minors) with chromaticism. Here's a solo that makes use of the scale options in a more chromatic way. The chromatic tones are circled.

Chapter **31**

Improvise over the II-V-I in C minor with all four approaches, using occasional chromatic tones.

Other options

In this chapter I've given you four scale options to explore over a minor II-V-I. There are still other options available to you, particularly over the G7(#5b9). Try the G auxiliary diminished scale or the G whole tone scale. Have fun exploring!

G auxiliary diminished: G Ab Bb B C# D E F G

G whole tone: G A B Db Eb F G

Part VI **Incomparable Comping**

While improvising a solo may be at the center of a jazz pianist's art, he probably spends much more of his musical life comping behind other soloists. If you want to work with the best musicians, take care to develop this side of your playing.

In this section of the book, you'll gain some valuable perspectives on the function of comping in an ensemble, In order to contribute to the sound of a group, it's vital to know not just what you're playing but why you're playing it. You'll also see how being able to play in all keys will improve both your comping and improvising. And you'll explore specifically the appropriate voicings for various musical environments. In the end you'll discover that comping is just another form of improvisation requiring every bit as much spontaneous creativity as soloing.

Chapter **32**

High Art

Are you ready? Here it is, the Key to Being a Great Accompanist:

> In order to accompany another musician well, you must genuinely want to hear his or her music.

That may sound simplistic, but it's amazing to me how many fine musicians never learn it. If you don't particularly care to hear what the other musician has to express, you won't listen in the right way and you won't accompany him or her well. In part, you need to function exactly as a member of the audience who just wants to hear every note, every idea, every nuance that the musician plays. If you don't feel that way, then you'll approach your accompanying role as a separate function in the music. You'll focus on your own concerns, and the music will not blend.

Years ago I learned a great lesson about accompanying bass solos by listening to an otherwise top-notch pianist do it badly. He played very softly and sparsely, which is usually the right approach. In fact, he hardly played at all; yet when he did, it was often at just the wrong time. He managed to cover up many of the bass player's best ideas. He was thinking of the music as piano comping, not as a bass solo.

Accompanying another musician is a high art. It requires tremendous control over one's musical resources to be able to listen closely to someone else while playing supportively behind him or her. Listen to the pianists who played with Miles in the fifties and sixties, from Red Garland and Wynton Kelly, to Bill Evans, Chick Corea, and Herbie Hancock: they were all first-rate compers. Listen to what pianists do behind singers: Tommy Flanagan behind Ella Fitzgerald, Jimmy Rowles behind Sarah Vaughan, Ralph Sharon behind Tony Bennett. Listen to Shirley Horn accompany herself.

The most fundamental error a pianist can make when he comps is to approach it without the proper focus. He goes in with this attitude: "It's the trumpet solo, so he's responsible for the creative music. I'm just here to do that comping thing that pianists always do behind solos. Basically it's a bunch of block chords." He will not only sound terrible himself, he'll also sabotage the trumpet player's efforts. I don't particularly like the word "comping." It makes the act sound like a mindless, utilitarian role, instead of the highly musical, creative act it should be.

Try taking this attitude toward comping: you and the soloist are collaborating composers. He has just handed you a score with only the trumpet part filled in. Now you need to write the piano part. This is not necessarily a jazz composition at all, nor is it classical, rock, or folk. You aren't bound by any stylistic limitations. You are free to write anything that sounds good to you (and sounds good with the trumpet part). If you hear syncopated block chords, fine; but if you prefer long quiet chords played right on the downbeat, write that. Perhaps you hear a unison line played with both hands, two octaves apart. Basically, the score is an open canvas. Comping behind another musician, then, is collaborative composing in real time.

How do you deal with a set of written chord changes and still use the composer's approach to comping? The answer is simply that the chord changes should influence what you play, but not when you play. If you don't want to play for four measures, don't—let the chords go by! Sometimes you may want to lay out for an entire chorus (for example, the first chorus of a bass solo) because it makes for a more interesting composition than if you fill in all the harmony.

Think of your collective performance as a process of transferring information, or data, to the listener (yes, I know that's a very sterile way to describe music). What information does the listener need to fully appreciate the music? I would say he needs to hear:

1. the melody
2. the harmony
3. the bass line
4. the time-feel and
5. the timbre of the various instruments

So when you comp, ask yourself this: what's missing if you don't play? Whatever it is, that's what you're there to provide.

You may think that this question has a simple answer: that your role as a comper is to provide the harmony. After all, if you don't provide the chordal information, who will? Well, in most cases the listener will hear the harmony accurately without any help from you. Consider this chord progression:

| FMa7 | BbMa7 | Ami7 D7 | Gmi7 C7 |

As soon as the bass player plays the roots of these chords, the listener will be able to fill in the harmonic information. Except for the F# in the D7 chord, every note of every chord is a member of the F major scale. As soon as the listener hears the Bb root, he'll naturally hear a Bb chord that is diatonic in the key of F major (BbMa7). The soloist will probably be playing a line that is based on an F major scale, so that will reinforce the same conclusion. If your only role as a comper were to provide the harmonic information, you would have no reason to play here at all. Now consider a slightly different progression:

| FMa7 | Bbmi7 | Ami7 D7 | Gmi7 C7 |

Now what's missing if you don't play? Some of the harmony may be missing—specifically, the Bbmi7. Without your input, the listener may still hear that chord as Bbmaj7. Nevertheless, there are still many reasons why you might choose not to play:

1. The soloist will probably improvise in a Bb dorian mode. The listener will then have all the information he needs to deduce that the chord is Bbmi7.
2. By including a Db in his line, the bass player may clinch the Bbmi7 harmony without your help.
3. You may choose not to clinch the harmony at all. It's a nice chord, but it gets boring if you delineate it every time.

Still, if you're approaching your comping from the standpoint I recommended (what's missing if you don't play?), you're probably more likely to play the Bbmi7 than the BbMa7.

Assuming that the harmony is already clear, though, what else is missing if you don't play? Obviously, the melody and the bass line are already provided, so you're off the hook there. So it must be the time-feel, right? Well, see what happens to the time if you stop playing: it's still there! The bass player and drummer are still cruising along, as well as the soloist, and there's no question where the time is (in fact, it may even get more solid when you lay out). One valid role that you could play, however, is that of a "second snare." Let me explain this. While the drummer generally uses his ride cymbal as an intrinsic part of the basic groove, he uses his snare differently—more sporadically, to provide occasional hits that add energy to the sound. You can use the piano in exactly the same way. Now, although you're not producing the time, you're still fulfilling a rhythmic function.

Sometimes, however, you may want to become a more basic cog in the rhythm "machine," rather than just adding a few hits here and there. At this point you should compare yourself more to a conga drum than a snare. In fact, try this exercise on a tune, either with a real band or just with a recording:

While the bassist, drummer, and melody instrument (horn, vocalist, etc.) are playing, play imaginary congas on the top of the piano. Just play along with the rest of the band as if you actually had a set of congas in front of you. Keep in mind, though, that the time is already there, so you can afford to play sparsely. Once you're getting the sound you want, then shift to the keyboard—but don't change a thing. Treat the keyboard just like a set of congas. Play both hands together sometimes, and then play one hand against the other to get the rhythms you want. Hit as many right notes as you can, but play wrong notes if you have to in order to maintain the groove. Remember: your primary role as a comper is more rhythmic than harmonic—so just be a drummer.

Sometimes you may decide to comp simply to add your timbre to the mix. All the basic elements (melody, harmony, bass line, time) are already in place without you, but you comp because you really think the timbre of the piano adds to the overall effect. That's a perfectly valid reason to play. It's also all the more reason to lay out sometimes: the listener will appreciate the sound of the piano more if it's not there all the time.

Chapter **32**

A good comper is always listening to the overall sound of the band. If he can add something valuable to that sound, he plays. If the sound is complete in every way without him, he doesn't. He can derive as much or more pleasure from just listening to the music around him as he can from playing. An inexperienced comper plays all the time, simply because he enjoys playing more than sitting. His focus is on his own playing rather than the sound of the band as a whole.

Here's something else, though, about a good comper: he doesn't play scared. I've put a lot of emphasis in this chapter on the virtue of listening and the sin of redundancy (i.e., duplicating functions). It might seem as if I'm saying that you should hardly ever play when you comp. While I do feel that most bad compers err on the side of busy rather than sparse, you can't second-guess yourself every time you reach for the keyboard. Just keep your ears open, be aware of the music around you, and play what you hear.

It may seem that my observations here about comping have been concerned solely with the role of a pianist in a combo (with a bass player and a soloist). Not at all—most of these comments would apply equally well to other playing environments. If you're playing in a duo with a singer, you still need to listen intently, think compositionally, and provide the missing essentials. If you're comping in the left hand for your own right-hand solo, you still need to avoid the predictable, utilitarian approach.

One way of thinking about left-hand comping is similar to the second snare idea. Think of the bottom half of the piano as a whole drum set. You've got the rootless voicing cymbal, the root-and-seventh shell snare, the root-and-tenth tom-tom, the root-and-fifth conga, the small-cluster gourd, the arpeggio chimes, the octave bass drum, and perhaps many more. Now simply play that drum set underneath your right-hand solo. Remember that these drums are primarily percussion instruments, not harmonic instruments. The harmony is to be found in many other places: in the bass player's line, in your solo line, and (most importantly) in your head. The same can be said for the time. Don't use your arsenal of drums to produce the time. Simply provide a light and varied collage of sounds with lots of space.

Chapter **33**

The Dirty Dozen

I frequently work with a vocalist who, in addition to her great sense of swing, authentic scatting ability and athletic voice, possesses an encyclopedic repertoire. She often begins a night's work with one or two set tunes, then tells the audience, "The rest of the night is up to you, folks. Just let me know what you want to hear." And for the next three hours, that's how it goes: someone in the audience asks for a tune and away we go. When it comes to the Great American Songbook, this singer is hard to stump.

But before we can perform a requested tune under these circumstances, a quick trans-action has to take place. Although she knows the keys for her standard repertoire, she has to quietly sing the first phrase or two of this new song to me in a comfortable range so that I can find her key. I pass it on to the bass player, she counts off the tempo, and we set her up with an appropriate intro.

I love working this way. I have to stay alert all night long, listening and thinking. Some-times I know the tune well and have played it in the singer's key. Occasionally, the tune is familiar to me but I've never played it in that key before. In many cases I've heard the tune, played it once or twice, but don't remember the chord progression. However, if I know the melody, I can generally come up with the right chords. From time to time, the singer will call a tune that I've never heard at all, but if the bass player knows it, we'll do it. I don't play during the first chorus but can usually join in the second time around. At the conclusion of a well-received performance, I often smile to think how amazed the audience would be if they could read my thoughts: Wow, that's a great tune—I should actually learn it sometime!

This may seem like an impressive skill, and, frankly, it impresses me that the human mind can respond in this way; however, this is just part of the job description for a profes-sional jazz pianist. I was completely unprepared for this when I first began working with singers. I couldn't believe that they didn't have charts for the tunes (how unprofessional, I thought). Then when I was expected to play a tune in a non-standard key, I was flabbergasted (did they think I was Einstein?) Well, I ran into several singers who worked in this way, and I began to get a queasy feeling. Was it me? Were these singers so used to working with pianists who could play in any key that they presumed anyone could do it? And that turned out to be the ugly truth.

So here I am, years later, and now I can play in any key without even thinking about it. By far, the single greatest factor in developing this skill was my on-the-job training. I learned to do it by doing it. But I also practiced in twelve keys—I still do—and I've discovered some very unexpected benefits from doing this. If you haven't ever done this, it can seem a formidable task at first—so I think it might help if you know in advance what the payoff will be. Here are the benefits:

1. Practical considerations: playing in twelve keys is a necessary skill for the professional jazz pianist. If you can do this, you can get work.

2. Understanding music: When you learn a tune in several keys, you become sensitized to its underlying structure. Instead of thinking of "All of Me" as a CMaj7 E7 A7 Dmi7, you begin to think of it as a I III7 VI7 II (or, more fundamentally, I V of VI V of II II). This, in turn, enables you to pick chords out by ear much more accurately. Notice, by the way, that I haven't used the word "transpose" in this chapter (until now). When you play a tune in a new key, you don't transpose it from the old key—you simply re-create it in the new one. At the end of "Harmonic Astronomy" (page 106) I compared this process to rebuilding a house. Once you have the blueprints, you can construct it on the same site (play the tune from memory) or another site (play it in another key)—it's all the same house.

3. Importing improvisational material: As much as you wish you had full access to your entire melodic repertoire when you improvise, the truth is that you probably play differently in Bb than you do in B. You may hear the same sound in both keys, but if it's not comfortable to your hands in B, you'll play a different line. If you always play "My Romance" in Bb, then, your ear will become accustomed to the sounds that are within your hand's "Bb stable." Very soon you may end up with the feeling that your solos all sound the same.

4. The solution may be as simple as moving the tune to a new key. Play it in B for a while, or A, or G. In each case, you'll end up playing some significantly different shapes. Entirely new melodic possibilities will open up to you and become part of what you naturally hear over that tune. When you return to the key of Bb, you'll find that you still hear all these new sounds. If you improvise slowly, you'll be able to get to them in real time. At first your fingering may be awkward—remember, if these patterns were inherently comfortable in Bb, you probably would have found them by now—but that will improve. In this way, you can greatly enrich your improvising in one key by importing melodic material from the others. In addition to improvising in all keys, you should practice melodies, licks, scales—even transcribed solos—in all keys.

So yes, as a pianist you need to be able to play in twelve keys for purely practical reasons so that you can be a good accompanist. And even if you're a horn player, you'll need this kind of flexibility in order to play with vocalists. But what if you don't aspire to play in other musicians' bands? What if you've made a decision that you will only write and perform your own music? First of all, I'd recommend against it. You'll become a much more flexible and versatile musician by playing other people's music, and your own music will be tremendously enriched by it. But even if you do elect to take the route of the isolated artist, you should still practice in twelve keys. The understanding of harmonic structure that you'll gain will be invaluable in your composing, and the melodic flexibility that you'll gain from improvising in twelve keys will tremendously enhance your ability to solo over your own tunes.

Chapter **33**

Every great journey begins with a small step. Take it now. Learn the first four bars of "It Could Happen To You" in F, then practice it in every key.

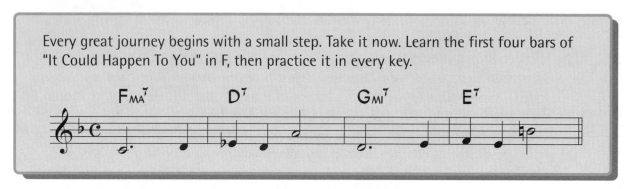

There—was that so hard? (Don't worry if the answer is yes—rejoice: you just took a giant leap.)

Voicings 101

Why do McCoy Tyner and Bill Evans sound so different? Does Oscar Peterson even play the same instrument as Thelonious Monk? And what about the difference between Chick Corea and Keith Jarrett? Well, there are certainly many reasons why these pianists get (or got) such different sounds out of the instrument, including touch, sense of time, and improvisational note choice. But another major factor that distinguishes each of these pianists is the way they voice their chords. McCoy's fourth-based colors, Chick's clusters, Keith's more open sounds--these decisions have a huge impact on the overall tone that each pianist gets from the instrument. In fact, I think that what distinguishes an advanced pianist is a wide palette of creative voicings, more so than a mastery of the single-note improvised line. You can learn more about voicings through transcribing, experimenting, taking lessons, and learning from texts such as Mark Levine's *The Jazz Piano Book.*

This chapter will not deal with the stylistic voicings of individual pianists. What I want to do here is help you organize your thinking about functional or stock voicings—i.e., the basic sounds that you'll need just to play tunes competently. While it's true that your music will not sound good without a spark of creativity, it will also never get off the ground if you have to reinvent the wheel every time you voice the chords for a tune. You might say that this chapter will deal with "craft" voicings rather than "art" voicings; in the end you'll need plenty of both.

I'm going to organize the discussion of voicings into various playing environments, distinguished from each other simply by the number of musicians present:

Environment #1: Solo piano voicings.
Environment #2: Duo voicings (a melody instrument and piano).
Environment #3: Trio voicings (piano, bass, and drums).
Environment #4: Quartet voicings (piano, bass, drums, and a melody instrument).

It's useful at first to think in terms of solo, duo, trio, and quartet voicings. Each of these sets addresses specific problems that are peculiar to that instrumentation. Once you've mastered them all, however, you'll find that you use a mixture of all the voicings, no matter what the environment. Imagine holding a palette with four dabs of paint on it, all different shades of the basic color known as Bb7. You bought one of those pigments at the Solo Piano Emporium, another at Duo Arcade, the third at the Trio Shop and the last at Quartets'R'Us. But now they're all just blobs of paint on your palette, and it's time to paint your picture using whatever combination best expresses your intent. If you're playing in a trio, you may use more of the trio shade, but only because it seems more appropriate--not because you consider the others off-limits.

Chapter **34**

Environment #1 – Solo voicings

The 2+2 approach

Here are the first four measures of the standard "But Beautiful":

Look at the chord symbols, then examine the way I've voiced each chord. The root is in the bass, the melody is on top, and in between there are two more notes: the 3rd and the 7th. In some cases the 3rd is in the left hand and the 7th is in the right; for other chords the order is reversed. Play these inner notes with your thumbs. This will enable you to stretch down with your left hand to play the roots, and it will leave four free fingers in your right hand for playing the melody. If you're playing a root and 7th in the left hand (such as for the first chord, BbMa7), play the root with the fifth finger. If you're playing a root and 3rd in the left hand (such as for the second chord, EbMa7), play the root with your second (index) finger. For the most part, then, you won't be using the third or fourth fingers of your left hand. You'll use a 5-1 or 2-1 fingering. I can't stress the importance of fingering enough here. If you use the correct fingering right from the beginning, your hands will embrace this way of playing much more quickly.

I call this the **2+2 approach** for the simple reason that you're playing two notes with each hand.

The Chromatic System

How do you know when to play a root and 7th in the left hand and when to play a root and 3rd? This decision must be based on a couple of criteria: the best range and the smoothest voice leading. The best range for the inner voices can best be described as "straddling middle C, with a slight bias to the left." It's fine if both thumbs are below middle C, but not too far below. Of course, if you place your inner voices in this range consistently, it follows that smooth voice leading between chords will happen as a matter of course.

I'd like to show you a clever system that automatically places your chords in the best position most of the time. Play the following chromatic scale from G to F#, and make sure to use the fingering written underneath.

Chapter 34

5   5   5   5   5   5   2   2   2   2   2   2

Memorize the fingering. It's not difficult: the scale runs from G to F#, and the dividing line between the six pinky notes and the six index finger notes is C to C#. Here's how to use this scale: simply play the root of each chord with the finger indicated by the scale, then set your thumbs on the 3rds and 7ths. If you play the root with the fifth finger, put your left thumb on the 7th and your right thumb on the 3rd. If you play the root with the second finger, put your left thumb on the 3rd and your right thumb on the 7th. Look again at the "But Beautiful" excerpt. You'll see that I used this chromatic system to select every voicing. Observe how each voicing straddles middle C (except for the Dmi7(b5) to G7, where the right thumb moves from C to B). Notice also how smoothly the thumbs move through the entire progression.

Now practice playing some solo piano voicings in this way, using the random 7ths chart in the appendix (page 302).

Chapter **34**

Solo piano voicings for the II-V-I

It's a good idea to learn solo piano voicings for the II-V-I progression in every key. Play these II-V-I progressions in D major and Ab major:

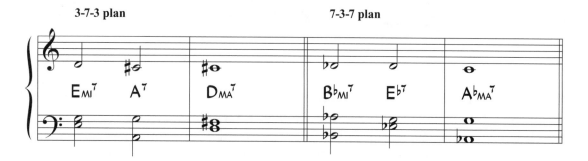

In the first case, the II chord is voiced with the 3rd in the left thumb. The V chord is voiced with the 7th, and the I chord is voiced with the 3rd again. This is why I call it the 3-7-3 plan. For the II-V-I in Ab major, the role of the left thumb is reversed. This is an example of the 7-3-7 plan.

You can learn your II-V-I's very quickly by using (apologies in advance) the Rule of Thumb:

As you go from II to V and from V to I, move one thumb at a time down a half step.

Now play both II-V-I's again. In the first case, the right thumb moves first, then the left thumb. This is always the case in the 3-7-3 plan. In the 7-3-7 plan, the left thumb is always the first to move. In both cases, the voice leading is very smooth.

Using the random II-V-I chart in the appendix (page 304), practice all twelve II-V-I's using both the 3-7-3 and the 7-3-7 plans. Some of the progressions will not be in the right range. Play them too high rather than too low, so that the chords don't sound muddy.

After you're comfortable with both plans, start mixing them as you practice the random chart. Choose the plan that places each II-V-I in the best range. Here's a good way to do that: use the chromatic scale system to choose the voicing for the II chord. Then use the Rule of Thumb to complete the progression. Almost all the voicings for the V's and I's will be in the correct range according to the chromatic system. A few will be slightly lower, but not enough to warrant breaking up the smooth voice leading:

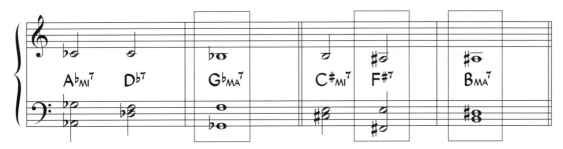

If you have large hands, you can replace the root-3rd voicings with root-10ths by dropping the root an octave. This is a great sound, because it creates a larger separation between the bass function (the root) and the chord function (the 3-7 shell) and adds some deeper sonorities to your playing:

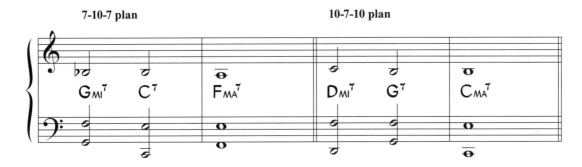

You'll need to adjust your left-hand fingering to incorporate the 10ths. Obviously, the only possible fingering for the root-10th stretch is 5-1. However, you should use a 3-1 fingering, not 5-1, for the root-7th voicings (4-1 is acceptable if you can't reach the notes otherwise). For example, the left-hand fingering for Gmi7 C7 Fmaj7 is 3-1, 5-1, 3-1. For Dmi7 G7 Cmaj7, the fingering is 5-1, 3-1, 5-1. This fingering will allow you to get from chord to chord with the most efficient hand movement.

Do you hear how much richer the sound becomes when you use 10ths instead of 3rds? For this reason, even many players with small hands work 10ths into their voicings by staggering the roots and the 3-7 shells:

Chapter **34**

Special Problems

The chromatic system is designed to place your chords in the best range and to insure smooth voice leading from chord to chord. Sometimes, however, it does just the opposite. Play this progression, a II-V in F major:

The chromatic system would suggest that you place your fifth finger on both roots. I'm sure you can see what's wrong here: the voice leading is not smooth at all. In this case it would make more sense to use the second finger on the root of the C7.

The chromatic system is merely a guide to help you in your voicing decisions. Don't hesitate to use a different solution if it places your chords in a better range or produces smoother voice leading. I do need to warn you, however, about a common hazard: I call it "harmonic gravity." If you always choose your voicings on the basis of smoothest voice leading, even in contradiction of the chromatic system, they may sink lower and lower on the keyboard until they sound too muddy. For example, don't voice this progression in this way:

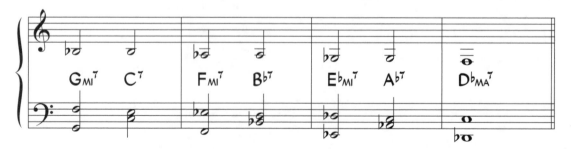

The thumbs move smoothly throughout, but only the first chord is voiced according to the chromatic system. By the third measure the progression starts to sound muddy. Try this solution instead:

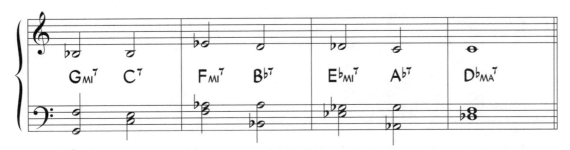

Every voicing except the C7 is voiced by the chromatic system, and the thumbs move smoothly except from C7 to Fmi7. Try to maintain smooth voice leading within the II-V's as I've done here. Jump up in between the II-V's, not within them.

Sometimes the melody note is the 3rd or 7th of the chord. If the melody note is high you should double it an octave down, but not if it's low:

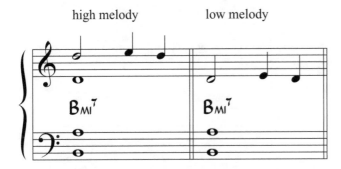

It's easy to tell when three notes are sufficient. Simply voice the chord (with no melody) according to the chromatic system. If you're already playing the actual melody note, then that's all you need. If the melody note is above that voicing, then you need the full four-note structure.

Why not use the 5th as an inner voice when the melody is the 3rd or 7th. Actually, you could do this, but be forewarned that your voice leading may suffer somewhat:

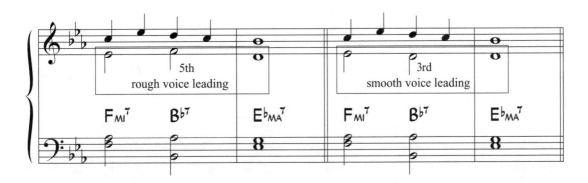

For that matter, why aren't we using 5ths in general? The answer is simply that the 5th doesn't contribute significantly to the chord's distinctive color. Play the following chord with and without the 5th and listen to how little difference there is:

Chapter 34

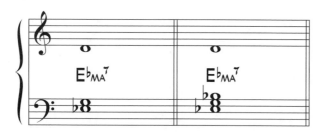

The 5th of a minor 7(b5) is more important, of course. But because it's still not as important as the root, 3rd, 7th, or melody, it will not occur in a standard four-note structure. Yes, you heard right: you'll play the same voicing for Ami7 and Ami7(b5) (Ex.1)! You can add the b5 as an extra note in either hand (Ex. 2). If the melody is the 3rd or 7th you can play the b5 as one of the two inner voices--but again, your voice leading may suffer (Ex. 3). Often the b5 will occur in the melody. In that case you could certainly omit it from the voicing (Ex. 4).

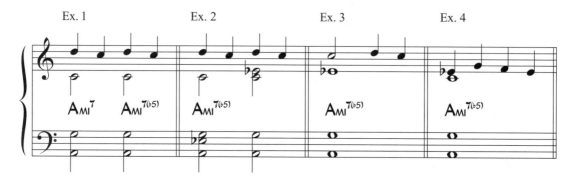

Sometimes the melody is actually lower than the highest note in the standard voicing (the right thumb note). There are several ways of handling this problem. You can choose a lower voicing than is indicated by the chromatic system, as long as it's not too muddy (Ex. 5). You can simply omit the right thumb note (Ex. 6). You can even play the melody underneath the voicing note (Ex. 7). Of course, you'll no longer play that voicing note with the thumb, and you'll need to play it softly enough that the melody is clearly heard.

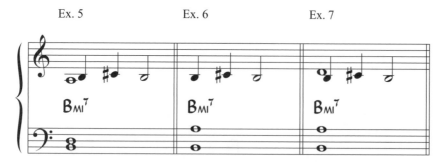

We've now examined several special problems that you'll encounter as you voice chords in solo piano style: harmonic gravity, low melodies, melodies that use the 3rd or 7th, mi7(b5) voicings, etc. The basic approach is quite simple, however: play the root in the bass, the melody on top, and the 3rds and 7ths with the thumbs (according to the chromatic system, generally). Before you continue, learn several tunes with this approach.

The 3+1 approach

Here again is the excerpt from "But Beautiful."

Compare the two versions. You'll see that the notes are exactly the same. The only difference is that you now play three notes with the left hand and one, the melody, with the right (hence the term **3+1 approach**). You may not have large enough hands to reach some of the chords. In that case, play the root on the downbeat, then come up and play the 7th and 3rd together on the upbeat (use the sustain pedal). For the small (root-3rd-7th) chords, play the root with the third finger; i.e., use a 3-2-1 fingering. If this is too wide a stretch, use your fourth finger on the root. Don't use your fifth finger on the root under any circumstances. Reserve that finger for the roots of the large (root-7th-3rd) chords.

It's very important that you understand that the notes are exactly the same for the 2+2 and the 3+1 approaches. You simply place your hands on those notes in a different way. Even the chromatic scale system still applies. Just replace the second finger with the third finger on the notes from C# up to F#:

What is the rationale for the 3+1 approach? If the notes are exactly the same as in the 2+2 approach, why bother to learn them in a second way? You probably know the answer: it leaves your right hand free to improvise. Furthermore, if the melody is especially high your right hand can play it without pulling the chord up with it.

Chapter 34

Improvising in solo piano style is actually done using an "x+1" approach: 3+1, 2+1, or 1+1. In the 2+1 approach your left hand plays the same root-3rd and root-7th shells as in the 2+2 approach. You simply omit the right thumb. In the 1+1 approach you improvise over the root only. Both of these approaches are harmonically incomplete, but it's not a problem. In many cases the harmonic scheme is straightforward enough that you don't need to supply all the information. It actually works better if you just imply it. If you do feel a need to hear the omitted chord tones (3rd, 7th, or both), you'll probably gravitate to those notes in your improvised line.

> Using the random 7ths chart again (page 302), practice playing solo piano voicings using just your left hand (root-3rd-7th and root-7th-3rd, according to the chromatic system). Then apply this approach to some tunes.

The 1+3 approach

Here is yet a third version of the "But Beautiful" excerpt:

This is the **1+3 approach**. Compare it to the previous versions. Again, the notes are exactly the same. The obvious difference is that you're now playing only one note, the root, in the left hand and everything else in the right. Unless you have exceptionally large hands you won't be able to play the right-hand part as I've written it. In the 3+1 approach you occasionally had to jump back and forth between the roots and the 3-7 shells. Now you may have to jump back and forth between the melody and those shells. You can use the sustain pedal, but not to the extent that it makes the melody sound muddy. In some cases you won't have time to squeeze a 3-7 shell in between the melody notes, so just omit it.

> Using the random 7ths chart again (page 302), practice playing solo piano voicings using this approach (playing only the root in the left hand and the 3rd and 7th in the right hand). Voice the chords according to the chromatic system. Then apply this approach to some tunes.

Advantages of each approach

As we discussed, 3+1 approach facilitates improvising and playing high melodies with your right hand. The 1+3 approach offers mirror-image advantages. It frees your left hand to play bass lines (walking, Latin, etc) and lower roots.

And what are the benefits of the 2+2 approach? At first glance, this appears to be the worst of both worlds. Your left thumb anchors that hand so it can't play complex bass lines, while your right thumb makes improvising difficult. The answer lies in the fact that you're only using two fingers on each hand to produce the fundamental sound of the tune. This frees the other three fingers to enhance that sound. You can add notes to a voicing:

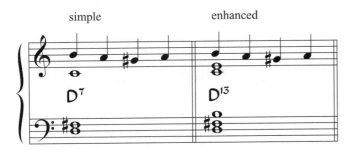

You can also add a moving inner voice (a countermelody) with your free fingers:

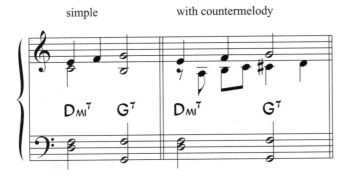

Now you have my story on basic solo piano voicings. Choose a tune and learn it using each distinct approach—the 2+2, the 3+1, and the 1+3. Don't mix the approaches at first, no matter how awkward it may be to play certain passages. For example, don't switch from a 1+3 to a 3+1 approach when the melody goes up high. You won't be able to use that solution in an actual tune if you're playing a walking bass line. Once you've learned to play the tune well using each approach, however, you should deliberately mix them. You could play four measures of 2+2, four of 1+3, four of 3+1—you could even switch measure by measure! Strive for an evenness of sound. A listener should not even be able to tell that you're switching approaches. The point of this is that no single approach will be appropriate for an entire tune. You'll need to be able to switch fluidly between approaches as you play. Eventually you'll be able to focus simply on what sounds you want from the piano, without thinking twice about your hands.

Chapter **34**

Environment #2 – Duo voicings

This section will be as short as the last one was long. It's not that you don't need a variety of voicing procedures in order to effectively accompany a singer or horn player in a duo format. But there is one strategy that is especially common here: left-hand bass lines and right-hand rootless voicings. Generally, place your voicings in the same range as you would if you were playing them in your left hand underneath your own solo. It's not my intention to discuss bass line construction in this chapter, and I'll save my discussion of rootless voicings for the next section. Let me conclude, then, with a short sample of the standard duo sound, applied to the first four measures of the tune "It Could Happen To You":

A walking bass line is not necessary. You can start with simple roots in the left hand.

Return to this practice box after you've learned rootless voicings. Then, using the random charts in the appendix (pp. 301-306), practice playing roots with your left hand and rootless voicings with your right hand. Then apply this approach to a few tunes.

Environment #3 – Trio voicings

For at least the past fifty years (more than half the entire history of recorded jazz), one of the most popular group formats has been the piano trio (piano, bass, and drums). Through the years, pianists have come up with a wide variety of solutions for voicing chords in this environment. Bud Powell used a lot of two-note voicings, especially the root-3rd and root-7th shells we discussed in the solo section. Decades later, McCoy Tyner favored modal voicings based on fourths. If there is one set of voicings, however, that almost every jazz pianist uses, it would have to be those that were developed in the late forties and early fifties by pianists such as Ahmal Jamal, Wynton Kelly, Red Garland, and especially Bill Evans. They are typically called "rootless voicings" (not a term I especially like, as I'll explain later). These voicings are no longer considered innovative, but they remain an ingeniously efficient way of incorporating extensions while leaving the right hand free to improvise. They have simply become part of the craft of jazz piano.

Some pianists play three-note rootless voicings, others prefer four-note. I think it's easier to take something out later than put something in, so I recommend that you learn the four-note voicings first:

The three-note voicings for major 7ths and minor 7ths are **379** and **735**. For dominant 7ths they are **379** and **736**. The only stock voicing for the mi7(b5) is the three-note one I presented above (**735**). Alternatives to the **4573** voicing include **5714** and **3579**. For the most part, diminished 7th chords are played as simple rooted chords in any inversion, although you can generate several good voicings by raising any one chord tone up a whole step.

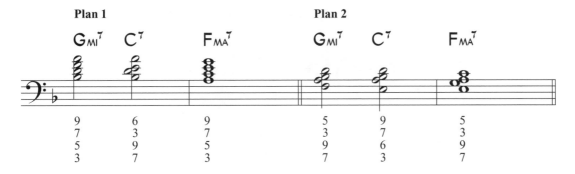

> Using the random note chart in the appendix (page 301), practice each of the eight primary voicings presented above. Then use the random 7th chart (page 302) to practice all the voicings at the same time. At first you'll find it easier to focus on one of the two voicings for each chord type (such as the voicings that are built on the 7ths), but ultimately you should use some of both for smooth voice leading.

Rootless voicings for the II-V-I

Just as with the solo piano voicings, you should learn rootless voicings for the II-V-I progression in every key.

Chapter 34

Notice how smooth the voice leading is from chord to chord. As you go from II to V, one note descends by a half step. That note then stays put as you go from V to I, while the other notes descend by various intervals.

Using the random II-V-I chart in the appendix (page 304), practice the Plan 1 progression with your left hand in every key. Then do the same for Plan 2. Then mix the plans to place the voicings in the best range (straddling middle C) and to achieve smooth voice leading. Here's an example:

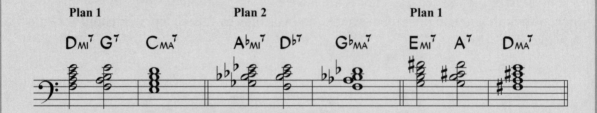

Also practice these progressions with your right hand (but in the same range), because you'll need them to play in a duo format. Play the roots with your left hand.

Selecting the appropriate plan for each II-V-I is not an exact science. While the choice is obvious in some keys, in others you'll find that either plan works well.

Rootless voicings for the minor II-V-I

Here are two rootless voicing plans for a II-V-I in the key of Bb minor:

Notice that the I chord has no 7th. You may add a minor 7th, a major 7th, or a major 6th if you like, but first learn the three-note voicing.

> Using the random minor II-V-I chart in the appendix (page 305), practice the Plan 1 progression with your left hand in every key. Then do the same for Plan 2. Then mix the plans as you did with the major II-V-I's. Practice the voicings with your right hand as well.
>
> Now review both your major and minor II-V-I voicings by using the random chart on page 306.

Special Problems

Practice applying these voicings to a few tunes. Most of them will work beautifully. Don't be surprised, however, if some of them sound wrong. Never forget this simple fact: when you play a rootless voicing for a chord written on a lead sheet, you're changing the chord. If the written chord is Cmi7 and you use a standard rootless voicing (such as 3579), you've changed the chord to Cmi9. The composer didn't ask for a 9th. If it turns out to be a bad note, he shouldn't feel compelled to warn you against it. If the written chord is Cmi7(b5) and you choose the 4573 voicing, you're adding a 4th that may or may not sound good in that particular case. It's almost a certainty that the problem notes in your voicings will be the new ones, the added notes that are not specified by the written chord (the 9ths, 6ths and 4ths).

When you find a troublemaker, the most straightforward solution is to omit it. You can also replace it with a more basic chord tone just underneath (for example, replacing a 9th with a root or a 6th with a 5th). For dominant 7ths, you can also alter it (#9, b9, b6). It's fine to include occasional roots in these voicings. If roots sounded that bad, we could no longer listen to the music of Bud Powell or Nat King Cole. These voicings grew more out of a need to include upper extensions than to exclude roots. If it didn't sound so odd, we would call them "9th-ful" or "13thful" voicings rather than "root-less" voicings.

Chapter 34

There are two scenarios that will result in the need to modify a standard rootless voicing.

1. **The voicings sound fine by themselves, but problems arise when you add the melody.** The melody is clashing with a new note in the voicing; i.e., it lies a half step or a minor 9th (an octave and a half step) above the voicing note.

These are the first four measure of Herbie Hancock's "Watermelon Man." The written chord is C7, but the standard rootless voicing (3679) makes it a C13. The long Bb in the melody clashes with the A (the 13th) in the voicing. It's not a very pleasant sound. I've written the voicing in whole notes. In reality, you'd probably comp the chord with a short hit or two in each measure. This would certainly mitigate the effect of the minor 9th interval. It might not bother you at all. If it does, however, you can easily fix the problem by omitting the 13th. Remember, Herbie never asked for that note in the first place!

2. **Some of the voicings sound wrong even before you add the melody.** Each chord in a progression serves a particular function and is in a specific key. The notes that comprise that chord are all members of that key scale, but the new notes in the rootless voicing may not be. If they're not, they will partially obscure the harmonic function of the chord. This explains why the voicing may sound odd to you.

There are two common examples of this problem. They both occur in the second measure of the tune "My Foolish Heart":

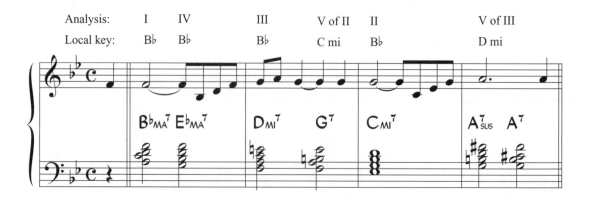

As the analysis indicates, the Dmi7 is a III chord in Bb major. All the notes in a basic Dmi7 (D F A C) are members of the Bb major scale, but the 9th (E) is not. While you can't flat the 9th, there are several solutions to this problem. You can omit the 9th or replace it with the root. The most surprising solution is that you can simply include the 9th. A note that is outside of the prevailing local key is not inherently bad—it's simply unexpected. It can sound wrong but it can also sound fresh and interesting. There's nothing wrong with playing an E here as long as you choose it for its sound. Just don't mindlessly include it as part of a standard rootless voicing because you think the composer asked for it.

The G7 is a V of II. The local key is C minor. All of the notes in a basic G7 (G B D F) are members of the C minor bebop scale (C D Eb F G Ab Bb B C), but the 9th (A) and the 6th (E) are not. The most straightforward solution here is to alter those notes. You can flat the 9th (Ab) or sharp it (Bb), and you can flat the 6th (Eb). You can also omit one or both of those notes. Or, as in the previous case, you can choose to include the unaltered 9th and/or 6th as fresh notes. The only unacceptable approach is to include the 9th and 6th automatically because you think the composer asked for them. You added those notes, and you're responsible for them.

The A7sus and A7 in the fourth measure are V of III. The local key is D minor. Once again, the 9th (B) and the 13th (F#) are not in the scale. I like the sound of those notes with the A7sus, however. I'd recommend flatting them only for the regular A7.

Compare this repaired version of "My Foolish Heart" with the previous one:

You may have wondered why I didn't present 3579 as a primary rootless formula for a minor 7(b5) chord. After all, that is the formula for a minor 7th voicing, and the two chords are quite similar. Here's the reasoning: Dmi7(b5) is almost always a II chord in the key of C minor. The 9th (E) is not in that scale. You can't simply flat the 9th, but you can omit it (hence the 735 voicing) or replace it with an 11th (hence the 4573 and 5714 voicings). Once again, though, you can choose the 9th as a fresh sound. Of course, you may want to adjust your improvised line to match that sound. A nice combination would be a 3579 voicing (F Ab C E) with an improvised line from the F melodic minor scale.

So what have you learned? First of all, you need to thoroughly familiarize yourself with the standard rootless voicings. You can use the random charts in the appendix to practice them in twelve keys, both as individual chords and in the context of II-V-I's.

Chapter **34**

Next, apply them to some of your favorite tunes, but be prepared to modify them if necessary. You'll need to alter a standard voicing either to avoid a clash with the melody or to make sure that it stays within the prevailing local key. The two most common examples of the latter problem are:

1. a minor 7th chord functioning as III in a major key: the 9th is a potential trouble-maker. Remove it, replace it with the root, or include it as a fresh sound. Notice that the 9th is not a problem when the minor 7th functions as a II or a VI.

2. a dominant 7th chord functioning as a V in a minor key: both the 9th and 13th (6th) could cause problems. Remove them, alter them (b9, #9, b13), or include them as fresh sounds. Notice that the 9th and 13th are fine when the dominant chord functions as a V in a major key.

You may be thinking, "I understand the principles here, but analyzing chord progressions is beyond me. How will I know when to alter a voicing if I can't tell how the chords are functioning in the progression?" First, analyze several tunes using the concepts you learned in "Harmonic Astronomy" (page 106) and the succeeding chapters. But also remember what I said earlier: you can solve many of these problems with your ear. Simply plug in the standard rootless voicings. Then, when you find one that doesn't sound right to you, round up the "usual suspects" (the 9ths, 6ths, etc.), find the bad notes and fix them. Yes, you can never know too much theory. In the end, however, theory is simply an after-the-fact description of what your ear will tell you anyway.

> Before you continue, apply rootless voicings to a couple of your favorite tunes.

Environment #4 – Quartet voicings

A solo pianist must constantly confront the challenge of performing three functions (bass line, chords, and melody) with two hands. The 3+1 approach allows him to fulfill the first two functions with his left hand and the third with his right. With the 1+3 approach, it's just the reverse. Finally, in the 2+2 approach, each hand performs one-and-a-half functions. No matter how the functions are distributed, it's a considerable feat.

The pianist in a quartet is primarily dealing with much kinder math: performing one function (chords) with two hands. Here the challenge is simply to take full advantage of the situation to create a rich palette of voicings, including many that are impossible to play in the other environments. Pianists through the years have devised a multitude of solutions to this problem, yielding a wide variety of colors and textures. It's far too big a subject for me to cover thoroughly in a few pages. Earlier in this chapter I referred you to Mark Levine's *The Jazz Piano Book*. I think his treatment of these voicings is particularly clear and informative. Here I will simply introduce you to a few approaches to get you up and running.

Approach #1 – Octaves over rootless voicings

This approach is very easy to understand, and it's relatively easy to execute. Simply play the same rootless voicings with your left hand that you would play under your own right-hand solo. Improvise with octaves with your right hand. Choose your notes freely, but always play in rhythmic unison with your left hand:

That's really about all there is to it. I should mention one technically challenging aspect of this approach, however: if you play a rhythm of consecutive eighth notes, you need to use legato articulation. This is much more difficult to do with octaves than with single-note lines. In order to achieve the correct articulation you'll need to use alternating fingering in your right hand:

Notice the articulation marks on the octave notes; they're essential to the correct execution. Play only the upper notes of each octave legato. The thumb notes are played short. Don't worry: the smooth sound of the upper line will mask the staccato notes underneath.

Although I'm presenting this as a comping approach, it's not hard to see that you could also use this texture in your own solo. In a sense, the difference lies in which hand is making the rhythmic decisions. If you're comping, you'll use sparser left-hand rhythms and match those rhythms with your right-hand octaves. If you're improvising, you'll focus on your right-hand rhythms and match those with your left-hand voicings.

Practice applying this approach to one of your favorite tunes.

Chapter **34**

Approach #2 – Open-position rootless voicings

This approach is also quite easy to understand but a little trickier to learn. Start with the same rootless voicings that you would normally play in your left hand under your right-hand solo, but spread them out by raising the next-to-the-lowest note by one octave. Play two notes with each hand.

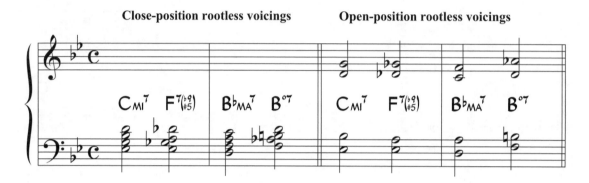

That's basically it. You're really just playing the same sound underneath the other soloists as you play underneath your own solo—just a little more spread out.

Major 7ths, minor 7ths, and dominant 7ths all sound great in open position. Diminished 7ths are usually played as rooted chords. Open them up in the same way: just raise the next-to-the-lowest note.

The mi7(b5) chord presents a special problem in this approach. Neither the 4573 voicing nor the 735 voicing works well in open position. (The 4573 voicing opens to 4735 and results in a minor 9th interval, and the 735 voicing simply becomes too spread out as 753.) Instead, start with any of these three close-position formulas: 1357, 3579, or 5714. You'll find that you can use these voicings in any inversion and open them up. Two of the resulting voicings contain minor 9th intervals and are consequently not so good (I've boxed them), but that still leaves ten good voicings:

Now practice applying open-position voicings to one of your favorite tunes.

Chapter **34**

Approach #3 – Upper-structure voicings

I'm using Mark Levine's name for these voicings so you'll know where to find out more about them (*The Jazz Piano Book,* by Mark Levine, Sher Music Co.). While it's of some importance to understand the theoretical basis for these voicings, it's more important to simply learn and incorporate them into your playing. Consequently, I'm going to begin with the "final result" voicings and suggest that you set upon the tasks of learning them in all keys and applying them to tunes. Then I'll go back and discuss the theory to support the results. (Note: the term "E4" refers to a stack of two perfect 4ths built on E.)

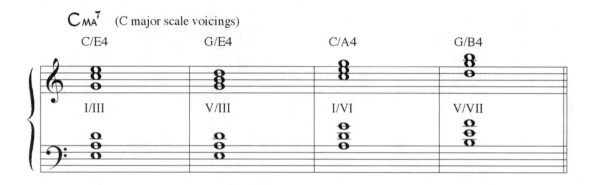

C𝗠𝗶⁷ (A♭ major scale voicings)

E♭/C4   E♭/F4   E♭/G4

♭III/I   ♭III/IV   ♭III/V

C𝗠𝗶⁷ (E♭ major scale voicings)

E♭/C4   E♭/F4   B♭/F4   E♭/G4

♭III/I   ♭III/IV   ♭VII/IV   ♭III/V

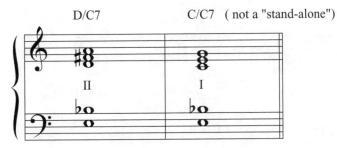

C⁷ (G melodic minor scale voicings)

D/C7   C/C7   (not a "stand-alone")

II   I

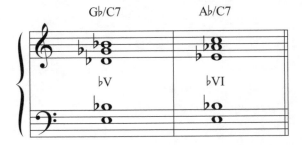

C⁷ (D♭ melodic minor scale voicings)

G♭/C7   A♭/C7

♭V   ♭VI

Chapter **34**

C⁷ (C auxiliary diminished voicings)

C/C7 (not a "stand-alone")   Eb/C7   Gb/C7   A/C7

I   ♭III   ♭V   VI

Cᴍɪ⁷⁽♭⁵⁾ (Eb melodic minor voicings)

Bb/R5   Bb/571   Bb/4573   Bb/735

♭VII   ♭VII   ♭VII   ♭VII

C°⁷ (C diminished scale voicings)

D/37   Ab/37   B/37   F/5R   B/5R

II/37   ♭VI/37   majVII/37   IV/5R   majVII/5R

Cᴍɪ⁶ (C melodic minor scale voicings)

G/36

V/36

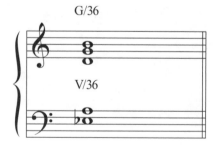

The basic format for these voicings is fairly straightforward. In the left hand, play a "fourth stack" (a structure in which the three notes are separated by perfect fourths) for major 7ths and minor 7ths. Play a left-hand tritone for dominant 7ths (3-7), diminished 7ths (3-7 or 1-5), and minor 6ths (3-6). There are various left-hand structures for the minor 7(b5) chord: 1-5 tritone, 571, 4573, and 735 (the last two are standard rootless voicings). The right-hand structure for all voicings is a major triad. You may invert any left-hand tritone or right-hand triad as you wish. You may also double the bottom note of the right-hand triad an octave up.

Practice approach for upper-structure voicings

Here's a way to get started learning these voicings. Pick one voicing for CMa7—G/E4, for example. That's V/III in any key. Using the random note chart in the appendix (page 301), practice that voicing in twelve keys until you've mastered it. Here's an example:

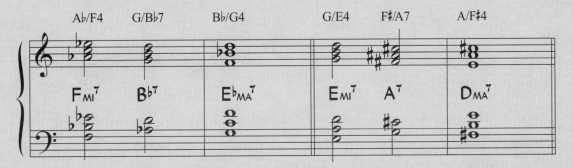

Do the same for a minor 7th voicing; try Eb/C4 for Cmi7 (that's bIII/I). Then learn a dominant voicing; try A/C7 (that's VI over the 3-7 tritone). Once you can find the voicings quickly, try them together as II-V-I's:

Learn this II-V-I progression in twelve keys, using the random II-V-I chart in the appendix (page 304). Then, using the random note chart, practice one minor 7(b5) voicing, one diminished 7th voicing, and one minor 6th voicing.

Chapter 34

At this point you are in control of one good voicing for each chord type, and you know one good II-V-I solution. The next step is to try these voicings out in a few tunes. True, your voice leading will not be very smooth, and some of your dominant 7ths will sound odd due to contextually inappropriate extensions, but it's a start. Just spend some time with a fakebook, applying these voicings to several tunes until you become comfortable with the process.

Now go back and get a second voicing for each chord type and a second II-V-I solution. What you want here are voicings that are roughly half an octave away from your first set:

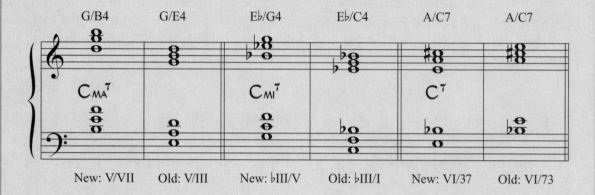

Learn the new voicings in twelve keys, individually and in a II-V-I context:

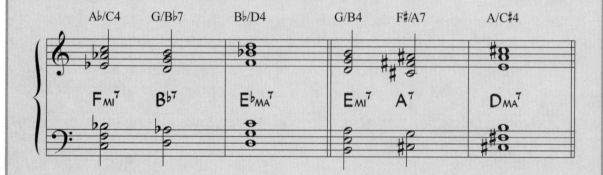

Finally, learn some more dominant 7th voicings in twelve keys. The A/C7 voicing is from the C auxiliary diminished scale. Learn D/C7 (from the G melodic minor scale) and Ab/C7 (from the Db melodic minor scale). Then revisit the tunes you worked on before. Now you'll be able to voice the chords more smoothly and choose dominant voicings that are more appropriate to the context. You'll encounter some situations where no upper-structure voicings sound good. Try open-position rootless voicings there instead.

Chapter **34**

Here are some good upper-structure voicings for the first 16 bars of "Like Someone In Love":

Chapter **34**

The theory behind upper-structure voicings

Are you ready for the theory behind these voicings? Fair warning: it's quite involved. Take it slowly, playing the voicings on the piano as you go. Remember, the most important thing is to get these voicings in your fingers and start using them. The theory is interesting, but don't worry that you're missing a vital piece of the puzzle if it doesn't come to you right away.

Every upper-structure voicing meets the following requirements:

1. **It fits within the appropriate scale.**

   As you know, there are several appropriate scales for a single chord. You should familiarize yourself with the various options and with the criteria for selecting between them. A C7 voicing that occurs in a G melodic minor context probably won't sound good in a Db melodic minor context and vice-versa.

2. **It consists only of valid chord tones.**

   Here's what you have to choose from:

   Major 7ths: 1 3 5 7 9 #11 13
   Minor 7ths: 1 3 5 7 9 11 13
   Dominant 7ths: 1 3 5 7 b9 9 #9 #11 b13 13
   Minor 7(b5)'s: 1 3 5 7 9 11
   Minor 6ths: 1 3 5 6 maj7 9
   Diminished 7ths: 1 3 5 7 9 11 b13 maj7

3. **It contains the essential notes of the chord.**

   Here they are:

   Major 7ths: 3-7 or 3-6
   Minor 7ths: 3-7
   Dominant 7ths: 3-7
   Minor 7(b5)'s: 3-5-7 or 4-5-7
   Diminished 7ths: 3-5-7 or substitute for any one of those. A note which is a whole step above a chord tone (4 above 3, b6 above 5, or Maj7 above 7) may substitute for that chord tone if it lies a major 7th above another note in the voicing. For example, a 4 will substitute for a 3 if there's a 5 underneath it. A b6 will substitute for a 5 if there's a 7 underneath it. And a maj7 will substitute for a 7 if there's a root underneath it.

4. **It includes no minor 9th clashes.**

   For example, C/B4 is not a good voicing for Cmaj7. Even though it meets the first three criteria, the C in the right hand clashes with the B in the left hand.

Upper-structure voicings for a minor 7th chord

Let's see how you can use this information to generate the voicings for Cmi7, using the Bb major scale. The format for this type of chord is a fourth stack in the left hand and a major triad in the right.

The first criterion is that all the notes in the voicing must fit within the appropriate scale. There are five fourth stacks and three major triads that fit within the Bb major scale:

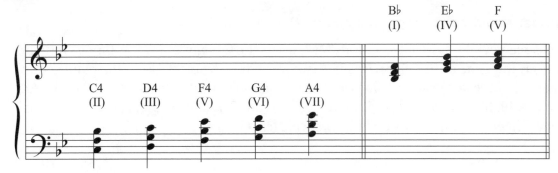

As you can see, diatonic fourth stacks are built on II, III, V, VI, and VII of a major scale. Diatonic major triads are built on I, IV, and V. From this raw material we can build fifteen voicings that fit within the Bb major scale:

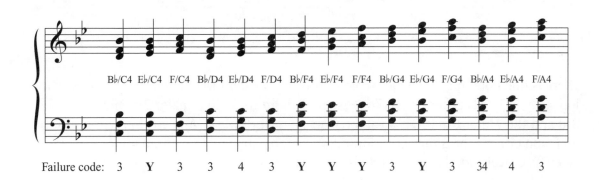

All fifteen of these voicings meet criterion #1 in that they fit within the appropriate scale. Criterion #2 requires that the voicing consist of valid chord tones. As it turns out, every note in the Bb major scale is a valid chord tone of Cmi7 (Bb=7th, C=root, D=9th, Eb=3rd, F=11th, G=5th, A=13th). So all fifteen voicings are still valid. Criterion #3 requires that the voicing contain the essential notes in the chord, which for a minor 7th chord are the 3rd and the 7th. A valid voicing for Cmi7 must have both an Eb and a Bb (both in the left hand, both in the right, or one in each). Eight of the above voicings (marked with a 3 underneath) fail this test. Criterion #4 prohibits minor 9th clashes. Three of the above voicings (marked with a 4 underneath) fail this test. Five voicings (marked with a Y) survive all four criteria:

Chapter **34**

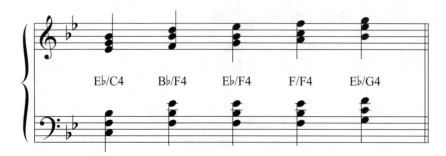

Eb/C4   Bb/F4   Eb/F4   F/F4   Eb/G4

Upper-structure voicings for a major 7th chord

Let's see how the system works for CMa7, using the C major scale. The format for major 7ths is the same as for minor 7ths (a triad over a fourth stack). Using the numbers we learned in the last example, we find that the diatonic fourth stacks are D4, E4, G4, A4, and B4 (II, III, V, VI, and VII). The diatonic triads are C, F, and G (I, IV, and V). Again we find fifteen voicings that fit within the scale (criterion #1):

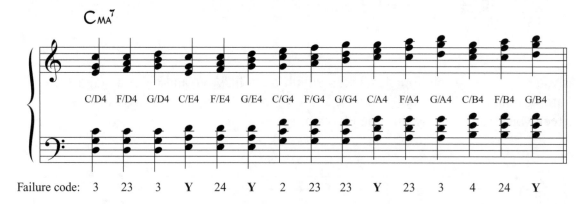

C/D4 F/D4 G/D4 C/E4 F/E4 G/E4 C/G4 F/G4 G/G4 C/A4 F/A4 G/A4 C/B4 F/B4 G/B4

Failure code: 3   23   3   **Y**   24   **Y**   2   23   23   **Y**   23   3   4   24   **Y**

There is one note in the C major scale that is not a valid CMa7 chord tone: F. Any voicing with an F fails criterion #2. The essential chord tones in a major 7th chord are the 3rd and the 7th or 6th (C6 is a valid replacement for CMa7). Any voicing without both an E and either A or B fails criterion #3. As before, any voicing with a minor 9th clash (such as C over B) fails criterion #4. Four voicings survive all four criteria:

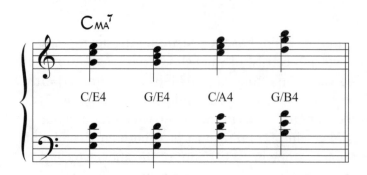

C/E4   G/E4   C/A4   G/B4

Upper-structure voicings for a dominant 7th chord

Now let's look at how the system can be used to generate voicings for C7, using a G melodic minor scale. The format for dominant 7ths is simpler, in that the left hand always plays the 3-7 tritone. The right hand still plays a major triad that fits within the scale. There are two major triads in a G melodic minor scale: C and D (IV and V). The field is immediately narrowed down to two voicings:

Notice how square the first voicing sounds. Don't use it as a stand-alone voicing. Instead, play it in conjunction with the other voicing:

For a C7 with a Db melodic minor scale, you'll still play the 3-7 tritone in your left hand, but the right-hand major triads are now Gb and Ab (IV and V of Db melodic minor).

Chapter 34

You may wonder why I selected the scales I did for C7 (G melodic minor, Db melodic minor, and C auxiliary diminished). After all, C7 is usually a V chord in F major or F minor. Why not use those scales to generate some voicings? Why not a C whole tone scale? Maybe there are some possibilities there.

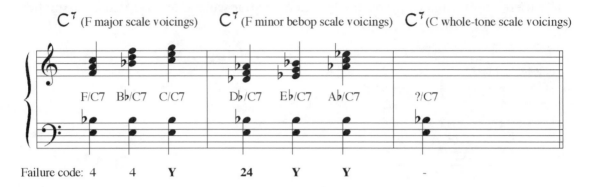

Three of these voicings fail due to the presence of invalid chord tones (criterion #2), minor 9th clashes (criterion #4), or both. Three voicings survive, but they're either too square (C/C7) or they were already generated by previous scales (Eb/C7 fits within C auxiliary diminished and Ab/C7 fits within Db melodic minor). The problem with the G whole tone scale is simply that there are no major triads within it. All the triads are augmented. That's why dominant 7th voicings must be generated by a melodic minor scale on the 5th, a melodic minor scale on the b2, or an auxiliary diminished scale on the root.

Look at the pattern of voicings that emerges if we consider the dominant 7th voicings from all three scale sources:

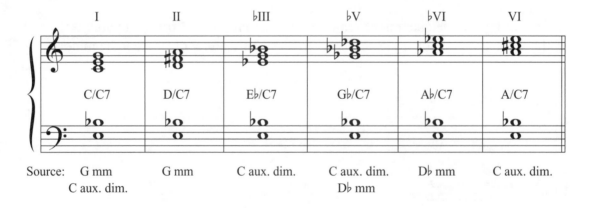

Observe that the last three triads (bV, bVI, and VI) are a tritone away from the first three (I, II, and bIII). This means that the same six voicings will work for Gb7, the tritone substitute for C7.

While it can be convenient to think of all six voicings as a group, it's important to remember which voicings belong to which scale. If you are dealing with a C7 that uses a G melodic minor scale, your major triads are C and D (I and II). If the C7 uses a Db melodic minor, the triads are Gb and Ab (bV and bVI). If the C7 uses a C auxiliary diminished scale, the triads are C, Eb, Gb, and A (I, bIII, bV, and VI). Notice that these four triads are a minor 3rd apart from each other.

The one constant among all these voicings is that there is a major triad in the right hand. As it turns out, however, there are many other structures that you can use in the right hand: minor triads, augmented triads, diminished triads, and even fourth stacks. I emphasized major triads up to this point because 1) jazz pianists have shown a small preference for major triads over the other structures, and 2) you need a manageable starting point. Here are some other voicings:

C7 voicings with minor triads in the right hand

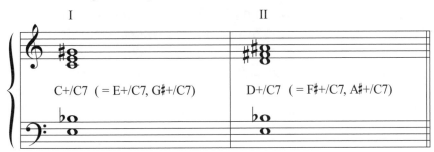

C7 voicings with augmented triads in the right hand

C7 voicings with diminished triads in the right hand

Chapter 34

C7 voicings with fourth stacks in the right hand

Several of these C7 voicings fit within the F major scale: Gmi/C7, Ami/C7, Edim/C7, D4/C7, E4/C7, and A4/C7. This is important because C7 so often functions as a V in F major. The two augmented triads (C+ and D+) yield voicings that belong to the C whole tone scale. In addition, the new right-hand structures result in some new G melodic minor voicings (Gmi/C7, Ami/C7, D+/C7, Edim/C7, F#dim/C7, D4/C7, E4/C7, and A4/C7), Db melodic minor voicings (Dbmi/C7, Ebmi/C7, C+/C7, Bbdim/C7, Cdim/C7, Eb4/C7, Ab4/C7, and Bb4/C7), and C auxiliary diminished voicings (Cmi/C7, Ebmi/C7, F#mi/C7, Ami/C7, and all eight diminished triad voicings!).

So that's the theory behind upper-structure voicings. In a nutshell: upper-structure voicings consist of various right-hand structures (major triads, minor triads, augmented triads, diminished triads, and fourth stacks) over various left-hand structures (mostly fourth stacks or tritones) that 1) fit within the appropriate scale, 2) consist of valid chord tones, 3) contain the essential chord tones, and 4) avoid minor 9th clashes. Now that I've boiled seven pages of material down to one sentence, it *still* sounds complicated, doesn't it? That's why I suggested at the beginning that you concentrate on the final-result voicings and not get hung up on the theory behind them. If you'll learn some of these voicings in twelve keys using the approaches I described earlier, you can begin making music with them in a relatively short time. You can go back later and fill in the gaps in your comprehension.

Obviously, these approaches to quartet voicings are applicable to groups larger than quartets—even big bands. I've covered octaves over rootless voicings, open-position voicings, and upper-structure voicings. There are other approaches (such as Shearing blocks) that would be worth your attention at some point, but these three should give you plenty of sounds to begin with. Strive for flexibility in the way you voice tunes.

> Apply all three approaches to a single tune, then practice shifting smoothly from one approach to the next, perhaps every four bars.

The Workout

At the beginning of this chapter I told you that the division of voicings into solo, duo, trio, and quartet environments is a useful but ultimately artificial strategy. All of these voicings are simply colors that you'll mix and match when you play a tune, whether by yourself or in a group. For example, you'll need all of these voicings for Fmi7:

Solo voicings

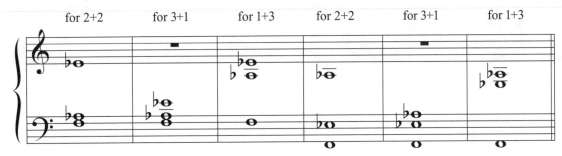

Duo voicings   Trio voicings

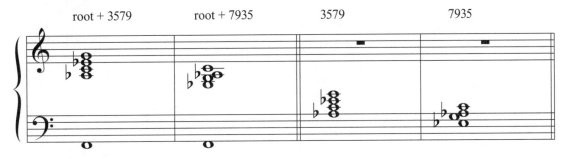

Quartet voicings

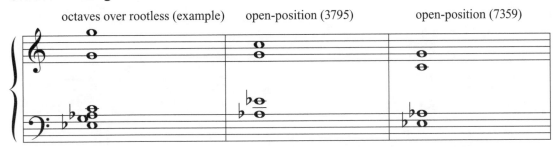

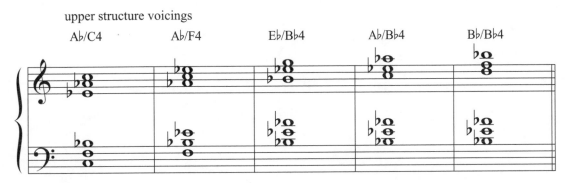

Chapter **34**

In order to gain the degree of flexibility that you'll need with these various voicings, pick a tune that you like and learn it with voicings from every environment. Keep each approach distinct and pure to begin with. When you've learned them all well, however, mix them deliberately. Practice until you can shift seamlessly from solo voicings to duo voicings to trio voicings to quartet voicings, back and forth. After considerable practice and playing experience, you'll be able to simply reach out and grab sounds from the piano as you hear them. For a jazz pianist, this is as important a form of improvisation as the single-note melodic line.

Chapter **35**

Scale Comping

A good jazz pianist approaches comping with as much creative fervor as he does improvising. While focusing primarily on the soloist, he selects from a seemingly endless array of voicings to provide the best accompaniment.

How can you achieve total spontaneity in your comping? To illustrate the nature of the problem, let me draw a parallel with improvisation. In "Notes That Work" (page 73) I discussed the concept of using licks. I referred to it as "improvisation by mosaic." Once you acquire enough tiles (licks), you can create an almost infinite number of patterns with them. The same is true of voicings. Once you've learned several voicings for each chord and can get from one to the next smoothly, your comping will take on a more spontaneous quality.

But just as there are several approaches to improvisation, there are other strategies for comping that don't involve learning preset voicings. There's a way of doing it that will result in new sounds every time you sit down to play. I call it scale comping.

Let's look at a II–V–I in the key of F minor. Here are a couple of standard voicing options from "Voicings 101" (page 227).

The most consonant scale for Gmi7(b5) is Bb melodic minor. Notice that all the notes in both Gmi7(b5) voicings belong to this scale. Likewise, all the C7 notes belong to its most consonant scale, Db melodic minor. And both the Fm voicings fit within an F melodic minor scale.

Chapter **35**

Improvise with these scales over the chords.

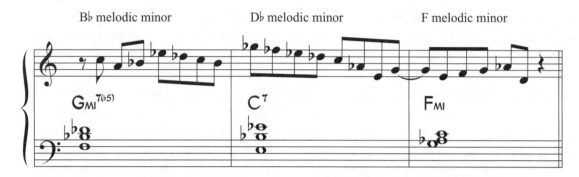

Now you're ready for scale comping. Simply put, improvise (softly and sparsely—remember, you're comping behind a soloist) with the notes of the three melodic minor scales, using mostly chordal textures (2-5 notes at a time). Don't concern yourself at first with stating the 3rd and 7th of each chord. In fact, don't think about the chords at all. Just think scales.

That's how it works. You simply play chord-like colors within the improvising scales rather than preset voicings. Obviously this approach will only work if:

1. You know your scales very well.
2. You can choose appropriate scales for the chords.
3. You can make smooth transitions from scale to scale.
4. Your time-feel is solid.
5. You listen to the soloist and play supportively.

It also helps if you can play the left hand off against the right. As you can see, I either use short single-note lines in the left hand in between the right-hand structures, or I play a block of notes using both hands.

What's so wonderful about this approach is that it invites you to think as improvisationally about your comping as you do about your soloing. You'll never again enter a section of a tune with a cast-in-stone voicing plan. When you comp with an anything-might-happen attitude, it brings a greater sense of immediacy, a higher energy, to your playing.

Here's how this approach might sound on the bridge of "Softly, As In A Morning Sunrise":

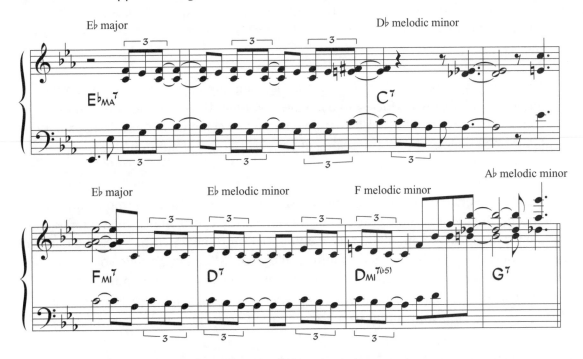

Practice scale comping over this progression.

Scale comping versus modal voicings

You might compare this approach to the well-known modal voicing strategy popularized by McCoy Tyner, Chick Corea, and others. Here are some two-handed modal voicings for Fmi7, using the notes of an F dorian mode:

Once again, these voicings are simply colors chosen from within the prevailing scale or mode. There are three differences between the two approaches, however:

1. Modal voicings are typically used over a static chord progression (a single chord or short vamp that lasts for a long time). Scale comping can be used even when the chords change every two beats.

2. Modal voicings are often built in fourths and played sequentially up and down the mode, as I've done here with the Fmi7. Scale comping can be done with a mixture of colors, not just fourths, and there's no need to go straight up or down the scale.

3. Modal voicings are usually created from the standard major scale modes (dorian, phrygian, lydian, etc.). When you use scale comping, there's no need to limit yourself to these modes. You can scale comp with melodic minor scales, auxiliary diminished scales, whole tone scales, any scales that you might choose for improvising.

Some of the colors that you create from these scales are sure to be harmonically ambiguous. In other words, either the 3rd or the 7th of the chord will be missing. But comping is more a rhythmic than a harmonic function to begin with. Since the harmony will generally be clear without your input, you're free to use any sounds you want that don't actually obscure the harmony. As you develop the ability to comp this way, you'll learn to control the amount of ambiguity in your colors. Eventually this becomes another way of varying your sound to make it more interesting.

Key scales versus most consonant scales

You can comp using colors from both key scales and most consonant scales. The good news about most consonant scales is that every note is safe. You can use the entire scale as your palette. When you use a key scale, however, you should remove the "avoid" notes at first. These are the same notes that would require special finesse if you were improvising with the scale because they clash with the underlying chord tones. For example, if you comp with an Eb major scale for EbMa7, remove the Ab. Assemble your colors using the other six notes.:

Eventually you can include the avoid notes, but you'll need to finesse them just as carefully as you do when they occur in your improvised solo.

Applications of scale comping

I use scale comping in a couple of different ways. I apply it to swing, Latin, and other such groove-oriented tunes by playing drums with the colors, using a lot of syncopation and crisp rhythmic figures, as the previous examples have demonstrated. But I also use it in ballads, often in a higher range, to create a beautiful wash of sound, using a more legato approach and careful pedaling. Here's how that might sound during the first four measures of "But Beautiful":

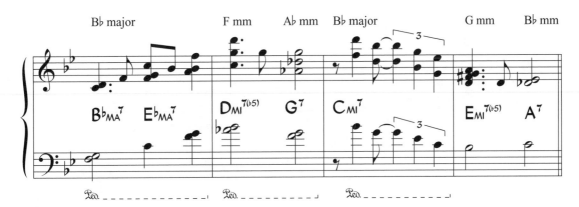

Practice scale comping over this progression.

Like many other comping approaches, scale comping can also be used in your own soloing, either interspersed between the melodic lines (comping for yourself) or elevated to primary status. Once you've become comfortable using it as a comping strategy, it will creep into your improvising naturally.

Part VII *At the Gig*

There's more to being a successful musician than just learning your instrument and mastering the intricacies of jazz. You have to be confident in your worth as a musician, know how to act around colleagues and the general public, and be prepared to handle the demands that accompany most performances.

Chapter **36**

Failsafe Performing

How would you feel if you knew now that you'll never bomb on a gig for the rest of your life, that every audience will thoroughly enjoy what you do, and that the only standards you'll ever have to be concerned with are your own? If you knew that, wouldn't you relax and have more fun on gigs? Wouldn't you play better?

If you're like most musicians, you take 98% of your talent for granted. You can't even remember when you learned most of what you know about music. It's in the dim past. Instead, you tend to focus on that last 2%. If that last, most advanced fraction of your musical ability shows up on the gig, you're thrilled. In your mind you scored 100. If only half of that part shows up, you feel mildly let down. You only scored 50. And if none of those advanced abilities manifest themselves on the bandstand, you feel miserable. You scored a goose egg.

This is when you need to remember that the audience is hearing all of your musicianship, not just what you've been working on for the past two weeks. They appreciate your beautiful tone, your mastery of bebop vocabulary, your basic sense of swing—all things which may have been a part of your playing for so long that you take them for granted. To that audience you just scored 98%! And because we're talking here about those abilities that you'll always be able to count on, you can never score less than 98%. You're bombproof! Of course you must continue to strive to meet your own standards, to get that last 2% in. But be aware that this is your own private game, that most audiences will not necessarily even hear any difference between 98% and 100%. And it's altogether possible that the audience's perspective on your playing is more accurate than your own.

This is how I came to this realization. There were gigs where I felt as if I couldn't face the audience at the end of the night. I thought I had played so badly that I was embarrassed to talk to anyone afterwards. Yet people told me, "That was wonderful" or "Beautiful piano playing!" At first I wondered if they were being sincere. When I learned that they were, I just wondered how they could have misheard my playing so badly.

Then there were other gigs where I just soared. Everything I wanted to play came effortlessly out of my fingers. Afterwards, I got the same comments as before: "Great job!" "That really swung." But it was evident to me that these people didn't really hear any difference in quality between the two performances—they just liked them both. When I tried to figure out how that could be, I realized that I had been considering the differences through a magnifying glass. I had been taking most of my musicianship for granted. Thereafter I began to lighten up on the bandstand, because I knew I was insulated against the possibility of really bombing. I put aside all thoughts of whether I was good or bad and just enjoyed the act of making music.

Chapter 37

What Is There to Say?

Music is a language in and of itself, and the ability to communicate with another musician without translating your feelings into words is a wonderful form of intimacy.

I frequently work with a very talented bass player. It often happens that we'll reach a certain spot in a tune, and I'll just give him a quick look without saying anything. From that look he intuits that I'm about to throw in a reharmonization. I haven't told him what the new chords will be because I know that he's familiar with my harmonic language and will probably guess correctly which way I'm going. And if he guesses wrong, he'll hear it so quickly that he can still match me within a beat or two.

Sometimes I don't look at him at all. I know that he's listening to what I play and will hear (or often anticipate) any new directions that I might take. It's not even important that he match what I do. I trust his judgment, and he's free to react to my new chords by staying with the original changes if he likes the contrast of one sound against the other. As long as we've both got our ears open, the music will be great.

You can relay a tremendous amount of information through your playing and through eye contact. But there will be times that verbal instructions are desirable. You may have a certain arrangement in mind. But be careful not to give the band too many instructions or they will be focused on following the details, and the flow of the music will be disrupted—the potential for "happy accidents" to occur will be squelched. If you feel strongly about an arrangement, either write it down so the musicians can read it on the spot or rehearse it in advance. Here are a couple of examples of how to talk down a tune:

ACTUAL ARRANGEMENT	WHAT TO SAY AND DO
My Shining Hour in Bb (piano trio) 1. Rubato piano solo 2. Intro: Latin vamp (BbMa7 B7) 3. Once through the head 4. Piano solo in swing 5. Bass solo in swing 6. Trade 8's with drums, then 4's 7. Last head (in Latin—ritard at bar 16, play bars 17-24 rubato, then back in tempo for last 8 8. Vamp out on BbMa7 B7	Pianist says: "My Shining Hour, Bb. Latin heads, swing solos." Then just play the opening piano solo and set up the intro vamp. Use eye contact to communicate the solo order, the trading, and the rubato section in the last head.

Chapter **37**

ACTUAL ARRANGEMENT	WHAT TO SAY AND DO

Polkadots and Moonbeams in F, ballad (vocalist and trio)
  1. Trio plays intro (last 4 bars of tune)
  2. Once through the melody
  3. Piano solo to the bridge
  4. Vocalist re-enters on bridge in double-time feel
  5. Back to single-time for last 8 bars
  6. Tag and ritard ending
	Vocalist says: "Polkadots and Moonbeams in F. Double-time feel on the last bridge."
	
	Then just count off the tune (You may not get the exact intro you wanted, but leave that decision to the band.) Signal the tag by singing a higher note and the ritard by using eye contact.

Just as overtalking a tune can inhibit the flow of the music, undertalking can result in tentative intros and clashing harmonies. Experience will teach you what needs to be said. As you become musically adept enough to communicate well non-verbally, you'll discover one of the most profound joys in making music.

How to Be and Not to Be

Certain rules of etiquette apply to musicians both on and off the bandstand:

1. **Hiring:** You're trying to line up musicians for a gig. You've got a list of ten bass players and you've already called the first nine, but they're all working. Now you call number ten. Don't start the conversation with, "Hi Joe, I'm really desperate. I've been calling bass players all afternoon but nobody's available. Can you do the gig?" Just ask him if he's available. If he says no, don't say, "Geez, I've tried everyone." Just ask him if he can suggest any other bass players. And if he does, don't respond with, "Nope, I already called him." There is no reason to let him know that you called him last even though, in some cases, the reason could be that he's the best bass player in town, and you assumed he's already booked.
2. **Booking:** Don't cancel a booked gig because you got an offer for another one that pays a few dollars more. This is only a legitimate practice if the gig is significantly more lucrative or if it represents a valuable career opportunity. Most bandleaders and club owners will understand in that case, but only if you give them plenty of advance notice. If you must cancel at the last minute, offer to find your own replacement.
3. **Gossiping:** Don't talk behind other musicians' backs. Most musical communities are small enough that you can't afford such behavior: it will come back to bite you. If you don't have something good to say about someone, just keep quiet. If you make a point of being supportive of musicians in your community, eventually people will begin to notice what a classy person you are.
4. **Accepting praise:** You just finished a terrible set. You're embarrassed to think that anyone would associate you with such a performance. Just then someone walks up to you and says, "I just wanted to thank you for the beautiful music—it was just great." Here's what you say: "Thank you." Not "Oh you must be kidding, I was just awful." That person didn't have to tell you he liked your playing. He chose to compliment you. Reward him by just saying, "thank you."
5. **For singers:** During an instrumental solo, stand relatively still and listen to the solo. Don't fiddle with your sheet music, don't leave the bandstand and strike up a conversation with a friend, and above all, don't begin to talk with the audience on the microphone. The solos are not to be thought of as background music. Acknowledge your instrumentalists a few times each set (introduce them to the audience). If you're sitting in with a band, thank them when you've finished singing. Think of the instrumentalists as fellow musicians, not as accompanists.
6. **For instrumentalists:** Singers are musicians too, and they're also people who deserve your full respect. It's not hip to look down your nose at vocalists: it's just uninformed. Many singers are well versed in the more technical aspects of music (such as theory), but those who aren't may still be fabulous musicians.

Chapter **39**

Keeping the Gig

One of the most common roles that a musician plays is that of a sideman—i.e., a member of a band led by someone else (often a vocalist). While it's important to do your own thing (form your own band, make your own recordings, etc.), there are certain invaluable aspects to being a sideman. You become a more versatile musician, because you constantly have to meet the musical requirements of very different leaders. You play different music every night with different musicians and in different locations, so you learn a lot of new tunes, network with many more musicians, and perhaps find more venues in which to book your own band—all without the stress that comes with the role of leader. You don't have to deal directly with club-owners, worry about publicity, etc. You just show up and play!

What skills do you need to be a successful sideman? Much of what I have to say here about being a sideman will apply whether the leader is a horn player, singer, or kazoo player. Let's assume, though, that your leader is a singer, because in this situation some additional issues arise. Also, please forgive my stereotypically sexist pronouns ("he" for the sideman, "she" for the singer)—it's a temporary convenience. After all, it's built in: have you ever heard of a "sidewoman?"

Gut feelings play a major role in most singers' hiring (and rehiring) decisions. They usually hire musicians who make them feel the most comfortable. If, at the end of a gig with you, the singer drives home thinking, "Man, that was so easy," you'll hear from her again. If instead she thinks, "Well, I can tell he's a great player, but for some reason I just didn't feel comfortable all night," then you need to start looking for work. So here, more or less in order of importance, are the assets a singer shops for in a sideman:

1. **Be nice.** I'm serious. The number one item has nothing specifically to do with your playing. Show up with a good attitude. Enjoy the music and the people you're playing with. Be flexible and willing to handle unexpected snags without losing your cool. Don't be short with the management or snobbish with the audience. If the gig requires more functional music (such as at a wedding or dance), don't grouse. You agreed to take the job. Now meet its requirements professionally and gracefully. Develop a reputation for being easy to work with.
2. **Play with solid time.** If your time-feel is erratic, it will infect every measure of every tune. By the end of the night the singer will feel like enlisting the services of a masseuse!
3. **Have a large repertoire.** Most singers want to have the freedom to call tunes as they feel them and not be limited to those tunes for which they have sheet music. In fact, some good singers will presume that you know hundreds of tunes and won't bring any sheet music with them at all.
4. **Be able to play in any key.** You may be able to play a knockout version of "My Romance" in Bb. That's great, but if your singer needs it in G and you can't do it, you're useless to her.

5. **Be able to read.** Most singers will bring some sheet music to the gig, either for non-standard tunes or for special arrangements. In fact, some singers have extensive, organized books of their material. Just as you don't want the singer to think, "Well, that was a drag: he didn't know any standards," you also don't want her to think, "Well, that was a drag: I was limited to calling standards all night because he couldn't read."

6. **Be able to play good intros and tags.** You need to be able to take the tempo from the singer's count-off accurately and then spontaneously and without hesitation create an intro that clearly gives her the key and lets her know when to come in. One of the most agonizingly awkward moments comes at the end of a bad intro, when the singer starts singing in the wrong key or doesn't come in at all. In addition to intros, you must also be able to play convincing tags and endings, and you must know about standard practices such as trading fours and double-time feel. And by the way, singers take note: if you're not completely confident about your starting note after an introduction, don't guess at it. It's much better to simply let the accompanists clean up their own mess by playing a clearer introduction than for you to come in wrong and have to adjust.

7. **Be able to comp chords that harmonically support the singer.** With an advanced singer you may be able to voice chords the same way you would behind a good sax player or during your own solo. A less experienced or more traditional singer may need to hear more conservative voicings.

8. **Be able to solo effectively.** Wow! Isn't this what you spend the bulk of your practice time on? Learning to improvise? And yet it's the last item on this list. Remember: from a purely practical sense of keeping the gig, you need the skills that make the leader most comfortable. But when you're taking your solo, the singer isn't even singing! Your ability to take effective, creative solos is far down on the list of priorities for most singers. Yes, in a musical community that has several very fine accompanists, your soloing ability could be the tiebreaker that gets you the gig. The most experienced singers will be the ones who care the most about it, but even with them other things will matter more.

Chapter **40**

Weddings and the Theory of Relativity

I know that it's hip to look down your nose at weddings, but I love playing them. Consider the typical elements: happy people, good food, often a grand piano, elegant surroundings, musicians whom you've hand-selected (assuming you're the leader), and considerably higher pay than the standard club gig. How could you not enjoy that? Supposedly you have to play a cornier brand of music at weddings than you would in a club, but I haven't found that to be true. Instead, in my trio we just turn down the volume to a background-music level and then play with just as much abandon and creativity as we would in a concert—often more, in fact, because we're more relaxed. Those guests who are not interested in the music are free to talk, and those who have an ear for good jazz invariably wander over to listen and appreciate.

Here's something that always amuses me at weddings. During the course of a reception, someone will invariably approach the bandstand and say, "I just wanted to come up and tell you guys how good you are. I'm embarrassed that no one else here is hip enough to appreciate what you're doing, but I'm digging it." Five minutes later, we get the same comment from someone else. By the end of the night, half the people in the room have both thanked us for the music and apologized on behalf of everyone else for being such squares.

Not all weddings and parties are fun to play. Occasionally I feel under-appreciated and wonder why they hired live music at all when recorded music would have served just as well. I do realize that it's a wedding, not a concert, and that the music is not the point. Yet no one likes to be completely ignored, much less resented.

At times like these I'm often struck by a curious phenomenon. Here we are, playing truly inspired, creative music. But the reaction we're getting from much of the audience is one of almost amused disdain, as if to say, "We know that your band is mediocre, simply by virtue of the fact that you're playing a wedding. The better musicians don't lower themselves to this." Yet I know from experience that if we were to play the next night in a concert hall instead of a banquet room, sell tickets for the event, and bill it as a very special jazz concert instead of a wedding reception, the same people would listen to the same music and be absolutely transported by its sheer artistry.

It's a matter of packaging—just trappings. Many people are unable to distinguish between mediocre and superior performances. They want to feel that the music is great, but they need to be told so by an authority before they feel safe in enjoying it. If the music is being presented in concert form, especially if it's performed by "big-name" musicians, it's probably safe to ooh and aah. If it's a club date by a local band, it could be good. If it's a wedding band, despite the fact that they appear to sound incredible, well, it's probably not safe to be blown away by how good they are, because maybe they're not.

Chapter **40**

There are plenty of people who can truly love music that hasn't been officially sanctioned by any authority. They know what's good without waiting to be told. But it's just human nature to need a little corroboration sometimes. Just be aware of that and don't take it personally.

As a musician, you should be prepared for the effect packaging will have on people's perceptions of you. If you take a society gig (wedding, party, bar mitzvah, etc.), put the same amount of emotional energy into the music as if it were a concert. Make every tune a special experience. Some of the guests will truly appreciate your music. And as for the rest, you can console yourself with the knowledge that they would also love your music if only it were packaged differently.

As far as that goes, put some thought into better ways of presenting yourself. Even something as simple as a well-crafted sign placed on the piano with your band's name on it can make a big difference. Don't allow a negative crowd to affect your self-image. If you think of yourself as a journeyman, then that's what you'll become.

Part VIII **Paths to Success**

The challenges to becoming a musician that I encountered are detailed in the chapter "Crooked Road." As you travel your own unique road, I hope that you can benefit from some of the insights I offer here regarding hard work, self-trust, and versatility.

Chapter **41**

The Answer

There's a point in almost every aspiring jazz musician's development (usually after a series of aborted attempts at real progress) when he asks this question:

"What's the answer?"

Translation: "I see all these successful, productive musicians around me, and I know that they must have done certain essential things to get where they are. Once I find the path they took, my days of confusion will be over and I'll be on the road to success."

Ah, if life were so simple. Wouldn't it be fascinating if you could interview ten or twenty of those musicians and ask them, "What did you do? What was the key that made it all work?" Well, let me save you some time and frustration. If you were to conduct such a set of interviews, the answers would be so diverse that they would make your head spin. Here's a sample:

"I just played a heck of a lot."

"I transcribed solos every day."

"I practiced pure technique drills. I never practiced improvising."

"Scales and theory, theory and scales..."

"I walked around with headphones on 24/7, just listening to all the classic recordings."

"I always played with superior musicians who pushed me."

"I worked on licks in twelve keys."

"Adrenaline is the answer. I was never much of a practicer. I always put myself in situations where I had to perform or else."

"It's really all about people. Networking, to be sure, but mainly just caring about the people around you. More than anything else, that's what opened doors for me."

"Organization is the key. There's a file on my computer where I keep a list of the lists I need to make."

And what if you were to ask each of these musicians about how he got his job? Most of their stories would be so convoluted and varied as to defy any attempt to find a common denominator.

Chapter 41

Through the years I've often gotten such questions from young musicians. I feel a sadness because I know that I can't give the student the type of answer he wants. If I could somehow show him the exact footprints that led to my success, his response would be, "Why, these footprints are going in three directions at once! Some of them seem to be going off in no meaningful direction, and others seem to be in direct opposition to each other. My feet don't fit comfortably in these footprints. I can't use them at all!"

The roads to progress and opportunity can be strangely twisted, as I well know. Years ago I read an article about John Coltrane that mentioned that he spent many hours practicing exercises from a specific book, Nicolas Slonimsky's *Thesaurus Of Scales And Melodic Patterns*. When I learned that both McCoy Tyner and Herbie Hancock had benefited from the same book, I knew my course was set.

I went through the book and identified 150 patterns that I particularly liked. My goal was to learn each of those patterns in two hands (two octaves apart) in twelve keys so well that they would flow effortlessly out of my fingers when I improvised. I soon settled into a practice routine in which I covered 50 patterns a day in six hours. Every three days I made it through the cycle. Then I started again. During this time I had my eyes closed almost continuously. My ears and fingers became sensitized to each and every pattern. I maintained this routine for almost six months. If this sounds to you like a monumental act of discipline, I need to tell you that it didn't feel that way at all. I felt obsessed, even addicted to what I was doing; or, to speak of it in lighter terms, it was fun. There was a Zen quality to that focused, quiet time I spent at the piano. It was immediately fulfilling to me. I probably logged over 750 hours in this endeavor, yet it never felt like drudgery.

But here's the catch: I failed miserably in my attempt to incorporate these patterns into my improvising. There were several reasons for this. For one, these patterns were atonal in nature, and I hadn't yet learned to improvise well within the confines of conventional tonality—I was trying to run before I could walk. Furthermore, I was so engrossed with my routine of practicing these patterns in their pure form that I never bothered to put them into an applied context. I never practiced them over chord progressions! Somehow in my naïveté I felt that if I just knew them well enough, they would flow out on their own when the time and the tonality were right. And the final reason that these patterns never made it into my improvising—believe it or not—is that I didn't work hard enough! I underestimated how thoroughly a pattern must be learned before it will happen on its own in one's playing. Basically, it must feel as if you press a single button and all the notes come flying out in a rush. If you have to send individual messages from your brain to your hands ("Remember to tuck the thumb under here; use the fourth finger here instead of the third," etc.), then you won't use that pattern when you improvise because your mind will be busy with other things. Even after several months of practicing, very few of the patterns had become buttons. I had simply chewed off too big a bite. Twenty-five patterns would have been more realistic.

Chapter **41**

But something strange and wonderful happened. Even though, after six months of work, I didn't sound like McCoy or Herbie or Coltrane, I discovered that I could play confidently without looking at the keyboard. I found that playing in octaves with both hands was no problem. And playing in twelve keys was a cinch! These are all tremendously important skills, yet I had considered them to be minor goals, very secondary to the acquisition of those specific patterns. Now here's my point: I expended a tremendous amount of energy doing something that felt very right at the time, and the end result was tremendous progress. The fact that I failed to achieve the specific goal that I had set for myself is unimportant. I put out the energy and something good happened.

Another twisted road is the one that led me to my teaching job at Cornish College of the Arts. (Had I known earlier how fulfilling the job would be, I would have submitted a necessarily modest resumé and been turned down.)

At the time Gary Peacock, the great bassist, was living in Seattle. I knew that Gary was quite a good pianist, so I called him up to set up some lessons. He taught at Cornish, but I was unaware of this. The lessons ultimately focused more on theory than piano. He introduced me to an interesting new concept and was pleased that I was able to comprehend it and turn it into music. A few months later, when he was preparing to head off to Oslo to make a record with Keith Jarrett, he called and asked if I would teach his classes at Cornish in his absence. I truly doubted that I was ready for such a responsibility, but I said yes.

But I was ready, and Gary hired me several times thereafter. Soon I was filling in for a couple of other teachers as well. So by 1983, when a full-time position became available, Cornish considered me a known quantity, someone whom they knew they could trust to do the job. They tendered an offer, and within a month I was on the faculty.

The goal of teaching at Cornish had never occurred to me. Perhaps I was just in the right place at the right time, but here's how I see it. I put energy into doing something that felt very right—taking lessons with Gary—and as a result a wonderful opportunity opened up. As in my Slonimsky story, it wasn't the result I had anticipated, but it was still a direct result of my putting out that positive energy.

So I think I actually do have an answer for that student who wants to know the key to success, and it's the elusive common denominator shared by almost all successful musicians. Find some things that you really enjoy putting your time and energy into—labors of love. If you're doing something because you should and you don't like it, stop! Find something that resonates with your spirit, and do a lot of what feels good every day.

These activities could include a regimented practice routine or learning tunes from a fake book; transcribing Bill Evans solos for six months or scat singing to Jamey Aebersold records. You could apprentice at a recording studio, sit in at every jam session in town, take drum lessons, teach privately, or devour biographies on Ellington or Mingus. Very simply, find those activities that feel right to you and fill up each day by dumping a tremendous amount of energy into them. Do these things because you love doing them, not as necessary evils in service of a distant goal, and do them with a feeling of obsession, of addiction. If you put out this much positive energy every day, it will come back to you in the form of progress and opportunities.

The sweet irony is that you won't care as much about what the future holds for you because you'll be enjoying your present so much. And because progress and opportunities occur in such wildly unpredictable ways, you'll realize that the only thing you can control is the present anyway.

In making such choices about how to fill up your day, you'll be opening some doors and closing others. You may have an idea about the type of musician you want to be (or should be), and it may be that the things that you love to do won't lead you in that direction. That's what you'll discover if you give yourself up to the type of hard work that feels most right to you. Have faith that the future will take care of itself. Not only will you enjoy your current musical life more, you'll also be on the quickest path to becoming the musician you were destined to be.

Chapter **42**

A Tale of Two Pianists

Pete and Roger lived next door to each other. Jazz was constantly in the air at Pete's household. His parents played instruments and encouraged Pete's interest in music, starting him with piano lessons at age five. He learned to play jazz by imitating what he heard on recordings and quickly developed his ear to a very high level. He studied theory but it seemed dry to him because he was already able to assimilate the sounds that he heard—the sounds that the theory described.

Pete could play like Jelly Roll, Tatum, Monk, Powell, Evans, Garner, Peterson and others. He was a walking compendium of jazz piano history. If there was a problem, it was that he sounded generic. Eventually a kind of internal logic kicked in, and Pete began to create sounds that, while derived from the musicians he'd heard, didn't sound specifically like any of them. He seemed to have found his own voice.

Roger, on the other hand, heard only pop and rock at home, and neither of his parents played an instrument. Roger hung out with his friends and gave little thought to his future. Eventually he went to college and majored in communications. He was a bright kid but lacked passion for his chosen major.

During his freshman year he began to fool around on a piano in his dormitory, composing simple songs and playing the blues. A friend introduced him to the recordings of Miles and Coltrane, and at this point something resonated in Roger's soul. He felt a passion for something outside of himself, and he knew he had to pursue music wherever it took him. He began piano lessons and eventually switched to a music school where he majored in jazz piano.

But unlike Pete, nothing came naturally to Roger. He struggled to overcome deficiencies in technique, time-feel, and melodic concept. He labored over transcribing and had to have the music in front of him for even the simplest tunes. He couldn't pick up sounds by osmosis like his friend Pete.

But Roger loved jazz and was willing to work. He was able to overcome his weak intuitive sense through the strength of his analytical mind. He loved theory, and he used it to reharmonize standards and develop interesting approaches to improvising. Because he understood the structure behind music, he became adept at memorizing and transposing.

Roger sounded good but not as natural as his friend Pete. Pete had virtually inherited his style while Roger had assembled his piece by piece. While Pete simply absorbed the music he heard, Roger had to create exercises for himself, almost mathematical in nature, which generated the rhythms, voicings, and melodic patterns that he heard on classic recordings. Sometimes Roger ended up with some unnatural combinations that didn't sound very good, so he threw them out. But he discovered others that sounded quite good and which he didn't recognize from any recordings.

Chapter **42**

Often Roger dissected a sound incorrectly. His ear was not as good as Pete's, so he thought he was hearing one sound on a recording when he was really hearing another. Using the inaccurately transcribed sound as the kernel of a new concept, he spun out similar patterns. Again he kept the ones that sounded good to him, falsely believing that he was simply imitating what he had heard.

As the years passed, Pete became a first-call pianist because he could always play in the appropriate style and he swung hard. But he found himself limited by his lack of technical knowledge. He could play everything he heard, but he couldn't go beyond that. Despite his success he envied the structurally based approach that allowed Roger to fully explore sounds that were not yet in his ear.

Roger's playing still didn't have the totally natural feel of Pete's, and he was unable to switch fluidly from style to style as Pete could. However, he was earning a local reputation for his distinctive style. People recognized Roger's performances as special because his brand of jazz piano couldn't be heard anywhere else. Roger had arrived.

There's a moral—or two—to this fable, and it's best stated by the great pianist, Bill Evans. "I always like people who have developed long and hard, especially through introspection and a lot of dedication. I think that what they arrive at is usually...deeper and more beautiful...than the person who seems to have that ability and fluidity from the beginning. I say this because it's a good message to give to young talents who feel as I used to. You hear musicians playing with great fluidity and complete conception early on, and you don't have that ability. I didn't. I had to *know* what I was doing. And ultimately it turned out that these people weren't able to carry their thing very far. I found myself being more attracted to artists who have developed through the years and become better and deeper musicians. I believe in things that are developed through hard work."

Also from Evans: "It's...a personality characteristic of putting things together in my own way, which is analytic. Rather than just accept the nuances or syntax of a style completely, I'll abstract principles from it and then put it together myself. It may come out resembling the (original) style, but it will be structured differently, and that may be what gives it its identity. I've often thought that one reason I developed an identity...is that I didn't have the facile talent that a lot of people have, the ability just to listen and transfer something to my instrument. I had to go through a terribly hard analytical and building process. In the end I came out ahead in a sense because I knew what I was doing in a more thorough way."

If you're a "Roger," take heart in Evans' words. Don't think less of yourself as a musician just because you have to assemble your music. Things may not come to you naturally, but all that matters is that they come.

If you're a "Pete" with abundant raw talent, rejoice and be grateful. But recognize that your talent can be developed even further.

Chapter **42**

It's worth emphasizing here one of the benefits of using your intellect to solve musical problems. It lies in the little "mistakes" that your analytical mind will make along the way—misinterpretations which survive in your playing because they sound good. I'm a firm believer that this error bank is one of the main sources of individual musical style.

Imagine transcribing—inaccurately—a Joshua Redman solo, then learning it well enough so that it has a major impact on the way you improvise. A year later Redman catches your performance and comes up afterwards. "Man, what you did on that last tune was so hip!" he says. "What were you doing and where'd you get that?" When you tell him where you learned it, he says, "No way! That wasn't what I was doing on that solo, but I really love what you made of it!"

So you've been playing it wrong all along? Well, who cares? The bottom line is that you're sounding great and you've developed a style all your own. That's a far better result than if you were playing just like Redman. No one will ever play his style as well as he does.

Chapter **43**

Compose Yourself

Composing is an indispensable part of developing one's musicianship.

1. It will help you become a much better improviser. Improvisation is composing in real time. By slowing the process down, you can zero in on the sounds that you like. When you approach your improvising in the same way as you do your composing, you'll find that you play with greater intensity and creativity.

2. It adds a new dimension to your musical identity. Instead of simply thinking of yourself as a tenor saxophone player, you can think of yourself as a composer as well. You can hold a body of work in your hands and say, "This is me. These are the sounds that are important to me, and they're down on paper, permanently." Musicians with multifaceted identities are more interesting, and they have many more opportunities.

3. Your technique might improve—odd, but true. When you compose a tune, you choose sounds very slowly, bending and shaping them until they're just right. However, once your tune is finished, you may find that you can't play parts of it very well: it's too high, too fast, or requires tricky fingering to get the right articulation. If you encountered these technical challenges in someone else's composition, you might struggle with them but never fully overcome them. You'd practice with the best of intentions, but if things got too difficult you'd switch to something easier. But if the tune is yours, you have an inherent incentive to practice it to perfection. You want to be able to present your music in the best possible light. As a result, you'll crash through technical barriers overnight that would otherwise seem insurmountable.

4. Original compositions are almost an obligatory part of any jazz recording project. Very few consist completely of standards. Why is this? In a word, because original compositions make a recording unique. If a CD includes some originals, the prospective buyer realizes that he can't get that exact music anywhere else. Yes, some very fine musicians such as Oscar Peterson have made their names almost entirely on their ability to play standards, but it's a particularly difficult way to go.

5. Composing music is a sure way to improve your ability to listen to and appreciate all music.

Sitting down to write your very first tune can be intimidating. You may think, "I have to know a lot more about music before I can even think about composing. There's so much theory, so many rules I don't know yet." There will always be more rules and more theory. Duke Ellington knew much more at age fifty than he did at thirty. You can't let that stop you. Instead, approach composing from a very personal standpoint. Explore sounds, throw out the ones you don't like, keep the ones you do, and make a tune out of them. That's all there is to it. Don't worry about whether a more experienced musician would like those same sounds or not, or whether your tune is theoretically valid. After all, theory is just an after-the-fact discipline that describes music that was written

Chapter **43**

by musicians who trusted their ears. If you don't know how to write music down precisely, that's all right—just put your sounds down on tape. Simply put, there's no valid reason to put off composing. Just get started—the more you do, the easier it gets.

Another common inhibitor among novice composers is the fear of being unoriginal: "I'm afraid my tune will sound like something that's been done before." Let me put your mind to rest on this one. I guarantee you that the most unique music you'll ever write will sound almost exactly like something that's been done before. You may have heard the other music in the past and been influenced by it, or you may have never heard it at all. In one sense, there really is nothing new under the sun.

In another sense, no two tunes really sound exactly the same. My advice is that you focus on composing music that sounds good and that expresses your musical feelings without giving a second thought to the question of originality. If the resulting music turns out to be overly derivative of someone else's style, so be it. By writing those sounds down, you'll take the first step toward moving beyond them to more personal ones. Ultimately, originality is an attribute that is largely out of your hands. All you can do is compose (and improvise, for that matter) from the heart. If you do that—and if you're very lucky—people may say, "I love that music: it's like nothing I've ever heard before." But at the very least, they'll say, "I love that music."

But how should you begin? Once again, there's also no single right way. You might begin with a melody, something that you improvised on your instrument or just sang. Perhaps you find a great chord progression on the piano. It might be the groove that you settle on first, or a bass line, or it could even be a lyric. Sometimes it's not even relevant to partition your music into melody, chords, bass line, etc. It might be more natural for you to simply put sounds together, to create a particular mood.

Some composers write at the piano (or another instrument), others do it solely with pencil and paper (then check the results later on their instruments). The rationale behind the latter approach is that you'll compose more freely if you're not constrained by the limits of your playing ability. I've never been able to do it that way, however. I need to hear the sound immediately so I can choose whether or not to keep it. If you do use your instrument when you write, I strongly recommend that you keep a tape recorder running the entire time. If you play something that you really like, it's right there on tape for you to refer to. There's no hazard of losing a good idea because you can't remember what you just played.

A tape recorder is also a great tool for keeping a log of your best ideas. Don't feel that everything you create has to become a finished product immediately. Just keep a running musical journal—on tape or on paper, or both—of little bits and pieces of music. When you get stuck in the middle of writing a tune—and every composer does—you'll have a huge backlog of ideas that you can use to get un-stuck.

Some composers find it helpful to have three or four tunes "under construction" simultaneously. If you're only working on one tune and you reach an impasse, you may force the issue and write something that doesn't quite work. But if you can escape the problem by switching over to another project, then you may find that the solution is waiting for you when you return.

One of my most successful periods as a composer resulted when I started by describing five tunes that I wanted to write. As I remember, it looked something like this:

1. A ballad with lyrics, with some major7#5 sounds
2. A waltz
3. A Bill Evans-ish, "Nardis"-like tune
4. A Chick Corea-esque samba
5. A funky, 16th-subdivision tune with gospel colors

Instead of starting with a blank slate, I went into each tune with a general framework. I found that this enabled me to join a tune, as if it were already underway and I were simply continuing the process. There was no sitting around, waiting for a bolt of inspiration to strike—I was able to hit the ground running. The music came quickly to me, and within a month I had written five good tunes. And by the way, neither the Evans tune nor the Corea tune came out derivative. As soon as I began the actual composing process, each tune took on a life of its own, and I simply allowed it to spin itself out (much like an improvised solo). Ultimately, the initial descriptive label for the tune served only as a catalyst to get the process rolling.

You can do this. You don't need to earn the right to compose. Get over the hump. It might even be fun.

Chapter **44**

Teaching

If you've never tried teaching music, you may be missing something. I've found it to be nearly as fulfilling as playing. Does the idea scare you? Maybe you're thinking, "Right— as if I could ever teach..." Perhaps several years down the road you'll be a sufficiently knowledgeable and talented musician that you might try it—just not now, right?

But think about it: exactly what must you have in order to be able to teach? A degree? A fully developed curriculum and a file cabinet full of handouts? A comprehensive knowledge of (and an ability to play) all musical styles? Many very fine teachers don't have degrees; curriculum develops with experience; and you probably have more to offer than you realize. You'll find, too, that good musicians don't always make good teachers. Some have trouble communicating their concepts clearly to students.

The qualities necessary to teach are the ability to play some type of music well and to show others how to do it. It's really that simple. If others find sufficient value in what you have to teach, then you're qualified.

In one respect, teaching is like playing an instrument; you'll be pretty bad at it at first. You'll be disorganized, you'll respond poorly to students' specific problems, or you'll recommend approaches that will prove to be ineffective. There's no avoiding this. You learn to teach by teaching. You mustn't allow your fear of these early growing pains to keep you from doing it.

One of the many benefits of teaching is that it shows you just what you know and what you don't. If you're struggling to explain a particular issue clearly to a student, it may well be that you're a little fuzzy on it yourself. Once you've identified a gap in your knowledge, you can more easily fill it in.

As a beginning teacher, I found it very unpleasant to tell a student, "I don't know" or "I can't teach you that." I thought, "This person is paying for my expertise, so I have to be an authority on everything or I'm ripping them off." In some instances I would respond to a student's question with apparent confidence when I didn't really know what I was talking about. What I should have done (and what I do now) is simply say, "You've got me there—I'm out of my league. If you find out the answer, let me know!" This serves my student well in two ways. First, he'll keep searching for the correct answer rather than be satisfied with my authoritative but essentially inferior response. Secondly, it can be a source of great encouragement to him to be able to see me as a work-in-progress like himself. If I present myself as a monolithic figure who never struggled along the way, it only makes it more difficult for him to see himself reaching his own potential as a musician.

I've come to realize that, as long as I'm working hard to further myself as a musician, I have no apologies to make for my current level. I'm much better than I was five years ago, but not nearly as good as I'll be five years from now. There are many things about music I don't know, and if one of those issues comes up I'll simply admit that I don't know it. There are many musicians in the world who can play better than I can in several respects, and occasionally one of them will come to me for lessons. If that happens, I'll teach him as well as I can. I'll try to fill in the holes in his playing, all the while learning from what he does well. I may not think that I have that much to show him, but I don't worry about it. It's really very simple: if he comes back for another lesson, then it's obviously worthwhile to him.

There are several possible models that can describe the student-teacher relationship. The most traditional one casts the teacher as an authority on music whose great wisdom qualifies him to evaluate the student's abilities, decide what is lacking, and create a program of study for him. The implied message from the teacher to the student is "I have an intimate relationship with music—it's like a secret of mine. In today's lesson I'm going to let you in on one small part of the secret." Most beginning students are comfortable working in this way, and I think it's fine for a while.

But as a student becomes more advanced, I try to change the dynamic between us so that the student begins to use me more as a consultant. Here, the message is from the student to the teacher: "I have my own personal relationship with music. If you can help me develop that relationship, great. If not, please don't get in the way."

In this relationship the student takes much more responsibility for setting the agenda for the lessons. He comes to a lesson with a veritable shopping list of areas he wants help with. I find that a student progresses more quickly when he's working on material of immediate concern to him, so I accommodate his requests as much as possible. Sometimes I have to say, "No, I can't teach you that until you've learned this," or "I can teach you that now, but frankly I think you need this more." But in general, I think that a student knows best what material is most relevant to him at a particular time, and this mode of learning encourages him to continually evaluate his relationship to music. That's a very healthy thing.

As a teacher you want to share your vision of the truth with your students. But there are those teachers who share too little of the truth. I call them "gurus." The guru derives an ego boost from being mysterious, and his worst nightmare is to be completely understood. He makes material much more complicated than need be. His response to student questions is to be cryptic, with the result that students become confused and learn nothing.

Then there are the "over-explainers" who share too much of the truth. The over-explainer doesn't want to get caught saying anything too simplistic for fear of incurring the scorn of students. Instead of offering a simple nugget of information, he will present a global perspective, complete with special cases and exceptions for which the student is unprepared. He is afraid that the student might discover more of the truth on his own and think the less of him as a teacher.

Chapter **44**

A good teacher will be willing to use a technique that I call "constructive dishonesty." He will present a small part of the picture as if it's the whole. The student feels that if he can just master that skill he'll have the answer. Buoyed by that incentive, he learns the material so well that it becomes a permanent skill—he can never un-learn it. Then the teacher can safely tell the student, "Well, that's not really the whole picture—this is the whole picture." Only when the student is ready for more of the truth does the teacher release it. The student makes steady progress and builds confidence. If a teacher is confident within himself and has the student's best interests at heart, he'll be willing to use this approach.

Constructive dishonesty is not an appropriate technique for all students. Some are only willing to master a series of small, sequenced steps if they know in advance where the steps are leading. They need the whole picture. Such a student is likely to feel insulted or patronized if he senses that the teacher is withholding information. A good teacher will respond by being as forthcoming as possible. The common denominator is this: a good teacher is concerned only with his students' welfare—not with boosting his status in their eyes.

Glossary

Coined terms are in italics

2-group — a section of a scale that is fingered 1-2 (in the right hand) and is followed by a thumb tuck-under.

3-group — a section of a scale that is fingered 1-2-3 (in the right hand) and is followed by a thumb tuck-under.

4-group — a section of a scale that is fingered 1-2-3-4 (in the right hand) and is followed by a thumb tuck-under.

Articulation — the legato or staccato execution of a series of notes. In legato articulation the notes are given their full value and played smoothly. In staccato articulation the notes are played short and crisp with space in between.

Chromatic — consisting in part of notes that do not belong to the prevailing key. For example, in the key of Eb major the melody D-Db-C-F#-G is chromatic.

Chromatic system — the procedure presented on page 229, by which the best solo piano voicing for a chord is chosen. Chords rooted on G, Ab, A, Bb, B, and C are played root-7-3. Chords rooted on C#, D, Eb, E, F, and F# are played root-3-7.

Color unity — the characteristic of any chord progression in which all the chords are of the same quality (for example, all major 7th chords), resulting in a sense of harmonic unity.

Comp — from the word "accompany": to play in support of a melodic instrument (including a singer). To play left-hand piano chords in support of a right-hand melody or improvisation. Comping also can refer specifically to the rhythmic aspect of chord playing.

Diatonic — consisting entirely of notes that belong to the prevailing key. For example, in the key of Eb major the melody D-Eb-Bb-G is diatonic.

Fourth-stack — a chord-like structure consisting of three notes separated by perfect 4ths, such as C-F-Bb. The term may also refer to larger stacks, such a C-F-Bb-Eb-Ab.

II-V-I progression — the most common chord progression in jazz, consisting of three chords, usually diatonic and built on the second, fifth, and first scale degrees, respectively. A II-V-I in F major is Gmi7 C7 FMa7. A II-V-I in F minor is Gmi7(b5) C7(#5b9) Fmi.

Inversion — the process of rearranging the notes of a chord so that the root is no longer in the bass; a chord that has been so rearranged. For example, in a second-inversion chord the fifth is in the bass.

Lick — a relatively short melodic fragment used for improvising. Licks may be used individually as motifs or strung together to form longer lines.

Modal progression — a chord progression characterized by the absence of traditional tritone resolutions, such as V to I. Typically (though not necessarily), each chord in such a progression is in effect for a significant duration (two measures or longer). Many modal progressions are characterized by color unity. Modal progressions are prevalent in the music of John Coltrane, McCoy Tyner, Chick Corea, Wayne Shorter, and many other modern composers.

Most consonant scale — a scale created for improvising over a chord that consists of the chord tones and the notes that are whole steps above those chord tones. To create a most consonant scale for a chord, begin on any chord tone and go up a whole step or to the next chord tone (whichever comes first), then proceed to the next chord tone and do the same until the scale is completed.

Motif — A brief fragment of music that is developed through repetition, pitch-shifting, and extension to create melodic unity.

Motivic development — the process by which a motif is repeated, pitch-shifted, and extended to create melodic unity.

Open-position voicing — a voicing that has been expanded by raising at least one note an octave. In this book, the term is applied specifically to a rootless voicing in which the next-to-the-lowest note is raised an octave.

Pitch-shifting — repeating a motif higher or lower within the same scale. For example, in the key of F major, the A-Bb-F motif can be pitch-shifted up to E-F-C.

Rhythmic displacement — the process by which a repeating rhythm changes its relationship to the measure. For example, in 4/4 time, a series of repeating dotted quarter notes will create a block of three rhythmically varied measures before the pattern repeats.

Rootless voicing — a voicing originally devised for left-hand piano accompaniment in which the root (and sometimes the 5th) is removed to allow for the inclusion of upper chord extensions and to avoid replication of the bassist's role. Introduced by such pianists as Bill Evans, Wynton Kelly, Red Garland, and Ahmad Jamal in the late forties and early fifties, these voicings came after the root-3 and root-7 shell voicings used by earlier bebop pianists such as Bud Powell and preceded the modal, fourth-based voicings pioneered by more modern pianists such as McCoy Tyner.

Rubato —played in a rhythmically free style, without a steady underlying beat.

Scale comping — a comping process in which "colors" are drawn freely from the appropriate improvising scale. Although these colors are usually chord-like in texture, they differ from standard chord voicings in that there are no pre-set formulas for any chord.

Scales and modes — refer to Common Scales, Modes, and Melodic Minor Modes (pp. 310-313).

Tonal progression — a chord progression characterized by the presence of traditional tritone resolutions such as V to I and typically the use of diatonic chords. This is the type of harmonic scheme described in "Harmonic Astronomy" (page 106) and is the basis of classical music, as well as that of such popular composers as Cole Porter, Rodgers and Hart, and Gershwin.

Transcribe — to duplicate a piece of music (on an instrument or on paper) from another source. In jazz the term usually refers to the aural process of learning music (such as an improvised solo) from a recording.

Transpose — to recreate a piece of music in a different key. All key relationships are maintained in this process. For example, in C major a D-E-G melody can be characterized by its scale degrees, 2-3-5. When this melody is transposed to Eb major, the result is F-G-Bb (also 2-3-5).

Tritone — an interval consisting of three whole steps. Augmented 4ths (such as Eb-A and C-F#) and diminished 5ths (such as D-Ab and B-F) are both tritones.

Upper-structure voicing (term coined by Mark Levine) — a voicing intended primarily for ensemble playing in which certain characteristic right-hand structures (such as major triads) are played over various left-hand structures (tritones, fourth-stacks, or rootless voicings, depending on the quality of the chord).

Vamp — a short section of music (such as a chord progression) that is repeated several times, usually until a cue is given to go on. Most vamps are either two measures or four measures long.

Voicing — the process of arranging the notes of a chord to adapt it to a particular musical situation (solo piano performance, big band writing, etc.). This process can include doubling, adding or removing notes, as well as inverting, compressing, or expanding the chord. The term also applies to any chord that has been so arranged.

Resources

Recordings of tunes in this book

Throughout this book I have referred to several tunes or excerpts of tunes. Here is a list of some of my favorite recorded versions.

TUNE	RECORDING	REFERENCED ON PAGE
"All The Things You Are"	Keith Jarrett: Standards, Vol. 1 (1983 ECM)	113
"Ask Me Now"	Fred Hersch Plays Monk (1997 WEA/Atlantic/Nonesuch)	211
"But Beautiful"	Getz/Evans: But Beautiful (1974 Fantasy/Milestone)	228, 235, 236, 267
"Do Nothing Till You Hear From Me"	Cootie Williams: Do Nothing Till You Hear From Me (1960)	49
"Embraceable You"	Nat King Cole: The Best of the Nat King Cole Trio (1942 Blue Note)	49, 142, 145, 326
"Everything I Love"	Fred Hersch: Live at Maybeck Recital Hall (1993 Concord)	14-17, 90-103, 154-5, 318-19
"How Long Has This Been Going On?"	Oscar Peterson: Paris Concertó Salle Pleyel (1978 Fantasy/Pablo)	158-9, 312-13
"I Love You"	Bill Evans: New Jazz Conceptions (1956 Fantasy)	113, 211
"I Should Care"	Abby Lincoln: When There Is Love (1992 Verve)	113-115, 314-15
"In A Sentimental Mood"	John Coltrane: The Gentle Side of John Coltrane (1961 Impulse)	177
"It Could Happen To You"	Chick Corea: A Week At The Blue Note (1998 Stretch)	44, 49, 83, 87-8, 110, 226, 238, 242-3
"Like Someone In Love"	John Coltrane: Lush Life (1957 Fantasy)	253
"Moment's Notice"	John Coltrane: Blue Train (1957 Blue Note)	211
"Mr. Clean"	Freddy Hubbard: Straight Life (1970 Sony/Columbia)	182
"My Foolish Heart"	The Tony Bennett/Bill Evans Album (1975 Fantasy)	49, 156-7, 242-3, 320-1
"My Funny Valentine"	Chet Baker: My Funny Valentine (1980 Blue Note)	120, 122-3, 316-17
"My Romance"	Brad Mehldau: Introducing Brad Mehldau (1995 Warner Bros.)	138
"Ruby My Dear"	Thelonious Monk: The Composer (1988 Columbia)	211
"Satin Doll"	Duke Ellington: Live At The Blue Note (1952 Blue Note)	211

"Since I Fell For You"	Red Garland Trio: It's A Blue World (1958 Fantasy)	160-1, 170-3, 324-5
"Softly As In A Morning Sunrise"	David Kikoski: Inner Trust (1998 Criss Cross)	178, 193-4, 265
"Someone To Watch Over Me"	Andy Bey: Ballads Blues and Bey (1995 Evidence Music)	177
"Stella By Starlight"	Keith Jarrett: Standards Live (1985 ECM)	142, 144
"Straight No Chaser"	Thelonious Monk: The Composer (1988 Columbia)	52
"The Nearness of You"	Eric Alexander: Up Over and Out (1993 Delmark)	133
"Watermelon Man"	Herbie Hancock: Headhunters (1973 Sony/Columbia)	242
"Whisper Not"	Wynton Kelly: Piano (1958 Fantasy)	119

Here's a great tip. If you have a computer and can access the Internet, go to a music website that sells recordings such as amazon.com. Locate the search engine and type in the name of the song you want to research. You'll then see an extensive list of recordings that include that song. In many cases you can click on a particular recording and listen to excerpts.

Recordings for general listening

Listening is as necessary to your musical health as nutrition is to your physical health. There's simply no substitute for it. Expose yourself to as many styles of music as you can, find what you love, and listen. If you would like some direction as to where to begin, I recommend the listening lists at the back of Mark Levine's books (*The Jazz Piano Book* and *The Jazz Theory Book,* both by Sher Music Co.)

Books and Periodicals

These books may fill in gaps in your knowledge, extend this book's material further, or simply offer a different point of view. All are available online.

Instructional and Conceptual

Creative Jazz Improvisation, by Scott D. Reeves (Prentice-Hall)
The Jazz Piano Book, by Mark Levine (Sher Music)
The Jazz Theory Book, by Mark Levine (Sher Music)
Inside Improvisation series, by Jerry Bergonzi (Advance Music)
The Charlie Parker Omnibook (Atlantic Music Corp.)
Improvising Jazz, by Jerry Coker (Simon and Schuster)
Patterns for Jazz, by Jerry Coker, James Casale, Gary Campbell and Jerry Greene (Columbia Pictures Publications)
The Lydian Chromatic Concept of Tonal Organization, by George Russell (Concept Publishing)

Thesaurus of Scales and Melodic Patterns, by Nicolas Slonimsky (Schirmer Books)
Jazz Piano: Creative Concepts and Techniques, by Jeff Gardner (HL Music)
CD: *"Dick Hyman's Century of Jazz Piano"* (order online at jssmusic.com)
The Great Jazz Pianists, by Len Lyons
Free Play: Improvisation in Life and Art, by Steven Nachmanovitch (Penguin-Putnam)
Jazz Improv Magazine (order online at jazzimprov.com)
The Jazz Piano Studyletter (order online at humboldt1.com/~jazz/index.html)
Music and Imagination, by Aaron Copland (Harvard University Press)
Notes and Tones, by Art Taylor (Da Capo Press)
Effortless Mastery, by Kenny Werner (Jamey Aebersold Jazz)
Thinking In Jazz, by Paul F. Berliner (The University of Chicago Press)
Reading Jazz, edited by Robert Gottlieb (Pantheon)

Collections of tunes

The New Real Book (Sher Music)
The Standards Real Book (Sher Music)
The All-Jazz Real Book (Sher Music)

Websites

The Internet is an inexhaustible resource for jazz instruction, access to recordings and books, and historical information. Good starting sites include allaboutjazz.com, jazzreview.com, and A Contemporary List of Jazz Links (riad.usk.pk.edu.pl/~pmj/jazzlinks).

To buy instructional material

shermusic.com
jajazz.com
drumdatabase.com
allmusic.com

Online instructional material

pgmusic.com/jazzpianomasterclass/lessons
outsideshore.com/primer/primer

Appendix

Random Notes

Use this chart to practice anything in 12 keys (chords, voicings, scales, etc.). The notes are arranged randomly, so you can go across or down.

	a	b	c	d	e	f	g	h	i	j
1	A	Ab	Bb	G	D	Db	A	Db	F	Gb
2	Gb	B	F	A	Bb	G	Eb	G	Bb	E
3	E	Db	C	F	B	Ab	Bb	Gb	D	Eb
4	Db	Ab	Eb	D	Ab	C	F#	C	Ab	A
5	A	Eb	C	G	E	B	D	Eb	B	F#
6	C	B	Gb	B	F	Ab	C	E	C#	E
7	F#	D	C	Ab	A	E	G	D	F	A
8	B	Eb	E	D	Bb	Db	D	Bb	B	G
9	E	A	C#	F	E	F#	Eb	C	Ab	C#
10	C	F	Eb	G	A	F	Ab	Gb	Bb	D

Random 7th Chords

	a	b	c	d	e	f	g
1	Emi7	Gdim7	C7	Dbmi7(b5)	F7	Bma7	Dmi7(b5)
2	Bb7	Ebmi7	Ab7	Ema7	Ddim7	Dbmi7	Fmi7
3	Edim7	Bbmi7	D#ma7	F#mi7	Cmi7(b5)	Gbdim7	C#ma7
4	Bbma7	Ebmi7(b5)	Ami7(b5)	Dma7	D#dim7	Gb7	Fma7
5	A7	Eb7	Gbmi7	D#7	F#ma7	Ami7	Abdim7
6	Cmi7	Dmi7(b5)	Db7	G#ma7	C#dim7	Ama7	Emi7(b5)
7	E7	F#dim7	A#mi7	Cma7	Abmi7(b5)	Adim7	Bmi7(b5)
8	G#mi7(b5)	Cdim7	Dmi7	F#7	Bdim7	F#mi7(b5)	Ebma7
9	Bbmi7(b5)	D7	Fmi7(b5)	Gma7	Bbdim7	Bmi7	G7
10	Ebdim7	B7	Abmi7	Gmi7(b5)	Fdim7	Gmi7	Abma7

Random major II-V's

	A	B	C	D
1	Dmi7 G7	Bmi7 E7	C#mi7 F#7	Ebmi7 Ab7
2	Gmi7 C7	Fmi7 Bb7	Emi7 A7	Bbmi7 Eb7
3	Ami7 D7	D#mi7 G#7	Gmi7 C7	Dbmi7 Gb7
4	F#mi7 B7	G#mi7 C#7	Fmi7 Bb7	Bmi7 E7
5	Bbmi7 Eb7	C#mi7 F#7	A#mi7 D#7	Gmi7 C7
6	Cmi7 F7	Dmi7 G7	Bmi7 E7	G#mi7 C#7
7	Dbmi7 Gb7	F#mi7 B7	Ebmi7 Ab7	Fmi7 Bb7
8	Ami7 D7	Emi7 A7	C#mi7 F#7	Cmi7 F7
9	Abmi7 Db7	Bbmi7 Eb7	F#mi7 B7	D#mi7 G#7
10	Bmi7 E7	Ami7 D7	Abmi7 Db7	Emi7 A7

Random major II-V-I's

	A	B	C	D
1	Dmi7 G7 Cma7	Bmi7 E7 Ama7	C#mi7 F#7 Bma7	Ebmi7 Ab7 Dbma7
2	Gmi7 C7 Fma7	Fmi7 Bb7 Ebma7	Emi7 A7 Dma7	Bbmi7 Eb7 Abma7
3	Ami7 D7 Gma7	D#mi7 G#7 C#ma7	Gmi7 C7 Fma7	Dbmi7 Gb7 Cbma7
4	F#mi7 B7 Ema7	G#mi7 C#7 F#ma7	Fmi7 Bb7 Ebma7	Bmi7 E7 Ama7
5	Bbmi7 Eb7 Abma7	C#mi7 F#7 Bma7	A#mi7 D#7 G#ma7	Gmi7 C7 Fma7
6	Cmi7 F7 Bbma7	Dmi7 G7 Cma7	Bmi7 E7 Ama7	G#mi7 C#7 F#ma7
7	Dbmi7 Gb7 Cbma7	F#mi7 B7 Ema7	Ebmi7 Ab7 Dbma7	Fmi7 Bb7 Ebma7
8	Ami7 D7 Gma7	Emi7 A7 Dma7	C#mi7 F#7 Bma7	Cmi7 F7 Bbma7
9	Abmi7 Db7 Gbma7	Bbmi7 Eb7 Abma7	F#mi7 B7 Ema7	D#mi7 G#7 C#ma7
10	Bmi7 E7 Ama7	Ami7 D7 Gma7	Abmi7 Db7 Gbma7	Emi7 A7 Dma7

Random minor II-V-I's

	A	B	C	D
1	Dmi7$^{(b5)}$ G7 Cmi	Bmi7$^{(b5)}$ E7 Ami	C#mi7$^{(b5)}$ F#7 Bmi	Ebmi7$^{(b5)}$ Ab7 Dbmi
2	Gmi7$^{(b5)}$ C7 Fmi	Fmi7$^{(b5)}$ Bb7 Ebmi	Emi7$^{(b5)}$ A7 Dmi	Bbmi7$^{(b5)}$ Eb7 Abmi
3	Ami7$^{(b5)}$ D7 Gmi	D#mi7$^{(b5)}$ G#7 C#mi	Gmi7$^{(b5)}$ C7 Fmi	Dbmi7$^{(b5)}$ Gb7 Cbmi
4	F#mi7$^{(b5)}$ B7 Emi	G#mi7$^{(b5)}$ C#7 F#mi	Fmi7$^{(b5)}$ Bb7 Ebmi	Bmi7$^{(b5)}$ E7 Ami
5	Bbmi7$^{(b5)}$ Eb7 Abmi	C#mi7$^{(b5)}$ F#7 Bmi	A#mi7$^{(b5)}$ D#7 G#mi	Gmi7$^{(b5)}$ C7 Fmi
6	Cmi7$^{(b5)}$ F7 Bbmi	Dmi7$^{(b5)}$ G7 Cmi	Bmi7$^{(b5)}$ E7 Ami	G#mi7$^{(b5)}$ C#7 F#mi
7	Dbmi7$^{(b5)}$ Gb7 Cbmi	F#mi7$^{(b5)}$ B7 Emi	Ebmi7$^{(b5)}$ Ab7 Dbmi	Fmi7$^{(b5)}$ Bb7 Ebmi
8	Ami7$^{(b5)}$ D7 Gmi	Emi7$^{(b5)}$ A7 Dmi	C#mi7$^{(b5)}$ F#7 Bmi	Cmi7$^{(b5)}$ F7 Bbmi
9	Abmi7$^{(b5)}$ Db7 Gbmi	Bbmi7$^{(b5)}$ Eb7 Abmi	F#mi7$^{(b5)}$ B7 Emi	D#mi7$^{(b5)}$ G#7 C#mi
10	Bmi7$^{(b5)}$ E7 Ami	Ami7$^{(b5)}$ D7 Gmi	Abmi7$^{(b5)}$ Db7 Gbmi	Emi7$^{(b5)}$ A7 Dmi

Random major and minor II-V's and II-V-I's

	A	B	C	D
1	Cmi7 F7	Abmi 7 Db7 Gbma7	Ebmi7 Ab7 Dbma7	Ami7 D7
2	Ebmi7$^{(b5)}$ Ab7 Dbmi	Bbmi7 Eb7	Gmi7$^{(b5)}$ C7 Fmi	Bmi7$^{(b5)}$ E7
3	Fmi7 Bb7 Ebma7	Abmi7$^{(b5)}$ Db7 Gbmi	F#mi7$^{(b5)}$ B7	Bbmi7 Eb7 Abma7
4	Cmi7$^{(b5)}$ F7	Gmi7$^{(b5)}$ C7	Fmi7$^{(b5)}$ Bb7 Ebmi	Abmi7$^{(b5)}$ Db7
5	Bmi7 E7 Ama7	Dmi7 G7 Cma7	Dmi7 G7	Emi7 A7 Dma7
6	Ebmi7 Ab7	Emi7$^{(b5)}$ A7 Dmi	Dbmi7$^{(b5)}$ Gb7	Dmi7$^{(b5)}$ G7 Cmi
7	A#mi7$^{(b5)}$ D#7 G#mi	Bmi7 E7	Ami7 D7 Gma7	Fmi7 Bb7
8	Dmi7$^{(b5)}$ G7	C#mi7 F#7 Bma7	Ebmi7$^{(b5)}$ Ab7	G#mi7$^{(b5)}$ C#7 F#mi
9	Fmi7$^{(b5)}$ Bb7	F#mi7$^{(b5)}$ B7 Emi	F#mi7 B7 Ema7	C#mi7 F#7
10	Gmi7 C7 Fma7	A#mi7$^{(b5)}$ D#7	Emi7 A7	Bmi7$^{(b5)}$ E7 Ami
11	Bbmi7$^{(b5)}$ Eb7	Abmi7 Db7	C#mi7$^{(b5)}$ F#7	Dbmi7 Gb7
12	Cmi7$^{(b5)}$ F7 Bbmi	Ami7$^{(b5)}$ D7	Cmi7 F7 Bbma7	Emi7$^{(b5)}$ A7
13	F#mi7 B7	G#mi7 C#7 F#ma7	Dbmi7$^{(b5)}$ Gb7 Cbmi	Ami7$^{(b5)}$ D7 Gmi
14	Abmi7$^{(b5)}$ Db7	Bbmi7$^{(b5)}$ Eb7 Abmi	A#mi7 D#7	D#mi7 G#7 C#ma7
15	Dbmi7 Gb7 Cbma7	D#mi7 G#7	C#mi7$^{(b5)}$ F#7 Bmi	Gmi7 C7

Scale type: _____ Construction:_____

C	
G	
D	
A	
E	
B	
F#	
C#	
A♭	
E♭	
B♭	
F	

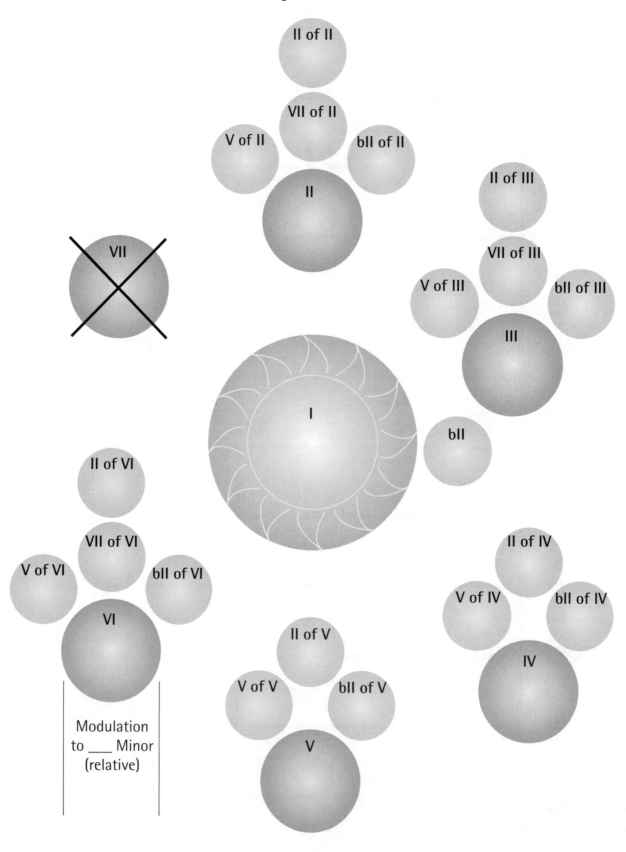

___ major "cosmic"

___ minor "cosmic"

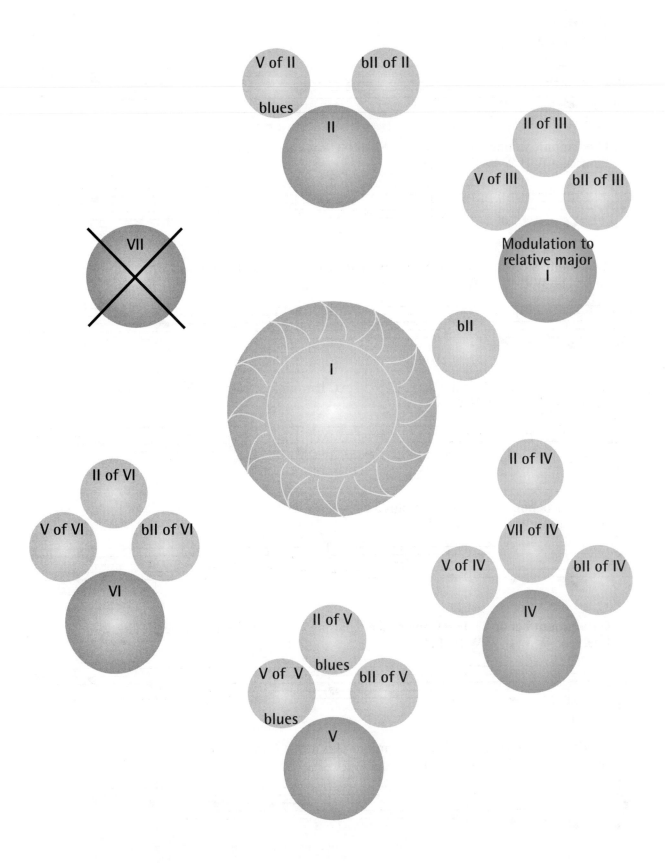

Common Scales

C major
Intervals: W W H W W W H

C harmonic minor = C major scale ♭3 ♭6 = C natural minor ♯7
Intervals: W H W W H aug2 H

C melodic minor (jazz form) = C major scale ♭3 = C natural minor ♯6 ♯7
Intervals: W H W W W W H

C natural minor = C major scale ♭3 ♭6 ♭7 = C harmonic minor ♭7 = E♭ major scale from C to C
Intervals: W H W W H W W

C major bebop = C major scale plus a ♯5
Intervals: W W H W H H W H

C dominant bebop scale = C major scale plus a ♭7 = C mixolydian mode plus a major 7
Intervals: W W H W W H H H

C minor bebop scale = C harmonic minor plus a ♭7 = C major scale ♭3 ♭6 plus a ♭7
Intervals: W H W W H W H H

C diminished
Intervals: W H W H W H W H (only 3 note-patterns)

C auxiliary diminished
Intervals: H W H W H W H W (only 3 note-patterns)

C pentatonic = 1 2 3 5 6 1 of a C major scale
Intervals: W W m3 W m3

C minor pentatonic = mode #5 of E♭ pentatonic = 1 ♭3 4 5 ♭7 1 of a C major scale
Intervals: m3 W W m3 W

C blues = C minor pentatonic plus a #4 = 1 ♭3 4 #4 5 ♭7 1 of a C major scale
Intervals: m3 W H H m3 W

C major blues = C pentatonic plus a #2 = 1 2 #2 3 5 6 1 of a C major scale
Intervals: W H H m3 W m3

C whole-tone
Intervals: W W W W W W (only 2 note-patterns)

Modes

C Ionian = Mode #1 of the C major scale = C major scale
Intervals: W W H W W W H

C Dorian = Mode #2 of the B♭ major scale = C natural minor scale ♯6
Intervals: W H W W W H W

C Phrygian = Mode #3 of the A♭ major scale = C natural minor scale ♭2
Intervals: H W W W H W W

C Lydian = Mode #4 of the G major scale = C major scale ♯4
Intervals: W W W H W W H

C Mixolydian = Mode #5 of the F major scale = C major scale ♭7
Intervals: W W H W W H W

C Aeolian = Mode #6 of the E♭ major scale = C natural minor scale
Intervals: W H W W H W W

C Locrian = Mode #7 of the D♭ major scale = C natural minor scale ♭2 ♭5
Intervals: H W W H W W W

Melodic Minor Modes

C Melodic Minor = Mode #1 of the C melodic minor scale
Intervals: W H W W W W H

C Dorian ♭2 = Mode #2 of the B♭ melodoc minor scale
         Also known as: C phrygi-dorian
Intervals: H W W W W H W

C Lydian Augmented = Mode #3 of the A melodic minor scale =C major scale ♯4 ♯5 =
         C lydian mode #5
Intervals: W W W W H W H

C Mixolydian ♯4 = Mode #4 of the G melodic minor scale = C major scale ♯4 ♭7
         Also known as: C whole-tone/diminished; C lydian ♭7; C lydian dominant
Intervals: W W W H W H W

C Mixolydian ♭6 = Mode #5 of the F melodic minor scale = C major scale ♭6 ♭7
         Also known as: C mixo-aeolian
Intervals: W W H W H W W

C Locrian ♯2 = Mode #6 of the E♭ melodic minor scale
         Also known as: C half-diminished
Intervals: W H W H W W W

C Altered = Mode #7 of the D♭ melodic minor scale
         Also known as: C diminished/whole-tone; C super-locrian
Intervals: H W H W W W W

314

I Should Care

Sammy Cahn
Axel Stordahl
Paul Weston

mcs = *most consonant scale*
mi = minor bebop scale
mm = melodic minor scale

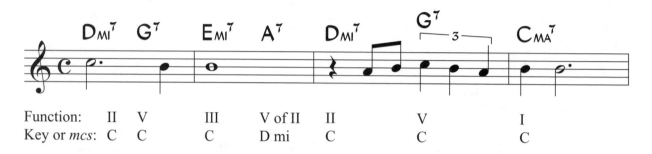

Function:	II	V	III	V of II	II	V	I
Key or *mcs*:	C	C	C	D mi	C	C	C

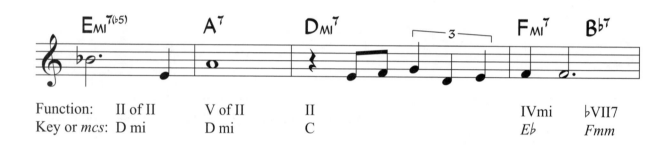

Function:	II of II	V of II	II		IVmi	♭VII7
Key or *mcs*:	D mi	D mi	C		*E♭*	*Fmm*

Function:	I	II of VI	V of VI	II of IV	V of IV	IV
Key or *mcs*:	C	A mi	A mi	F	F	C

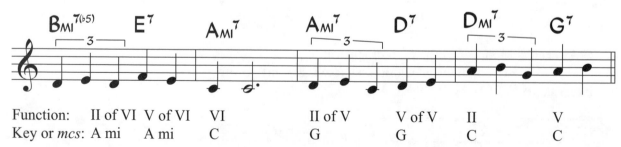

Function:	II of VI	V of VI	VI	II of V	V of V	II	V
Key or *mcs*:	A mi	A mi	C	G	G	C	C

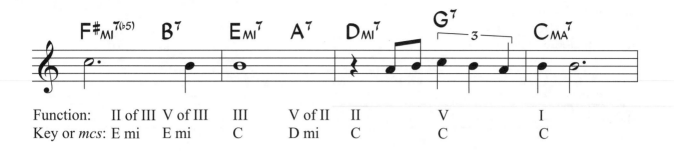

Function:	II of III	V of III	III	V of II	II		V		I
Key or *mcs*:	E mi	E mi	C	D mi	C		C		C

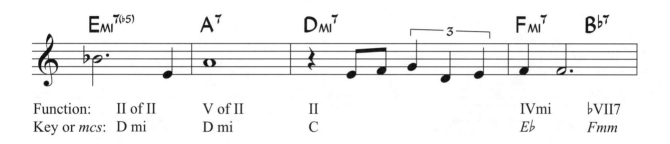

Function:	II of II	V of II	II			IVmi	♭VII7
Key or *mcs*:	D mi	D mi	C			*E♭*	*Fmm*

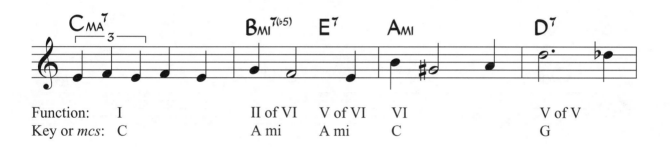

Function:	I		II of VI	V of VI	VI		V of V
Key or *mcs*:	C		A mi	A mi	C		G

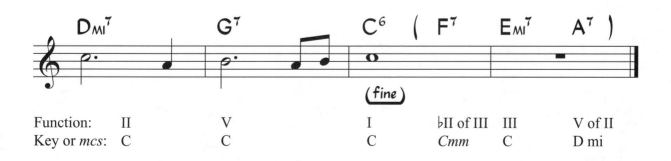

Function:	II	V	I	♭II of III	III	V of II
Key or *mcs*:	C	C	C	*Cmm*	C	D mi

My Funny Valentine

Rodgers/Hart

mcs = *most consonant scale*
mi = *minor bebop scale*
mm = *melodic minor scale*

Function: I
Key or *msc*:   C mi

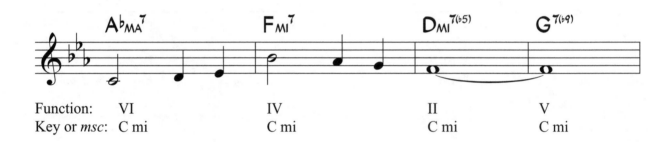

Function:	VI	IV	II	V
Key or *msc*:	C mi	C mi	C mi	C mi

Function: I
Key or *msc*:   C mi

Function:	VI	IV	Eb:	IVmi6	V
Key or *msc*:	C mi	C mi		*Abmm*	Eb

Function:	I	II	III	II	I	II	III	II
Key or *msc*:	E♭	E♭	E♭	E♭	E♭	E♭	E♭	E♭

Function:	I	**C mi:**	V	I	II of VI	♭II of VI	VI	II	V
Key or *msc*:	E♭		C mi	C mi	A♭	*Emm*	C mi	C mi	C mi

Function:	I
Key or *msc*:	C mi

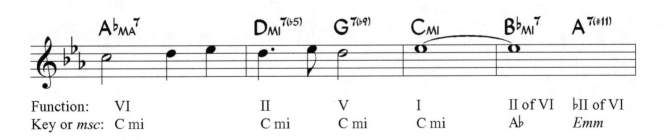

Function:	VI	II	V	I	II of VI	♭II of VI
Key or *msc*:	C mi	C mi	C mi	C mi	A♭	*Emm*

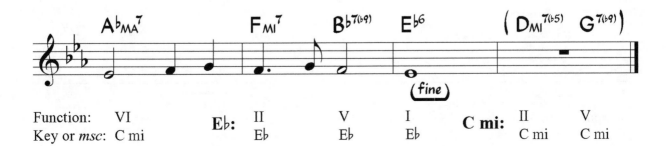

Function:	VI	**E♭:**	II	V	I	**C mi:**	II	V
Key or *msc*:	C mi		E♭	E♭	E♭		C mi	C mi

Everything I Love

Cole Porter

mcs = *most consonant scale*
mi = minor bebop scale
mm = melodic minor scale

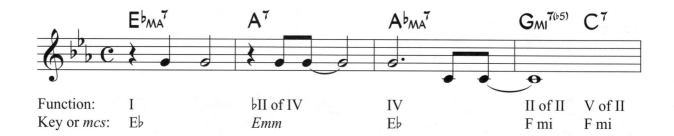

Function:	I	♭II of IV	IV		II of II	V of II
Key or *mcs*:	E♭	*Emm*	E♭		F mi	F mi

Function:	II	V	I	IV
Key or *mcs*:	E♭	E♭	E♭	E♭

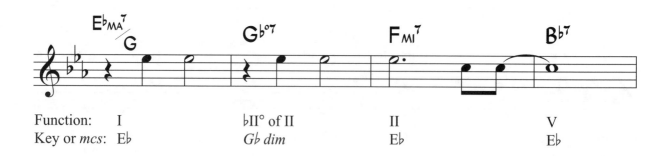

Function:	I	♭II° of II	II	V
Key or *mcs*:	E♭	*G♭ dim*	E♭	E♭

Function:	II	V	I		II	V
Key or *mcs*:	G♭	G♭	G♭		E♭	E♭

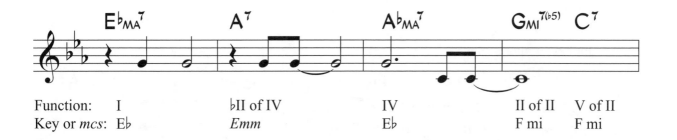

Function: I   ♭II of IV   IV   II of II   V of II
Key or *mcs*: E♭   *Emm*   E♭   F mi   F mi

Function: II   V of III   V of VI
Key or *mcs*: E♭   G mi   C mi

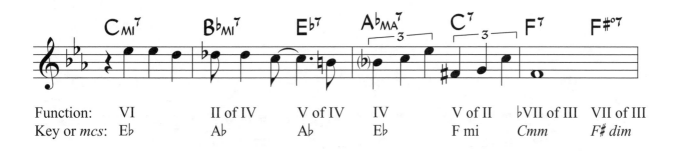

Function: VI   II of IV   V of IV   IV   V of II   ♭VII of III   VII of III
Key or *mcs*: E♭   A♭   A♭   E♭   F mi   *Cmm*   *F♯ dim*

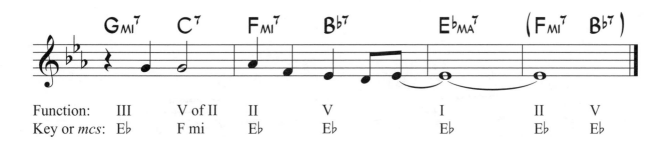

Function: III   V of II   II   V   I   II   V
Key or *mcs*: E♭   F mi   E♭   E♭   E♭   E♭   E♭

320

My Foolish Heart

Washington/Young

mcs = *most consonant scale*

mi = *minor bebop scale*

mm = *melodic minor scale*

Function:	I	IV		III	V of II	II		V of III
Key or *mcs*:	B♭	B♭		B♭	C mi	B♭		D mi

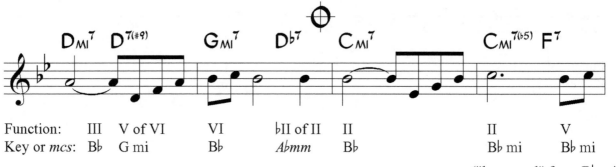

Function:	III	V of VI	VI		♭II of II	II		II	V
Key or *mcs*:	B♭	G mi	B♭		*A♭mm*	B♭		B♭ mi	B♭ mi

("borrowed" from B♭ mi)

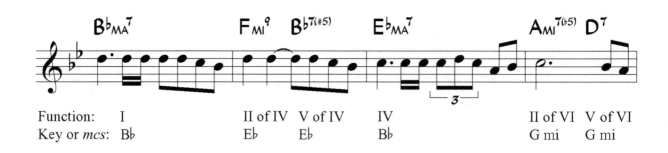

Function:	I		II of IV	V of IV	IV		II of VI	V of VI
Key or *mcs*:	B♭		E♭	E♭	B♭		G mi	G mi

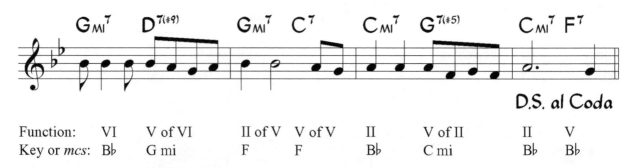

D.S. al Coda

Function:	VI	V of VI	II of V	V of V	II	V of II	II	V
Key or *mcs*:	B♭	G mi	F	F	B♭	C mi	B♭	B♭

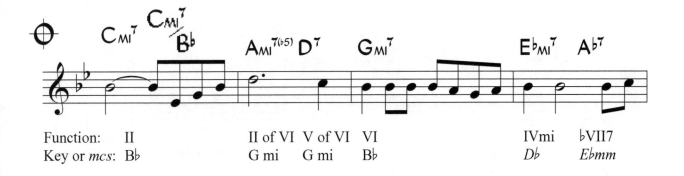

Function: II   II of VI V of VI VI   IVmi   ♭VII7
Key or *mcs*: B♭   G mi   G mi   B♭   *Db*   *Ebmm*

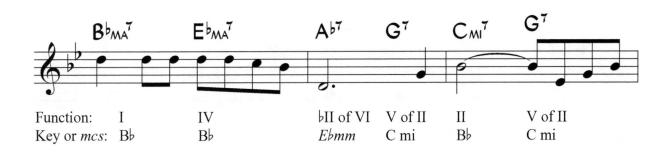

Function: I   IV   ♭II of VI V of II   II   V of II
Key or *mcs*: B♭   B♭   *Ebmm*   C mi   B♭   C mi

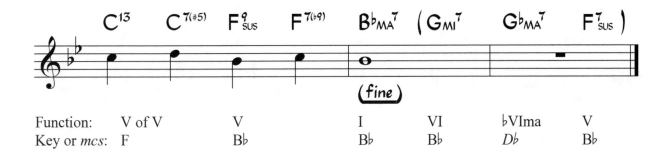

(fine)

Function: V of V   V   I   VI   ♭VIma   V
Key or *mcs*: F   B♭   B♭   B♭   *Db*   B♭

How Long Has This Been Going On?

George and Ira Gershwin

mcs = *most consonant scale*
mi = *minor bebop scale*
mm = *melodic minor scale*

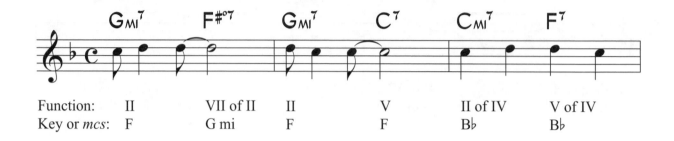

Function:	II	VII of II	II	V	II of IV	V of IV
Key or *mcs*:	F	G mi	F	F	B♭	B♭

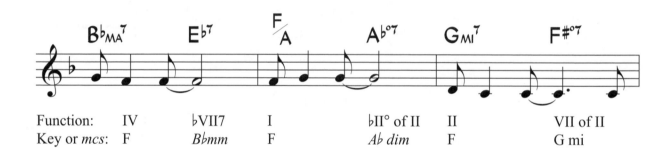

Function:	IV	♭VII7	I	♭II° of II	II	VII of II
Key or *mcs*:	F	*B♭mm*	F	*A♭ dim*	F	G mi

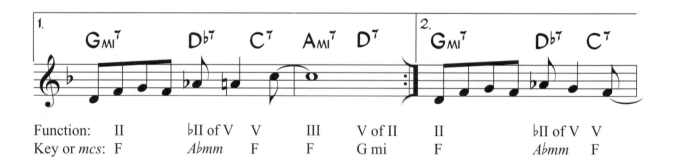

Function:	II	♭II of V	V	III	V of II	II	♭II of V	V
Key or *mcs*:	F	*A♭mm*	F	F	G mi	F	*A♭mm*	F

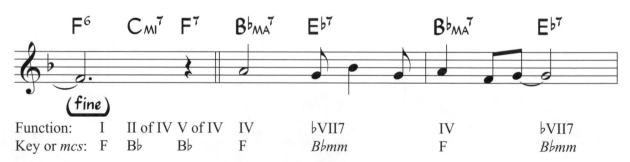

Function:	I	II of IV	V of IV	IV	♭VII7	IV	♭VII7
Key or *mcs*:	F	B♭	B♭	F	*B♭mm*	F	*B♭mm*

323

Function:	IV	♭VII7		IV	**A mi:** II	V	I	II	V
Key or *mcs*:	F	*B♭mm*		F	A mi	A mi	A mi	A mi	A mi

D.C. al 2nd ending al fine

Function:	I	II	V	I	II	V	I	**F:**	VII of II
Key or *mcs*:	A mi	A mi	A mi	A mi	A mi	A mi	A mi		G mi

Since I Fell For You

Buddy Johnson

mcs = *most consonant scale*
mi = *minor bebop scale*
mm = *melodic minor scale*

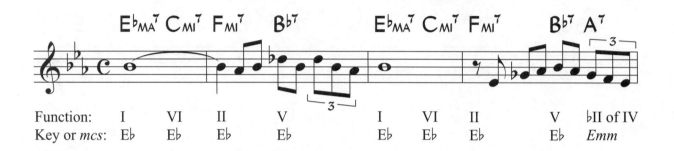

Function:	I	VI	II	V	I	VI	II	V	♭II of IV
Key or *mcs*:	E♭	E♭	E♭	E♭	E♭	E♭	E♭	E♭	*Emm*

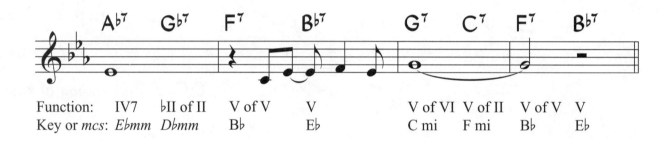

Function:	IV7	♭II of II	V of V	V	V of VI	V of II	V of V	V
Key or *mcs*:	*E♭mm*	*D♭mm*	B♭	E♭	C mi	F mi	B♭	E♭

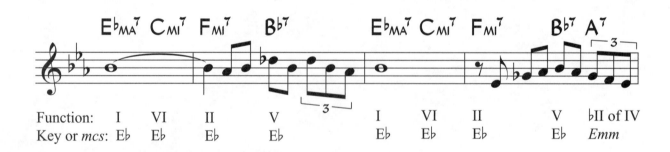

Function:	I	VI	II	V	I	VI	II	V	♭II of IV
Key or *mcs*:	E♭	E♭	E♭	E♭	E♭	E♭	E♭	E♭	*Emm*

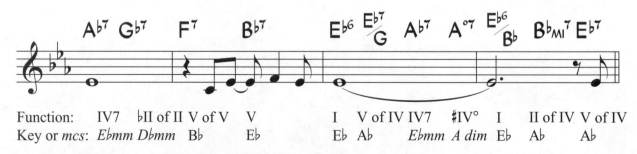

Function:	IV7	♭II of II	V of V	V	I	V of IV	IV7	#IV°	I	II of IV	V of IV
Key or *mcs*:	*E♭mm*	*D♭mm*	B♭	E♭	E♭	A♭	*E♭mm*	*A dim*	E♭	A♭	A♭

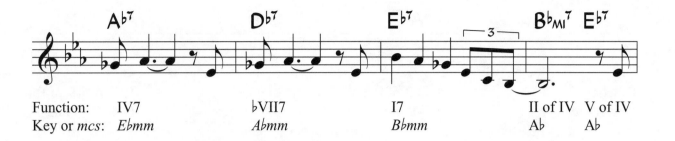

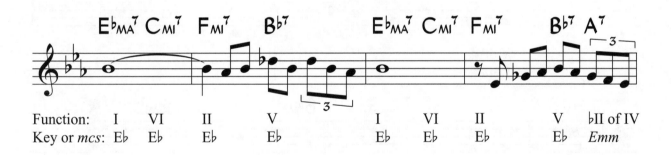

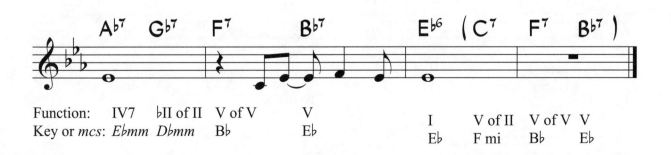

Embraceable You

Gershwin-Gershwin

mcs = *most consonant scale*
mi = *minor bebop scale*
mm = *melodic minor scale*

Index

continued next page

Index

About the Author

Randy Halberstadt lives in Seattle, Washington, with his wife Chris and daughter Robin. A moderate health nut and avid juicer, Randy enjoys movies, Sonics basketball, and reading science books that don't require any knowledge of science.

He also enjoys being a part of the Northwest jazz scene. In addition to teaching privately and at Cornish College of the Arts, Randy performs throughout the area, both as a leader and a sideman. He has performed with Herb Ellis, Buddy DeFranco, Terry Gibbs, Jay Clayton, Ernestine Anderson, Sheila Jordan, Marlena Shaw, Slide Hampton, Pete Christlieb, and Bobby Shew.

Randy has made two recordings of his own music. "Inner Voice" (Pony Boy, 1990) is a trio album, while "Clockwork" (Pony Boy, 1995) adds alto sax and five vocalists singing Randy's original lyrics. He is also featured on Jay Clayton's "Circle Dancing" (Riverside, 1997). Randy has also arranged and produced music for vocalist Janis Mann and Greta Matassa.

Randy Halberstadt is available for clinics and performances.

randy@randyhalberstadt.com
www.randyhalberstadt.com

Latin Music Books & CDs from Sher Music Co.

The Latin Real Book (C, Bb or Eb)

The only professional-level Latin fake book ever published! Over 570 pages. Includes detailed transcriptions of tunes, exactly as recorded by:

Ray Barretto
Eddie Palmieri
Fania All-Stars
Tito Puente
Ruben Blades
Los Van Van
NG La Banda

Irakere
Celia Cruz
Arsenio Rodriguez
Tito Rodriguez
Orquesta Aragon
Beny Moré
Cal Tjader

Andy Narell
Mario Bauza
Dizzy Gilllespie
Mongo Santamaria
Manny Oquendo & Libre
Puerto Rico All-Stars
Issac Delgaldo

Ft. Apache Band
Dave Valentin
Paquito D'Rivera
Clare Fischer
Chick Corea
Sergio Mendes
Ivan Lins

Djavan
Tom Jobim
Toninho Horta
Joao Bosco
Milton Nascimento
Leila Pinheiro
Gal Costa
And Many More!

Muy Caliente!

Afro-Cuban Play-Along CD and Book
Rebeca Mauleón - Keyboard
Oscar Stagnaro - Bass
Orestes Vilató - Timbales
Carlos Caro - Bongos
Edgardo Cambon - Congas
Over 70 min. of smokin' Latin grooves!
Stereo separation so you can eliminate the bass or piano. Play-along with a rhythm section featuring some of the top Afro-Cuban musicians in the world!

The Latin Real Book Sampler CD

12 of the greatest Latin Real Book tunes as played by the original artists: Tito Puente, Ray Barretto, Andy Narell, Puerto Rico Allstars, Bacacoto, etc. $16 list price. Available in U.S.A. only.

101 Montunos

by Rebeca Mauleón
The only comprehensive study of Latin piano playing ever published.
• Bi-lingual text (English/Spanish)
• 2 CDs of the author demonstrating each montuno
• Covers over 100 years of Afro-Cuban styles, including the danzón, guaracha, mambo, merengue and songo—from Peruchin to Eddie Palmieri.

The True Cuban Bass

By Carlos Del Puerto, (bassist with Irakere) and **Silvio Vergara**, $22.
For acoustic or electric bass; English and Spanish text; Includes CDs of either historic Cuban recordings or Carlos playing each exercise; Many transcriptions of complete bass parts for tunes in different Cuban styles – the roots of Salsa.

The Brazilian Guitar Book

by Nelson Faria, one of Brazil's best new guitarists.
• Over 140 pages of comping patterns, transcriptions and chord melodies for samba, bossa, baião, etc.
• Complete chord voicings written out for each example.
• Comes with a CD of Nelson playing each example.
• The most complete Brazilian guitar method ever published! $28 list price.

Joe Diorio – "Nelson Faria's book is a welcome addition to the guitar literature. I'm sure those who work with this volume will benefit greatly"

The Salsa Guide Book

By Rebeca Mauleón
The only complete method book on salsa ever published! 260 pages. $25

Carlos Santana – "A true treasure of knowledge and information about Afro-Cuban music."
Mark Levine, author of The *Jazz Piano Book*. – "This is the book on salsa."
Sonny Bravo, pianist with Tito Puente – "This will be the salsa 'bible' for years to come."
Oscar Hernández, pianist with Rubén Blades – "An excellent and much needed resource."

The New Real Book Series

The Standards Real Book (C, Bb or Eb)

Alice In Wonderland
All Of You
Alone Together
At Last
Baltimore Oriole
A Beautiful Friendship
Bess, You Is My Woman
But Not For Me
Close Enough For Love
Crazy He Calls Me
Dancing In The Dark
Days Of Wine And Roses
Dreamsville
Easy To Love
Embraceable You

Falling In Love With Love
From This Moment On
Give Me The Simple Life
Have You Met Miss Jones?
Hey There
I Can't Get Started
I Concentrate On You
I Cover The Waterfront
I Love You
I Loves You Porgy
I Only Have Eyes For You
I Wish I Knew
I'm A Fool To Want You
Indian Summer

It Ain't Necessarily So
It Never Entered My Mind
It's You Or No One
Just One Of Those Things
Love For Sale
Love Walked In
Lover, Come Back To Me
The Man I Love
Mr. Lucky
My Funny Valentine
My Heart Stood Still
My Man's Gone Now
Old Folks
On A Clear Day

Our Love Is Here To Stay
Secret Love
September In The Rain
Serenade In Blue
Shiny Stockings
Since I Fell For You
So In Love
So Nice (Summer Samba)
Some Other Time
Stormy Weather
The Summer Knows
Summer Night
Summertime
Teach Me Tonight

That Sunday, That Summer
Then I'll Be Tired Of You
There's No You
A Time For Love
Time On My Hands
'Tis Autumn
Where Or When
Who Cares?
With A Song In My Heart
You Go To My Head
Ain't No Sunshine
'Round Midnight
The Girl From Ipanema
Bluesette
And Hundreds More!

The New Real Book - Volume 1 (C, Bb or Eb)

Angel Eyes
Anthropology
Autumn Leaves
Beautiful Love
Bernie's Tune
Blue Bossa
Blue Daniel
But Beautiful
Chain Of Fools
Chelsea Bridge
Compared To What
Darn That Dream
Desafinado
Early Autumn
Eighty One

E.S.P.
Everything Happens To Me
Fall
Feel Like Makin' Love
Footprints
Four
Four On Six
Gee Baby Ain't I Good To
You
Gone With The Wind
Here's That Rainy Day
I Love Lucy
I Mean You
I Should Care
I Thought About You

If I Were A Bell
Imagination
The Island
Jersey Bounce
Joshua
Lady Bird
Like Someone In Love
Line For Lyons
Little Sunflower
Lush Life
Mercy, Mercy, Mercy
The Midnight Sun
Monk's Mood
Moonlight In Vermont
My Shining Hour

Nature Boy
Nefertiti
Nothing Personal
Oleo
Once I Loved
Out Of This World
Pent Up House
Polkadots And
Moonbeams
Portrait Of Tracy
Put It Where You Want It
Robbin's Nest
Ruby, My Dear
Satin Doll
Search For Peace

Shaker Song
Skylark
A Sleepin' Bee
Solar
Speak No Evil
St. Thomas
Street Life
Tenderly
These Foolish Things
This Masquerade
Three Views Of A Secret
Waltz For Debby
Willow Weep For Me
And Many More!

The New Real Book - Volume 2 (C, Bb or Eb)

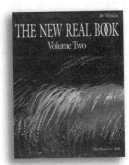

Afro-Centric
After You've Gone
Along Came Betty
Bessie's Blues
Black Coffee
Blues For Alice
Body And Soul
Bolivia
The Boy Next Door
Bye Bye Blackbird
Cherokee
A Child Is Born
Cold Duck Time
Day By Day

Django
Equinox
Exactly Like You
Falling Grace
Five Hundred Miles High
Freedom Jazz Dance
Giant Steps
Got A Match?
Harlem Nocturne
Hi-Fly
Honeysuckle Rose
I Hadn't Anyone 'Til You
I'll Be Around
I'll Get By

Ill Wind
I'm Glad There Is You
Impressions
In Your Own Sweet Way
It's The Talk Of The Town
Jordu
Killer Joe
Lullaby Of The Leaves
Manha De Carneval
The Masquerade Is Over
Memories Of You
Moment's Notice
Mood Indigo
My Ship

Naima
Nica's Dream
Once In A While
Perdido
Rosetta
Sea Journey
Senor Blues
September Song
Seven Steps To Heaven
Silver's Serenade
So Many Stars
Some Other Blues
Song For My Father
Sophisticated Lady

Spain
Stablemates
Stardust
Sweet And Lovely
That's All
There Is No Greater Love
'Til There Was You
Time Remembered
Turn Out The Stars
Unforgettable
While We're Young
Whisper Not
Will You Still Be Mine?
You're Everything
And Many More!

The New Real Book - Volume 3 (C, Bb, Eb or Bass clef)

Actual Proof
Ain't That Peculair
Almost Like Being In Love
Another Star
Autumn Serenade
Bird Of Beauty
Black Nile
Blue Moon
Butterfly
Caravan
Ceora
Close Your Eyes
Creepin'
Day Dream

Dolphin Dance
Don't Be That Way
Don't Blame Me
Emily
Everything I Have Is
Yours
For All We Know
Freedomland
The Gentle Rain
Get Ready
A Ghost Of A Chance
Heat Wave
How Sweet It Is
I Fall In Love Too Easily

I Got It Bad
I Hear A Rhapsody
If You Could See Me Now
In A Mellow Tone
In A Sentimental Mood
Inner Urge
Invitation
The Jitterbug Waltz
Just Friends
Just You, Just Me
Knock On Wood
The Lamp Is Low
Laura
Let's Stay Together
Litha

Lonely Woman
Maiden Voyage
Moon And Sand
Moonglow
My Girl
On Green Dolphin Street
Over The Rainbow
Prelude To A Kiss
Respect
Ruby
The Second Time Around
Serenata
The Shadow Of Your Smile
So Near, So Far
Solitude

Speak Like A Child
Spring Is Here
Stairway To The Stars
Star Eyes
Stars Fell On Alabama
Stompin' At The Savoy
Sugar
Sweet Lorraine
Taking A Chance On Love
This Is New
Too High
(Used To Be A) Cha Cha
When Lights Are Low
You Must Believe In Spring
And Many More!

Other Jazz Publications

The Jazz Theory Book

By Mark Levine, the most comprehensive Jazz Theory book ever published! $38 list price.
- Over 500 pages of text and over 750 musical examples.
- Written in the language of the working jazz musician, this book is easy to read and user-friendly. At the same time, it is the most comprehensive study of jazz harmony and theory ever published.
- Mark Levine has worked with Bobby Hutcherson, Cal Tjader, Joe Henderson, Woody Shaw, and many other jazz greats.

The Jazz Piano Book

By Mark Levine, Concord recording artist and pianist with Cal Tjader. For beginning to advanced pianists. The only truly comprehensive method ever published! Over 300 pages. $32

Richie Beirach – "The best new method book available."
Hal Galper – "This is a must!"
Jamey Aebersold – "This is an invaluable resource for any pianist."
James Williams – "One of the most complete anthologies on jazz piano."
Now available in Spanish too! ¡El Libro del Jazz Piano!

The Improvisor's Bass Method

By Chuck Sher. A complete method for electric or acoustic bass, plus transcribed solos and bass lines by Mingus, Jaco, Ron Carter, Scott LaFaro, Paul Jackson, Ray Brown, and more! Over 200 pages. $16

International Society of Bassists – "Undoubtedly the finest book of its kind."

Eddie Gomez – "Informative, readily comprehensible and highly imaginative"

Concepts For Bass Soloing

By Chuck Sher and Marc Johnson, (bassist with Bill Evans, etc.) The only book ever published that is specifically designed to improve your soloing! $26
- Includes two CDs of Marc Johnson soloing on each exercise
- Transcriptions of bass solos by: Eddie Gomez, John Patitucci, Scott LaFaro, Jimmy Haslip, etc.

"It's a pleasure to encounter a Bass Method so well conceived and executed." – **Steve Swallow**

The Yellowjackets Songbook

Complete package contains six separate spiral-bound books, one each for:
- Piano/partial score • C melody lead sheet
- Synthesizer/miscellaneous parts
- Bb & Eb Horn melody part • Bass • Drums

Contains 20 great tunes from their entire career. Charts exactly as recorded – approved by the Yellowjackets. World famous Sher Music Co. accuracy and legibility. Over 400 pages, $38 list price.

The Jazz Solos of Chick Corea

Over 150 pages of Chick's greatest solos; "Spain", "Litha", "Windows", "Sicily", etc. for all instrumentalists, single line transcriptions, not full piano score. $18

Chick Corea – "I don't know anyone I would trust more to correctly transcribe my improvisations."

The World's Greatest Fake Book

Jazz & Fusion Tunes by: **Coltrane, Mingus, Jaco, Chick Corea, Bird, Herbie Hancock, Bill Evans, McCoy, Beirach, Ornette, Wayne Shorter, Zawinul, AND MANY MORE!** $32

Chick Corea – "Great for any students of jazz.'
Dave Liebman – "The fake book of the 80's."
George Cables – "The most carefully conceived fake book I've ever seen."

African Percussion, The Djembe

The first comprehensive djembe method book ever published.
- CD included of the author, Serge Blanc, playing each section of the book.
- Includes 22 great standards of traditional djembe music.
- Duet and trios writtten out so you can start playing and practising in groups.

The New Real Book Play-Along CDs (For Volume 1)

CD #1 - Jazz Classics - Lady Bird, Bouncin' With Bud, Up Jumped Spring, Monk's Mood, Doors, Very Early, Eighty One, Voyage **& More!**
CD #2 - Choice Standards - Beautiful Love, Darn That Dream, Moonlight In Vermont, Trieste, My Shining Hour, I Should Care **& More!**
CD #3 - Pop-Fusion - Morning Dance, Nothing Personal, La Samba, Hideaway, This Masquerade, Three Views Of A Secret, Rio **& More!**
World-Class Rhythm Sections, featuring Mark Levine, Larry Dunlap, Sky Evergreen, Bob Magnusson, Keith Jones, Vince Lateano & Tom Hayashi

Recent Sher Music Publications

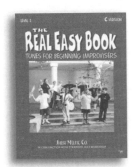

The Real Easy Book Vol. 1
TUNES FOR BEGINNING IMPROVISERS

Published by Sher Music Co. in conjunction with the Stanford Jazz Workshop. $19 list price.
The easiest tunes from Horace Silver, Eddie Harris, Freddie Hubbard, Red Garland, Sonny Rollins, Cedar Walton, Wes Montgomery Cannonball Adderly, etc.

Get yourself or your beginning jazz combo sounding good right away with the first fake book ever designed for the beginning improviser.
Available in C, Bb, Eb and Bass Clef.

The Real Easy Book Vol. 2
TUNES FOR INTERMEDIATE IMPROVISERS

Published by Sher Music Co. in conjunction with the Stanford Jazz Workshop. Over 240 pages.$29.
The best intermediate-level tunes by: Charlie Parker, John Coltrane, Miles Davis, John Scofield, Sonny Rollins, Horace Silver, Wes Montgomery, Freddie Hubbard, Cal Tjader, Cannonball Adderly, and more!

Both volumes feature instructional material tailored for each tune. Perfect for jazz combos!
Available in C, Bb, Eb and Bass Clef.

The All Jazz Real Book

Over 540 pages of tunes as recorded by:
Miles, Trane, Bill Evans, Cannonball, Scofield, Brecker, Yellowjackets, Bird, Mulgrew Miller, Kenny Werner, MJQ, McCoy Tyner, Kurt Elling, Brad Mehldau, Don Grolnick, Kenny Garrett, Patitucci, Jerry Bergonzi, Stanley Clarke, Tom Harrell, Herbie Hancock, Horace Silver, Stan Getz, Sonny Rollins, and MORE!
Includes a free CD of many of the melodies (featuring Bob Sheppard & Friends.). $44 list price.
Available in C, Bb, Eb

The Latin Bass Book
A PRACTICAL GUIDE

By Oscar Stagnaro
The only comprehensive book ever published on how to play bass in authentic Afro-Cuban, Brazilian, Caribbean, Latin Jazz & South American styles.
$34 list price
Over 250 pages of transcriptions of Oscar Stagnaro playing each exercise. Learn from the best!

Includes: 3 Play-Along CDs to accompany each exercise, featuring world-class rhythm sections.

Metaphors For The Musician

By Randy Halberstadt
This practical and enlightening book will help any jazz player or vocalist look at music with "new eyes." Designed for any level of player, on any instrument, "Metaphors For The Musician" provides numerous exercises throughout to help the reader turn these concepts into musical reality.
Guaranteed to help you improve your musicianship.
330 pages - $29 list price. Satisfaction guaranteed!

Inside The Brazilian Rhythm Section

By Nelson Faria and Cliff Korman
This is the first book/CD package ever published that provides an opportunity for bassists, guitarists, pianists and drummers to interact and play-along with a master Brazilian rhythm section. Perfect for practicing both accompanying and soloing.
$28 list price for book and 2 CDs - including the charts for the CD tracks and sample parts for each instrument, transcribed from the recording.. Satisfaction guaranteed!

The finest in Jazz & Latin publications
SHER MUSIC CO.
www.shermusic.com

See **www.shermusic.com** for more information, including a complete list of tunes in all our fake books.
To order, call (800) 444-7437 or fax (707) 763-2038